Ton und Wort
The Lieder of Richard Strauss

Studies in Musicology, No. 15

George Buelow, Series Editor
Professor of Musicology
Indiana University

Other Titles in This Series

Ton und Wort

The Lieder of Richard Strauss

by
Barbara A. Petersen

RESEARCH PRESS

Produced and distributed by
UMI Research Press
an imprint of
University Microfilms International
Ann Arbor, Michigan 48106

Library of Congress Cataloging in Publication Data

Petersen, Barbara Ellingson, 1945-
   Ton und Wort.

      (Studies in musicology series ; no. 15)
      Bibliography: p.
      Includes index.
      1. Strauss, Richard, 1864-1949. Songs.   I. Title.
II. Series.

   ML410.S93P35   784'.3'00924   79-24415
   ISBN 0-8357-1072-6

To my parents,
Mary Ross and Rudolph C. Ellingson

CONTENTS

vii

Contents

ILLUSTRATIONS

TABLES

xi

ABBREVIATIONS

Asow   E. H. Mueller von Asow. *Richard Strauss. Thematisches Ver-zeichnis. Nach dem Tode des Verfassers vollendet und heraus-gegeben von Alfons Ott und Franz Trenner.* 3 vols. (vols. I and II edited by Asow, III by Ott and Trenner). Vienna, 1955–74.

AV   *ohne Opus Asow Verzeichnis* numbers. These are works to which Strauss did not assign opus numbers and which are in-dexed by Trenner and Ott in vol. III of Asow. AV 1–150 are works without opus numbers including youthful works; AV 151–182 are lost works; AV 183–192 are arrangements of works by other composers; AV 193–306 are fragments, plans, and ideas for works not carried out; and AV 307–391 are prose writings and editions.

DM   Norman Del Mar. *Richard Strauss. A Critical Commentary on His Life and Works.* 3 vols. London, 1962–72.

GL   Franz Trenner, editor. *Richard Strauss. Gesamtausgabe der Lieder.* 4 vols. London, 1964–65. Vols. I, II, and the first part of III contain all the lieder with piano accompaniments to which Strauss assigned opus numbers. Vol. III continues with the songs without opus numbers (most of which were published previously) and then with a supplement of "Jugendlieder" (most of which are presented here in print for the first time). Vol. IV contains the orchestral lieder and orchestrations by the composer of lieder originally written with piano accompani-ments. (The orchestral lieder appear in the earlier volumes with piano reductions, not all of which are by the composer.)

Grasberger, *Briefe*
    Franz Grasberger, editor, in collaboration with Franz and Alice Strauss. *"Der Strom der Töne trug mich fort." Die Welt um Richard Strauss in Briefen.* Tutzing, 1967.

IRSGM   *Internationale Richard-Strauss-Gesellschaft. Mitteilungen.* Nos. 1–62/63 (October 1952–December 1969).

NL   Willi Schuh, editor. *Richard Strauss. Nachlese. Lieder aus der Jugendzeit und Verstreute Lieder aus späteren Jahren.* London, 1968. This edition includes eighteen songs already printed in GL III, three newly discovered songs, and three fairly complete sketches of songs.

RSB   *Richard Strauss-Blätter. Herausgegeben von der Internationalen Richard Strauss-Gesellschaft (Wien).* At first irregular; semi-annual since 1976; Nos. 1–12 (June 1971–December 1978) and continuing.

Strauss, BuE
        Richard Strauss. *Betrachtungen und Erinnerungen.* Edited by Willi Schuh. Second, enlarged edition. Zurich, 1957.

Strauss/Eltern, Strauss/Gregor, Strauss/Thuille, etc.
        Collections of correspondence between Strauss and the persons named; see Bibliography under Richard Strauss.

PREFACE

During the course of my work on the lieder of Richard Strauss, this book has evolved from what was first intended to be a style-analytical study to the present collection of chapters on widely differing aspects of the composer's songs. It gradually became clear to me over the years that a comprehensive analysis of such a large body of works would be an impossibly ambitious undertaking. At the same time, I recognized that the characteristics of Strauss's style found in the songs *in nuce* were expanded to larger dimensions in the more extended symphonic and stage works. While the composer's harmonic vocabulary, for instance, did not change drastically from one musical genre to another, a truly accurate evaluation of his harmonic style should not be limited to the lied, which is, after all, the smallest genre in which he composed a number of works.

Each of the chapters presented here, then, treats an aspect of the composer's lieder: their texts, creation, sources, performance, and, finally, critical reception. No other study has heretofore covered these aspects of Strauss's songs in such detail. Other analytical topics could certainly have been added to these: the harmonic style mentioned above, the transformation of piano accompaniments into orchestral versions, the relationship of voice and piano, and a fuller comparison of Strauss's text setting in opera and lied. In choosing to concentrate my analysis on Strauss's choice and setting of lied texts, I hope I have indeed supported the Olivier-Flamand claim that in vocal music "Ton *und* Wort sind Bruder und Schwester."

ACKNOWLEDGMENTS

Facsimiles from Strauss's sketchbooks (Illustrations 5–8) are reproduced in this study by permission of Franz and Alice Strauss of the Richard Strauss Archive and of Dr. Renata Wagner of the Bayerische Staatsbibliothek. Boosey & Hawkes has generously given permission for the inclusion of those music examples for which they hold copyright: the songs of opp. 22, 46, 47, 48, 51, 66, 68, 69, AV 34, 43, 120, 150, and the operas *Salome* and *Intermezzo*.

I wish to express my thanks to Martin Bernstein and Elaine Brody of New York University for inspiring my interest in German romanticism in general and the lied in particular, as well as to James Haar for seeing this project through its many stages. To those who allowed me access to sketches and manuscripts I am greatly indebted: the Strauss family in Garmisch, Dr. Robert Münster of the Bayerische Staatsbibliothek, the late Dr. Alfons Ott of the Städtische Musikbibliothek, and Mr. James G. Roy, Jr., of BMI, New York. The mutual sharing of information on the subject of Strauss's lieder with Dr. Franz Trenner has been a source of encouragement to me. I am also grateful to Mrs. Nancy Bennett for her verification of a few details in the German. Finally, Dr. Elise B. Jorgens deserves my thanks for her contribution to Chapter III in the form of general criticisms and valuable suggestions about the interpretation of poetry in solo song as well as for the time and reassurance she gave during its preparation.

I

AN HISTORICAL-BIBLIOGRAPHIC SURVEY
OF STRAUSS'S LIEDER

The lieder of Richard Strauss stand at the end of a tradition which had begun in the late eighteenth century with relatively simple compositions and continued through the nineteenth century with increasingly complex and diversified works. Some writers in the present century have defined this lied tradition rather narrowly, choosing not to consider Strauss's slightly over two hundred songs a part of it. Few people, however, held this attitude at the end of the nineteenth century, when Strauss was writing the majority of his lieder. Beginning with his first group of published songs—op. 10, which he wrote in 1885 and had published by 1887—his lieder enjoyed an immediate popularity that is attested to by their prompt appearance in print, widespread performance, frequent arrangements and orchestrations, and early recordings.

Editions of the Lieder

Nearly all of the lieder Strauss composed between 1885 and 1901—twenty-two groups from op. 10 to op. 49—were published within two years (and in some instances within only a few months) of their completion. Throughout the years, Strauss has been accused by some of his most vehement detractors of producing merchandise for publishers rather than creating works of art under inspiration. In the extant correspondence with or about his publishers, there is no evidence to support this view in connection with the composition of lieder. Furthermore, the publication of his songs brought Strauss rather little financial reward compared with the sums he obtained for orchestral works (and later for the operas). If he had been writing to earn money, he certainly would have chosen a genre more profitable than that of the lied. It was Strauss's philosophy that one does not compose in order to earn money, but takes in money in order to be able to pursue composition.[1] In only two instances did he ever write works on commission; neither of these is a song.[2]

As a young composer, Strauss was fortunate in having a wealthy family to assist in the first few publications of his works. In 1881 Breitkopf & Härtel brought out his first work to appear in print, the *Festmarsch*, op. 1; the expenses were paid by Strauss's uncle Georg Pschorr, the owner of the prosperous Pschorr brewery in Munich. Shortly thereafter Breitkopf & Härtel rejected Strauss's String Quartet, op. 2. He then submitted it to the Munich publishing house of Joseph Aibl, of which Eugen Spitzweg was the proprietor.[3] Spitzweg's acceptance of the quartet began a series of some thirty publications with Aibl. From op. 2 (composed in 1881) to the songs in op. 37 (completed in 1898), Aibl was Strauss's principal, though not exclusive, publisher. Beginning with op. 10, Strauss entrusted to Aibl the publication of nine groups of songs (opp. 10, 19, 21, 26, 27, 29, 32, 36, and 37).

With the exception of Strauss's Symphony in F minor (op. 12), for which his father paid the engraving and printing costs, Aibl paid the composer a one-time fee for the rights to the works they agreed to publish. The earliest of these compositions were sold to Aibl when Strauss's annual salary as a conductor was only two to three thousand German marks. Examples of the amounts he received from Aibl (in German marks, worth approximately U. S. $0.20 just before 1900) show that the larger works commanded considerably greater sums than the lieder:

Aus Italien, op. 16	500
Don Juan, op. 20	800
Tod und Verklärung, op. 24	1600
Guntram, op. 25	5000
Till Eulenspiegels lustige Streiche, op. 28	1000
Zwei Gesänge für 16stimmigen gemischten	
Chor a cappella, op. 34	2000
Lieder:	
op. 10 (8 songs)	200
op. 21 (5 songs)	200
op. 29 (3 songs)	500

Some of Strauss's letters from this period respond to or comment on Spitzweg's apparently constant reminders that the songs were expensive to issue because of the large numbers of them, the translations they required, and other details relating to their production.

During his years of negotiation with Aibl, Strauss turned to the firm of Daniel Rahter in Hamburg for two groups of songs, opp. 15 and 17.[4] The publication of op. 22 by Adolph Fürstner (Berlin) in 1891 began his long association with that firm, which continued to publish his works for many years.[5] Upon selling the four songs of op. 22 to Fürstner for 800 marks, Strauss expressed to Spitzweg his surprise at their acceptance of the high fee.[6] Fürstner had apparently approached Strauss for a group of songs and was offered the "complicated and experimental" songs which he had promised Spitzweg he would try out on another publisher. Fürstner at first wanted to bargain, but Strauss stood firm, even though he admitted to Spitzweg that he had named such a high sum out of pure bravado.[7]

By 1900 Strauss had informed Spitzweg that Fürstner was to be his new publisher; he was, however, still investigating other possibilities.

Illustration 1

Cover of Strauss's op. 22 (Berlin: Fürstner, [1891]).

Two Leipzig houses appear as song publishers: Robert Forberg (op. 39 in 1898; op. 44 in 1899), and F. E. C. Leuckart (op. 41, 1899; later op. 77). The Berlin firm of C. A. Challier & Co. (Richard Birnbach) issued op. 43 in 1899, having purchased the group of three songs from the composer for 1200 marks. Both Forberg and Leuckart published a few other Strauss works, but Challier's appearance here is unique. By the turn of the century Strauss was clearly an important enough figure to command higher fees than Spitzweg was willing to pay. He began searching for a replacement for the Aibl firm, which was in any case soon to be absorbed by Josef Weinberger's Universal-Edition (founded in 1901). Under the terms of his agreements with Aibl, Strauss had surrendered all rights to—and thus any future opportunities to earn money from the sale of—his works. One of the main reasons for this break with Aibl was probably his attempt to secure better terms by beginning anew with another publisher. In early 1904, Spitzweg tried (unsuccessfully) to interest the Berlin firm of Bote & Bock in taking over the Aibl catalogue. After Hugo Bock turned down the offer, Strauss expressed his displeasure that no German publisher had wanted his works (which were among the most important in the Aibl catalogue) and that he had had to settle for an Austrian firm's taking them over.[8] This probably explains Strauss's decision never to give the Vienna-based Universal-Edition any new works during his lifetime. (All of his compositions previously published by Aibl were, however, reissued under the Universal imprint.)

Before he began to use the Fürstner firm exclusively for the five groups of songs from op. 46 to 51 [excluding op. 50], Strauss was able to interest Bote & Bock in the orchestral songs of op. 33. In addition to later printing the songs of opp. 56 and 67, they were the party responsible for the creation of op. 66, the satirical *Krämerspiegel*. After agreeing to publish the *Symphonia domestica* (op. 53) and the six songs of op. 56, Bote & Bock convinced Strauss to reserve for them his next group of songs as well. Their demands may have been a contributing factor in the composer's refraining from song-writing for almost twelve years after 1906. Always concerned for the composer's rights and privileges—in both copyright and performance—Strauss decided firmly against entrusting any more works to Bote & Bock. Thus the possibilities narrowed, and Adolph Fürstner (1833–1908), head of the firm bearing his name, took over as Strauss's principal publisher. Fürstner issued eight of the operas (from *Feuersnot* to *Die schweigsame Frau*), much choral and instrumental music, and several groups of songs (opp. 22, 31, 46, 47, 48, 49, 51, 68, 69, and 71).

Strauss's business and personal dealings with the Fürstner family were mutually beneficial. Their initial contract of 1900 practically guaranteed the composer an annual income; when the option for renewal came in 1903, Strauss turned it down because he did not want to feel compelled to produce for his publishers.[9] Both this decision and the unsatisfactory outcome of the obligation to Bote & Bock provide not only strong arguments against Strauss's composing merely for financial gain but also a good defense against critics such as Ernest Newman, who charged him with creating merchandise, not music.[10]

In 1913, Otto Fürstner (1886–1958), son of Adolph, opened a branch of the publishing house in Paris in order to secure longer copyright protection for Fürstner's composers, among whom Strauss was a major figure. At that time, German copyright protection lasted only thirty years beyond the author's death, while in France a copyright was valid for fifty years after his death. The Fürstners further promoted Strauss's career by helping to get performances of his works in France (until their materials and documents were confiscated in World War I) and by issuing his music with covers of higher artistic quality and more interest than those of Aibl. (For examples of Fürstner's illustrated covers, see Illustrations 1–4.) In Germany, Otto Fürstner served for many years on the board of directors of the Genossenschaft deutscher Tonsetzer (of which Strauss was in 1898 a founding member) and worked with Strauss to assure composers of protection for their works and rights. When the political situation in Germany forced Otto to leave the country, he established Fürstner Ltd. in London and continued to be successful with the publication and sale of Strauss's music. His German interests were looked after until 1950 by the Berlin firm of Johannes Oertel, who became the publisher of Strauss's last four operas. During World War II, Fürstner was forced to sell the rights for certain countries to a number of works in his catalogue. He chose Boosey & Hawkes, under the leadership of Ernst Roth, for the assignment of many of Strauss's lieder.[11] After Otto Fürstner's death in 1958, the firm was continued by his wife, Ursula, who cooperated with Boosey & Hawkes in the 1964–65 publication of the four-volume *Gesamtausgabe der Lieder.*

Regardless of who the publisher was, the first editions of Strauss's lieder sometimes (and second editions almost always) included singable English translations of the texts, the majority prepared by John Bernhoff, Paul England, or Constance Bache. Other reprints sometimes added or substituted French, Italian, or Russian translations. The initial edition of a group of songs was often comprised of versions for high, medium, and low voices. If only one version was at first printed, by the time a reprint was needed the other voice ranges were issued as well. Although Strauss wrote the majority of his songs for high voice, many of the manuscripts he prepared for his publishers include his own indications of suitable transpositions (which were then carried out by the engraver, probably without intermediate manuscript copies). Strauss determined the transpositions separately for each song, not for the entire opus. The transpositions he suggested for op. 47, for example, have nos. 1, 4, and 5 a major third lower, no. 2 a half step lower, and no. 3 a whole step lower.[12] Whether for high, medium, or low voice, almost all editions gave the voice in the treble clef. Except for one youthful song, *Soldatenlied,* Strauss did not write his vocal parts for lieder in the bass clef again until the orchestral op. 33, nos. 3 and 4 (1895–96).

Illustration 2

Cover of Strauss's op. 46 (Berlin: Fürstner, 1900).

Illustration 3

Inside cover of Strauss's op. 46, no. 1 (Berlin: Fürstner, 1900).

Illustration 4

Cover of Strauss's op. 68, no. 4 (Berlin: Fürstner, 1919).

At first Aibl issued the songs of opp. 10 and 19 in two volumes (*Hefte);* each *Heft* of op. 10 sold for 1.80 marks, each of op. 19 for 1.50. Upon Strauss's insistence Aibl began to publish subsequent songs individually as was, the composer reminded Spitzweg, the practice of other publishers (Rahter and Fürstner included).[13] According to listings in *Ernst Challier's grosser Lieder-Katalog* supplements, in the 1890's the prices of Strauss's individual songs ranged from .60 marks for some of the shorter songs in opp. 15 and 17 to 3.00 for the longer works in op. 33. Reprints of the most popular Strauss songs in some or all voice ranges followed at approximately eight- to twelve-year intervals.

Since op. 10 appears to have been one of his more widely known collections, its publishing history can be considered representative of other well-liked songs as well. The songs in op. 10 were completed on 12 November 1885 (13 November if the ninth song, which remained unpublished until recently, is included).[14] The earliest extant letter from Strauss's correspondence with Spitzweg concerning Aibl's publication of op. 10 dates from 5 January 1886. The eight songs were first issued in two volumes of four songs each in 1887 (plate numbers 2602a–d and 2602e–h), for high voice with German text only.[15] The prints examined for the present study show that in 1897 op. 10 was re-issued, again in two volumes, but with German and English texts and in versions for both high and low voice. After having taken over the Aibl firm, Universal-Edition reprinted the songs individually in 1907, added a version for medium voice in the same year, and again reprinted them in 1912. The 1907 publications were newly copyrighted, and renewal of the copyright was claimed in 1925.[16] By this time, all the songs in op. 10 (along with all those in opp. 15, 19, 21, 22, and 56) had appeared in a first American edition, James Huneker's *Richard Strauss. Forty Songs* (Boston, 1910). In addition, many of them—especially the ever popular *Zueignung, Die Nacht,* and *Allerseelen* (op. 10, nos. 1, 3, and 8)—had been transcribed for piano solo and other instrumental media.

In 1912 Universal-Edition issued in four volumes (each available in versions for high, medium, and low voice) all of Strauss's songs that had originally been published by Aibl. The forty-three lieder included are not presented in chronological or numerical order in these volumes, nor does the arbitrary arrangement seem to have a musical or poetic justification. Later additions to this series include volumes 5 through 10/11, each devoted to a single opus: 15, 17, 33, 41, 43, and 56 (the last group in the double volume 10/11). At about the same time another multi-volume *Lieder Album* was issued (in versions for high and low voice) by Fürstner.[17] Three of these eight volumes are devoted to reprints of single opus groups, while the five others include opp. 46–49 in an inexplicably strange order.

Strauss himself was responsible for determining the numbering of songs within an opus. With the exception of op. 10, the order in which the songs appear in the *Stichvorlagen* (the manuscript copies from which the engraver worked) is retained in the publications. Since most of the songs were to be published separately rather than as groups, and since the order in which they were composed is seldom reflected by the numerical sequence in the opus, little importance should be attached to the order within groups, except in the case of a few "cycles" (see Chapter II, p.26). Thus the random order of publication of his songs in the Universal and Fürstner collections probably did not concern Strauss. In fact, the songs may have been so arranged in an effort to conform to his ideas about lieder programs and to prevent singers from feeling that an entire opus ought to be performed as a song cycle. In his own lieder performances with his wife Pauline and other singers, Strauss usually presented a selection of songs from different groups. He aimed at variety rather than unity—and consciously emphasized the diversity of expression in his lieder, an aspect of them that he felt his detractors ignored. A list of songs performed at a typical Strauss *Liederabend,* this one held in Brunswick in late October 1908, is enumerated by Alan Jefferson: twenty-one songs are divided among five groups on the program.[18] They represent fourteen different opus numbers, none of which was sung in its entirety. Op. 21, nos. 2, 3, and 1, were sung together (in that order), but no other adjacent selections are from the same opus. (For examples of other varied programs which Strauss accompanied, see Table 6 and Illustration 9 in the present study.)

Between the turn of the century and World War I, other Strauss anthologies—both large and small—appeared in Munich (some intended for the foreign, especially French, market) and in foreign cities (among them Budapest and New York). These numerous reprints are evidence not only of the great popularity and widespread appeal of Strauss's songs, but also perhaps of the attempt to summarize or finalize in print a genre which both the composer and the musical world in general appeared to be abandoning. This view is supported in the evaluations of Strauss's lieder writing by such authors as Ernest Newman and Henry T. Finck, who assumed that they were discussing a completed *oeuvre* to which the composer would not add.

Performance of the Lieder

The performances by Strauss and his wife—thoroughly discussed in Chapter VI—are our best evidence that his lieder were heard throughout the musical centers of Germany and elsewhere in Western Europe, as well as being available in editions there. During the Strausses' concerts in America during 1904, they received favorable reviews and often performed songs a second time ("da capo") for their enthusiastic audiences. Announcements and reviews of other performances of Strauss's lieder in America prove that some of the songs were well known to concertgoers by 1904. The composer-accompanist-conductor's concert programs with other singers on tours through major European cities are also documented. During the 1890's the songs were performed by various singers both in *Liederabende* and at orchestral concerts; in the latter, either piano or orchestral accompaniments were provided. After the turn of the century, it was considered aesthetically more pleasing to include only orchestral songs in orchestral concerts. As more composers wrote orchestral songs or arranged their own and other composers' piano accompaniments for orchestral forces, orchestral lieder came to be heard more frequently than the operatic arias that had often appeared in orchestral concerts of the late 1800's. At the same time, *Liederabende* with works by a variety of composers continued to be popular.

An early example of a "Strauss marathon" was presented in Vienna by the well-known baritone Franz Steiner, who sang all of the composer's songs in recitals during January and February 1920.[19] Presumably, Steiner gave a complete cycle of all songs published with opus numbers from op. 10 to op. 56, but not the early songs or other miscellaneous occasional songs now catalogued with AV numbers. The total number of songs he performed would have been 112. Although described as an "Aufführungszyklus des gesamten Liedschaffens," these recitals probably did not include the rather new songs in opp. 66–69.[20]

Arrangements, Orchestrations, and Transcriptions

The earliest arrangement of a song from Strauss's op. 10 to appear in print was Max Reger's piano version of *Allerseelen* (no. 8), published by Universal-Edition in 1904. Robert Heger's orchestration of this song dates from the early 1930's, as do his other four orchestrations of Strauss's lieder. Heger's orchestration of *Zueignung* (no. 1) was published by Universal in 1932 and recorded by Gerard Hüsch in 1933.[21] Strauss's own orchestration of the song for Viorica Ursuleac was created much later, on 19 June 1940; it was not published until 1965.[22] Even earlier than Heger, Leopold Weninger and Felix Mottl had both orchestrated Strauss's *Ständchen* (op. 17, no. 2). Mottl's version was published in 1912 by Daniel Rahter, the original publisher of op. 17, and Weninger's (an orchestration in which there is no voice part, this line having been taken over by Violin I) in 1903, also by Rahter. Weninger's orchestration of *Heimkehr* (op. 15, no. 5, this time with the vocal line retained) was published by Rahter in 1920. As Strauss's songs became better known, versions for various sized orchestras—many without the vocal soloist (and thus without the words)—appeared in print. In all cases the original publishers were responsible for the arrangements; work on them was probably done by editors and arrangers who worked for hire, perhaps without Strauss's consent or knowledge. Once these works had been purchased, the publisher was quite free to do as he wished. Issuing the same works in multiple versions was clearly a less expensive proposition for the publisher than extracting new works from the composer, paying a high fee for them, and hoping that they would sell. Universal-Edition issued arrangements of some of Strauss's songs for chamber orchestra in its Vindibona-Collection. Bote & Bock printed a group for chamber orchestra, arranged by A. Wilke, in their Walhalla series; Giuseppe Becce's full-orchestra arrangements of the same songs appeared in their Pantheon series. Leuckart and Challier each issued arrangements of one song, and Fürstner three arrangements of three different songs.[23]

Besides the orchestrations and orchestral arrangements without voice, there have long been other arrangements of Strauss's lieder. Some of these depart quite far from the original idea of the lied, and certainly would have surprised the composer. There are arrangements for female chorus, mixed chorus, male chorus, piano and a melody instrument (usually violin or violoncello, but also trumpet or trombone), symphonic band, and even saxophone quartet and Hammond organ. Five songs in particular have been drawn on most frequently: *Zueignung* (op. 10, no. 1), *Allerseelen* (op. 10, no. 8), *Ständchen* (op. 17, no. 2), *Morgen!* (op. 27, no. 4), and *Traum durch die Dämmerung* (op. 29, no. 1). Performances, arrangements, and recordings all indicate that these five lieder were and have remained Strauss's most-loved songs in the eyes of the musical public.

Like the orchestrations, most other arrangements of these songs were published individually; there are, however, three significant collections of piano arrangements. The first, a group of six songs transcribed for piano solo by Max Reger, was published in 1899 by Joseph Aibl and reprinted in 1904 by Universal-Edition, who issued six additional transcriptions along with the reprint (see Table 1 in Chapter II).[24] All of the transcribed songs are in their original key, and the original accompaniment is quite faithfully retained. German and English texts appear over the righthand staff, which includes the vocal melody, usually as the uppermost voice. The significance of this collection in relation to Reger's own lieder writing is pointed out in Chapters II and III. All of the songs in his collection had originally been published by Aibl; Otto Taubmann made another series of transcriptions for solo piano of songs first published by Fürstner.[25] This collection, published by Fürstner in 1903, consists of twenty-five lieder (all those in Strauss's opp. 22, 31, and 46–49), again with German and English texts, in the original keys, and following quite closely the music of their models. The piano figurations are somewhat more elaborate than Reger's so that the vocal line is often embedded in the texture rather than floating on top of it. Close examination reveals that this is not so much a feature of any changes Taubmann made in the music as it is a result of the nature of the songs themselves. The gradual influence of Strauss's other compositions is at work on these later songs, causing the vocal and instrumental lines to become interwoven. The melodic motives shared by piano and voice provide the structural elements of these lieder just as other motives form the basis of his tone poems and operas. Some critics, in fact, have gone so far as to consider Strauss's treatment of the voice in such passages as more instrumental than vocal.[26]

The third set of piano transcriptions, by no less a virtuoso than Walter Gieseking, likewise remains faithful to the original songs. Gieseking's *Ausgewählte Lieder. Richard Strauss. Freie Bearbeitungen* (Berlin: Fürstner, 1923) includes arrangements of five songs which were originally published by either Fürstner or Rahter. Gieseking's main additions are extensive phrasings, fingerings, and other performance directions.[27]

None of the piano transcriptions examined for this study is a fantasy or improvisation on the songs in the grand manner of Liszt, Thalberg, Tausig, or other nineteenth-century keyboard virtuosos. In considering the orchestrations against a nineteenth-century background, it appears that they reverse the earlier trend of making available symphonies and operatic excerpts in piano reductions for performance in the home. In the early twentieth century, lieder formerly intended for the home or other intimate surroundings came to be heard in large concert halls with full orchestras and other ensembles. Having the songs available in as many editions as possible was clearly to the publisher's financial advantage and insured the performance of these works in one medium or another.

Recordings of the Lieder

At the same time Strauss's lieder were being made available in various printed versions, the new recording industry was beginning to provide performances of them for a wider public. The first documented recording of one of his songs is appropriately that of *Zueignung*. This is a cylinder recording made in 1898 by Anton van Rooy, who was among the earliest of all singers to make recordings.[28] Strauss himself accompanied Heinrich Schlusnus and Robert Hutt in recordings of his lieder in the early 1920's. Recordings taken from the Österreichischer Rundfunk programs in 1942 include his accompanying of lieder sung by Anton Dermota, Lea Piltti, and Maria Reining. As an orchestral conductor, he led Julius Patzak and the Vienna Philharmonic in four lieder, recorded during a concert. In addition, Strauss's renditions of the accompaniment alone for three songs (*Zueignung, Allerseelen,* and *Traum durch die Dämmerung*) have been preserved, each in two different keys.[29]

By 1970, the year in which Dietrich Fischer-Dieskau's nine-record album of 134 songs by Strauss was released, every one of the composer's 138 lieder for voice and piano that had been published during his lifetime was available in at least one recorded version. Robert Craft appropriately labeled Fischer-Dieskau's monumental undertaking "a barometer of the Strauss boom"; other new recordings of the songs continued in the 1970's. The most complete international discography of Strauss's lieder, that of Morse and Norton-Welsh in RSB, no. 5, lists a total of 80 recordings of *Morgen!* between 1899 and 1972. It is followed closely by *Ständchen* with 79, *Zueignung* with 78, *Traum durch die Dämmerung* with 76, and then *Allerseelen* with 53. Shortly after Anton van Rooy made his

Zueignung cylinder, three of these favorites appeared in 1899 recordings, with the first recording of *Allerseelen* following in 1903.[30]

Even now, however, there are still no recordings of some of the *Jugendlieder* or of a few occasional pieces from Strauss's later years. Of the fifteen lieder originally written with orchestral accompaniment, the two in op. 44 remain unrecorded, while *Das Thal* (op. 51, no. 1) and the three Hölderlin hymns of op. 71 have been recorded only as private undertakings. The orchestrated versions of five songs originally written with piano accompaniment are still unavailable.[31] As Robert Craft laments, some of these songs contain "virtually unknown orchestral music"; good orchestral writing from a master of the orchestral palette remains unheard because of all the songs with orchestra only the *Four Last Songs* are performed with any regularity.[32] Meanwhile, new issues of the *Four Last Songs* continue: they were recorded in 1974 by Gundula Janowitz and in 1975 by Leontyne Price; in 1976 Lisa Della Casa's 1953 recording was re-released; Monserrat Caballé's interpretation can be heard on the Erato label. The latest artist to record the set is Kiri Te Kanawa (with Andrew Davis and the London Symphony Orchestra, Columbia Masterworks 76794).

Although some of Strauss's own orchestrations are not yet included in the discography, some of the orchestrations by other composer-conductors are represented. Two of Robert Heger's orchestrations (*Heimliche Aufforderung* and *Ich trage meine Minne*) and Mottl's *Ständchen* are conducted by Strauss along with his own orchestration of *Morgen!* in the Patzak concert mentioned above. To have programed these orchestrations and permitted the recording, Strauss certainly must have approved of them. In his correspondence, conversations, or the writings of his contemporaries are almost no references to his opinions about or reactions to any of these recordings, performances, or arrangements of his music. In a rare example of a reference to one of the arrangements, he is said not to have approved of Mottl's orchestration of *Ständchen* because it made more popular a song he already considered too well known. His comments do not include, however, any statement on the quality of Mottl's orchestration or on his attitude toward such alterations by someone other than the original composer. It seems unlikely that he would have objected to such work in view of his own creation of cadenzas for a Mozart concerto (K. 491), keyboard reductions of chamber and orchestral works, orchestrations of lieder by Beethoven and Ritter, editions of Gluck's *Iphigénie en Tauride* and Mozart's *Idomeneo,* and the other works now catalogued as AV 183–92 ("Bearbeitungen fremder Kompositionen").[33]

Recent Publications of and about the Lieder

In the years since Strauss's death—and even more so since the revival of interest brought about by the celebration of his centenary in 1964—

there have been new discoveries of lieder manuscripts, new publications of songs in facsimile and engraved editions, and frequent appearances of new biographies and other books as well as recordings. An Internationale Richard Strauss-Gesellschaft was formed in Berlin shortly after the composer's death. Its purposes were to hold international meetings and seminars, to encourage performances and publications of the composer's works, to compile a comprehensive bibliography, and to collect all pertinent letters, scores, and other memorabilia for the Richard Strauss Archive in the Strauss home at Zoeppritzstrasse 42, Garmisch-Partenkirchen, Bavaria. After several years of disagreement among the leadership, the society was dissolved in 1970. The *Mitteilungen* they published from 1952 to 1969 (IRSGM, nos. 1–52) continued up to the final issue to report on performances, new publications, and recordings. Their articles and reviews were usually brief but contained valuable information, often in the form of reminiscences or letters to and from poets, publishers, conductors, and singers. Almost immediately after the dissolution of this society, a successor was established at the Vienna State Opera, also under the name Internationale Richard Strauss-Gesellschaft. The new society's *Blätter* (nos. 1–12 published between June 1971 and December 1978) have concentrated less on current news or short reports; instead each issue has been devoted to a major work or genre, or to a collection of correspondence.[34] *Blatt* no. 5 (August 1974) is an issue concerning Strauss's lieder; it contains the Morse and Norton-Welsh discography and my brief essay "Richard Strauss and the Performance of His Lieder."[35] As part of the society's annual meeting in Salzburg during August 1974, Norton-Welsh gave the premiere of *Wer hat's gethan?*, the recently rediscovered ninth song of op. 10. *Wer hat's gethan?* entered the Strauss discography in 1975.[36] The youngest Strauss society is the Richard-Strauss-Gesellschaft München e.V., established in 1977 for the purpose of research, publication, performance, and recording. Under the leadership of Wolfgang Sawallisch, President, and Franz Trenner, Principal Editor, the society has begun publishing monographs, correspondence, and catalogues by and about Strauss. It aspires to the eventual establishment of a Richard-Strauss-Institut in Munich.

Recent developments concerning Strauss's manuscripts include those mentioned in Chapter IV: the acquisition of the *Stichvorlage* for op. 10 by New York's Pierpont Morgan Library, the announcement of the inclusion of Schumann-Heink's manuscript of *Notturno* (op. 44, no. 1) in the Carl Haverlin/Broadcast Music Inc. Archives, and the transfer of manuscripts from the firm of Fürstner Ltd. to the Staatsbibliothek and the Städtische Musikbibliothek in Munich.[37] The acquisition by the Pierpont Morgan Library of part of the Robert Owen Lehman collection, housed there since 1973 as the "Lehman Deposit," includes the original manuscripts for the piano versions of op. 27 and the orchestral score of op. 27, no. 4, as well as some important instrumental works. The orchestral manuscripts of op. 68, nos. 1–5, have passed from Strauss's heirs via

Eugen Antosch to Musikantiquariat Hans Schneider, where, at last report, they remain.[38]

Strauss's lieder manuscripts are from time to time for sale:
Schneider's *Katalog Nr. 194 . . . 1. Teil,* for example, offers a four-page
autograph of the early lied *Waldesgesang* (AV 55) for 7500 German
marks (ca. $3,000).[39] Since Schneider does not give the source from which
he obtained this manuscript, it is unclear whether or not it is the dated
clean ink copy formerly owned by Dr. Eric Fiala of Vienna, of which a
photocopy provided the basis for the GL edition. Evidence in favor of its
being Fiala's is provided by the fact that two other works formerly owned
by him are offered on the subsequent pages of Schneider's catalogue. In
addition, although Schneider says there are a few tiny variants from the
printed edition, his facsimile of the last page of music (on his p. [7])
reveals no substantial variants except at the right edge of the second
system, where either the manuscript or a copy thereof was trimmed too
close and three notes of the accompaniment cut off. The only other tiny
variants concern notational details (stemming, beaming, etc.) that would
naturally have been normalized by the editor or engraver. On the other
hand, the description of the manuscript in Asow, p. 1170, argues against
Schneider's offering being Fiala's copy. The editors of Asow as well as
Schneider list the manuscript as two sheets (title page and three pages of
music); the Asow description of the paper calls it sixteen-lined folio size,
while Schneider's facsimile (greatly reduced) shows three systems of three
lines each, laid out for vocal/piano music.

Facsimile editions published recently include the original piano version of *Morgen!* as well as the short score of *Im Abendrot.* The latter first
accompanied articles by Joachim Herrmann in 1959 and 1964, then in
1967 was issued separately.[40] Schneider has produced facsimile editions of
Wir beide wollen springen, AV 90 (in 1968), and *Wer hat's gethan?,* AV
84A (in 1974). In addition, facsimiles (usually of selected pages from
autographs) have appeared in catalogues such as Schneider's or those for
exhibitions as well as in books by Grasberger, Schuh, and others.

Modern editions published after the centenary *Gesamtausgabe der
Lieder* include *Wer hat's gethan?,* printed with the facsimile mentioned
above, and the collection *Nachlese. Lieder aus der Jugendzeit und Verstreute Lieder aus späteren Jahren,* edited by Willi Schuh (London:
Boosey & Hawkes, 1968), which forms a sort of supplement to the GL.
In addition to reprints of twenty-six songs found in GL III, NL contains
three early songs, one short (five-measure) Goethe setting from 1930, and
three early song sketches.[41] One of the three early songs, *Der Spielmann
und sein Kind,* is the earliest known example of an orchestral (or perhaps
orchestrated?) lied by Strauss.[42] Its orchestral version, in manuscript at
the Strauss Archive, has yet to be published. As of this writing, the only
other Strauss lieder known to be extant but unpublished are *Malven* (see
Chapter IV, n. 7) and the unfinished sketches listed in Appendix B of the
present study.

Since 1964, several collections of Strauss's correspondence have been published: these include the voluminous *Briefe* edited by Grasberger, a fourth edition of Hofmannsthal correspondence, and letters to and from Willi Schuh, Ludwig Thuille, Ludwig Karpath, and Ernst Roth. Strauss biographies have proliferated, especially English language ones, including those by Norman Del Mar, Alan Jefferson (two), Michael Kennedy, and George Marek. Except for Del Mar, who concentrates more on the works than on the life of the composer, these authors devote rather little attention to the lied. Jefferson's *The Lieder of Richard Strauss,* the only monograph to date dealing exclusively with the lieder, discusses forty-seven of the songs in some detail. For the most part, Jefferson chose the same songs about which much has already been written. Along with recording and performing artists, he has neglected here opp. 22, 26, 33, 43, 47, 51, 66, 67, 69, 71, 77, and most of the later occasional pieces. Rather than present the songs in chronological order or by vocal type (lyric, declamatory, coloratura, etc.), Jefferson has divided them into groups according to such text topics as songs of love, sentiment, and seasons and times of day. There are also brief chapters on Strauss's milieu, Strauss as composer and performer, and the early songs. The appendices do not take into account the most up-to-date information available as of their writing, and are full of inaccuracies. Del Mar's appendices are somewhat better, but like Jefferson's are constructed from sometimes inaccurate secondary sources rather than from any firsthand knowledge of the manuscripts.

Jefferson's three books and Marek's *Richard Strauss. The Life of a Non-Hero* recall Ernest Newman's early Strauss biography: each author has several negative opinions to voice, especially where money, Pauline, and the Nazis are concerned. As is the case with Newman, neither writer has been able to overcome his prejudices in order to provide a lucid, objective evaluation of the lieder. Willi Schuh's recently published *Richard Strauss. Jugend und frühe Meisterjahre. Lebenschronik 1864–98* (Zurich, 1976) certainly does Strauss and his works more justice. This is the first volume in Schuh's "authentic" and complete study of Strauss, who designated Schuh, one of his closest friends in later years and a prolific writer on his works, as his "official" biographer. It is to be hoped that Schuh will devote attention in the remaining volume(s) to Strauss's sketches for incomplete works, especially in the years just after 1900. The two sections on lieder in the present volume, "Strauss und die Dichter seiner Lieder" and "Das Liedschaffen" (pp. 445–74), do not treat the sketches.[43]

If the present rate of publication of works on Strauss continues, bibliographic control of the sources may become nearly impossible. The bibliography begun by Oswald Ortner and intended to cover all monographs and articles relating to the composer from 1882 onward has progressed slowly. Part I (1882–1944), listing well over a thousand items, was begun by Ortner and completed by Grasberger for publication in Strauss's centenary year. Part II (1944–1964), edited by Günter Brosche and published in 1973, covers over seventeen hundred titles. A supplement to Part II lists an additional thirty-five books that appeared between 1965 and 1972; comprehensive coverage for these years will presumably follow. Writings specifically about the lieder represent only a very small portion of the titles listed (in Part II some forty titles, as opposed to over seven hundred for the operas).

Bibliographic control over Strauss's own works will also require constant updating as manuscripts are discovered and sold or sketches identified. Although the editors of the thematic catalogue have not announced their intention to issue supplements on a regular basis, the catalogue is already in great need of correction and updating. Since it was in preparation for over three decades, from Asow's first efforts in 1942 to the appearance of the end of the last volume in 1974, a section of *Corrigenda et Addenda* was essential. The *Corrigenda* remedy a number of errors (though hardly all, even failing to correct obvious typographical errors) found in the previous 1,634 pages. The *Addenda* include new citations for four musical works, one arrangement, ten fragments, and eleven prose writings by Strauss. These are assigned AV numbers with letter suffixes so that they can be keyed into the appropriate chronological order, which in itself suggests the possibility of future revisions of the catalogue. To the *Addenda* should now be added the twenty-seven unfinished works listed in Appendix B of the present study. Since these sketches cover only the vocal and choral works, they may represent only a small portion of the hitherto undiscovered works that were abandoned by Strauss before their completion.

II

THE POETS AND POETRY OF STRAUSS'S LIEDER

It has often been stated that Strauss's choice of poems to set to music seldom included the type of poetry selected by the better-known lied composers who were his predecessors or contemporaries. Although this claim is perhaps true for some of his settings—of poems by Felix Dahn (1834–1912), John Henry Mackay (1864–1933), Otto Julius Bierbaum (1865–1910), Count Adolf Friedrich von Schack (1815–94), and the other poets he drew on in the 1880's and 1890's—it is on the whole a misleading generalization. In many cases, Strauss did choose texts by poets who enjoyed some vogue at the time and who were not neglected by other composers. A list of the poets whose works were set by Strauss would have many names in common with similar lists for Schumann, Brahms, Reger, Pfitzner, and other lesser known composers. Strauss's decision to use the same poets and the same types of poetic expression as other composers reveals his attitude and taste just as much as does the coincidence of settings of the same poem by two or more composers. The latter is actually of greatest interest for the specific purpose of comparing the settings, even if—as is often true—no influence from one to another can be traced.

At least two factors contribute to the fact that Strauss's lieder on the same poems set by other composers have not been recognized as such. First, his settings originated too late in the century to be indexed in *Ernst Challier's grosser Lieder-Katalog* (Giessen, 1885) or other nineteenth-century catalogues; further, they appeared too late in the history of the lied to be considered by some twentieth-century writers as belonging to this Romantic tradition.[1] Second, some of Strauss's songs—those lacking opus numbers and falling outside the repertoire of his well-known lieder—are early works and later "occasional" songs, most of which remain largely unheard and undiscussed today. A third possible explanation for the lack of recognition of texts used by several composers is that sometimes Strauss or the others created their own titles for the songs (rather than using the poet's title or the first line, if the poet did not have a separate title), and thus complicated the identification of identical poems.

With the exception of certain poems from the folk tradition or imitations thereof (including Dahn's poetry in op. 21) and the Shakespeare and Goethe songs in op. 67, very few of Strauss's songs use the first words of their text as the title. In the majority of his lieder, Strauss retained the poet's title. Among the exceptions are Hermann von Gilm's *Habe Dank*, which became *Zueignung* (op. 10, no. 1); Richard Dehmel's *Lied der Mutter*, which Strauss retitled *Wiegenliedchen;* and Dehmel's *Venus Mater*, which the composer changed to *Wiegenlied*. These Dehmel verses present a good example of the confusion that composers' titles can cause. Dehmel's *Lied der Mutter* (first line "Bienchen, Bienchen wiegt sich im Sonnenschein") from his collection *Der Kindergarten* was set by Max Reger as *Wiegenlied*, op. 43, no. 5 (ca. 1899–1900), then by Strauss as *Wiegenliedchen*, op. 49, no. 3 (1901). *Venus Mater* ("Träume, träume du mein süsses Leben!") from Dehmel's *Die Verwandlung der Venus* was used for Strauss's *Wiegenlied*, op. 41, no. 1 (1899). In the works of Reger it appeared with the title *Träume, träume du mein süsses Leben. Wiegenlied*, op. 51, no. 3 (1900), while Hans Pfitzner retained the original title in his op. 11, no. 4 (1903). Other examples include Rückert's (and Strauss's) *Vom künftigen Alter* (AV 114), called by Schubert *Greisengesang;* and Henckell's *Winterweihe*, set by Strauss as *Winterweihe*, op. 48, no. 4, but by Schoenberg as *In diesen Wintertagen* (the first line of the poem). Alban Berg's unpublished early song *Nachtgesang* actually has the same text as Strauss's *Nachtgang*, op. 29, no. 3: Berg himself wrote the title incorrectly.[2]

Reliance on song titles for identification of the texts has caused confusion in the opposite direction as well, not only for the casual observer, but also for the cataloguer. An example of misleading coincidence is the folk poem *All mein Gedanken* and Felix Dahn's poem of the same title. The former, which is found in sources as early as the Lochamer Liederbuch, was set by Brahms in his collection of *Deutsche Volkslieder;* the latter appeared as Strauss's op. 21, no. 1, and Reger's op. 75, no. 9. The seeming coincidence results from Dahn's having used incipits from folk poems in his collection *Schlichte Weisen*, from which this poem comes. Beyond the incipits, the two poems continue differently:

> All mein Gedanken, die ich hab,
> die sind bei dir,
> du auserwählter einger Trost
> . . .
>
> (Volkslied)

> All mein Gedanken,
> mein Herz und mein Sinn,
> da, wo die Liebste ist,
> . . .
>
> (Felix Dahn)

The other four Dahn poems from *Schlichte Weisen* set by Strauss in op. 21 could also be confused with actual folk poems because of their incipits.

Except for the noticeable absence of Eichendorff and Rückert, the list of well-known poets whose works Strauss set in his youth reads not unlike a list of Schumann's favorite poets.[3] The writers represented in

Strauss's *Jugendlieder* (songs dating from 1871 to 1884) were mostly Romantics active between 1790 and 1860; they include Burns, Byron, Geibel, Goethe, Heine, Hoffmann von Fallersleben, and Uhland. Schumann had set works by all of these poets, and Brahms by four (Goethe, Heine, Fallersleben, and Uhland). Wolf later used the poetry of the same four as Brahms, along with Strauss also choosing from among the Romantics poems by Lenau and translations by Geibel. The works of some of these poets (Burns, Byron, Heine, Schiller) served the young Strauss as the inspiration for only one song. Other names appeared more often: Geibel (nine early songs), Goethe (three), Fallersleben (seven), and Uhland (five). Strauss set certain poets' works not only in his youth, but also in later years, when they provided words for either songs or choral works; these include Goethe, Heine, Lenau, Schiller, and Uhland. Although he drew on Goethe's *West-östlicher Divan* several times, notably absent from Strauss's lieder texts are verses from *Wilhelm Meisters Wanderjahre* and *Faust*. *Wilhelm Meisters Wanderjahre* inspired lieder composers from Zelter—whose five settings appeared in 1795, the very year in which the novel was published—and Reichardt to Wolf and later composers, while *Faust* proved a favorite of opera, symphonic, and vocal composers of several nationalities throughout the nineteenth century.

At this writing, at least eighty-five poems set by Strauss, or more than one third of the poems appearing in his songs and incomplete song sketches, are known to have been used by at least one other composer. There exist at least ninety settings of one poem, Goethe's *Gefunden,* which is the basis of Strauss's op. 56, no. 1 (dating from 1903). The only currently available printed list of lieder texts set by Strauss and other composers is that of Alan Jefferson in *The Lieder of Richard Strauss,* Appendix D (p. 125). Jefferson includes only twenty-one of Strauss's songs, omitting all of the Goethe settings as well as several others.[4] His listing of settings by Pfitzner and Reger is fairly complete, but not without errors in opus numbers, dates of composition or publication for all three composers, and the omission of one song. No mention is made of the interesting fact that Reger also transcribed a number of Strauss's lieder for solo piano and that many of these poems were the very ones that Reger chose to set subsequently.[5] Table 1 lists the twelve transcriptions, of which seven of the poems were reset by Reger. A comparison of some of these lieder appears in Chapter III. Six of the seven other poems used for lieder by both composers (but not to our knowledge arranged for solo piano by Reger) appeared in Strauss's version first. Jefferson's list includes a single song by each of four other composers, Schubert, Berg, Schoenberg, and Conradin Kreutzer, and two each by Eduard Lassen and Frederick Delius. Certainly the handful apiece of settings by Loewe, Schumann, Brahms, Zelter, and Robert Franz should have been included. There are also noteworthy settings of one or two of the same poems by Wolf, Berlioz, and Mendelssohn in the nineteenth century, and by Ernst Pepping and Lukas Foss in the twentieth.

Table 1

Reger's Transcriptions of Strauss's Lieder
and His Own Lieder on the Same Texts

Max Reger. *Richard Strauss. Ausgewählte Lieder. Piano Solo. (Mit beigefügten deutschen und englischen Text)*. English translations by John Bernhoff. Volumes I (Munich: Joseph Aibl, 1899; reprinted Vienna: Universal-Edition, 1904) and II (Vienna: Universal-Edition, 1904). (Also available as twelve separate numbers.)

Title	Strauss's op. no. and date	Reger's op. no. and date
(Volume I)		
1. *Breit über mein Haupt*	19,2 (1 February 1888)	----
2. *Morgen!*	*27,4 (21 May 1894)	66,10 (1902)
3. *Traum durch die Dämmerung*	29,1 (4 May 1895)	**35,3 (1899)
4. *Ich trage meine Minne*	32,1 (26 January 1896)	----
5. *Glückes genug*	37,1 (8 February 1898)	* **37,3 (1899)
6. *Meinem Kinde*	*37,3 (7–8 February 1897)	*43,3 (1900)
(Volume II)		
7. *Allerseelen*	10,8 (31 October 1885)	----
8. *All mein Gedanken*	21,1 (12 February 1889)	75,9 (1903–04)
9. *Du meines Herzens Krönelein*	21,2 (7 April 1889)	76,1 (1909)
10. *Cäcilie*	*27,2 (9 September 1894)	----
11. *Heimliche Aufforderung*	27,3 (22 May 1894)	----
12. *Nachtgang*	29,3 (7 June 1895)	51,7 (1900–01)

*   Also orchestrated by the composer.
** Reger also transcribed his own settings of these songs for harmonium, in which version they were published by Aibl in 1903.

Admittedly, many of the other composers who set the same poems as Strauss are scarcely—if at all—known today, and even Strauss would not have been aware of their settings. There is no solid evidence to show that he paid attention to or was influenced by the settings of other composers that would have been available to him. (A possible exception might be provided by the work of his boyhood friend, Ludwig Thuille, with whom Strauss is known to have exchanged not only ideas for early compositions but actual manuscripts as well.) Strauss's published correspondence and other writings contain no references to other settings of the texts he chose. Except for the youthful performances given at Aunt Johanna Pschorr's in the 1880's, he probably had rather little contact with other composers' lieder. As an accompanist and a conductor of orchestrated lieder, Strauss almost always performed his own songs. His programs with his wife did not include lieder by other composers.

There are isolated references in Strauss's published letters to the performance of songs by Lassen, Schubert, Brahms, and Ritter (all with piano), and by Mahler (with orchestra), but never are these works mentioned in relation to their composition or their texts. Even these references to the songs are insignificant, since they may have been a result of the singer's choice of repertoire and not of Strauss's choosing at all. Strauss and Mahler, who knew and promoted each other's works, did not set any of the same poems; the closest link between their lieder texts is that both used poems by Rückert and verses from *Des Knaben Wunderhorn*. Although it has been claimed that Strauss consciously avoided texts that had been set by other composers, this opinion is hard to support without evidence that he was indeed familiar with the lieder of other composers.[6]

Strauss's choice of poets for his mature lieder (beginning with op. 10 in 1885) reveals a distinct change from his earlier preference for late eighteenth and early nineteenth-century poems of the type set by Schubert, Schumann, and his other predecessors. Strauss was not alone in favoring the lesser poets of his day over the early masters: Brahms as well chose to set poems by his contemporaries, some of whom also happened to be his friends. Among Brahms's poets, works by the following are known today through his music: Franz Kugler, Adolf Frey, Karl Candidus, Josef Wenzig, Ludwig Hölty, and Carl Lemcke. Both Brahms and Strauss set poems by Adolf von Schack, Detlev von Liliencron, August von Kopisch (Strauss in choruses, not lieder), and Karl Simrock (Strauss only in his translation from *Hamlet*). Most of these poets would be forgotten today were it not for their musical settings.

Jack M. Stein laments the indiscriminate choice of poetry on the part of composers (including Schubert, who "composed anything in sight"):

One of the saddest trials for the literary-minded lover of nineteenth century songs is the seemingly irresistible urge great composers had to write beautiful settings of

poems which weren't worth the effort. Brahms and Richard Strauss especially seem
not to have known a good poem from a poor one, and the genius they lavished on the
settings of mediocre poetry or worse, such as Daumer's "Wie bist du meine
Königin"; . . . Hermann von Gilm's "Zueignung"; and his "Allerseelen"; or Otto
Julius Bierbaum's "Traum durch die Dämmerung" has given these poems an immor-
tality they scarcely deserved.[7]

At nearly age sixty, Brahms set his first and only poem by Liliencron
(1844–1909), one of the new generation of poets on whose works
Strauss was to concentrate. Other younger members of this generation—
born up to the 1860's and thus Strauss's contemporaries—whose works
were set by Strauss include Dehmel, Bierbaum, Mackay, Heinrich Hart,
and Emanuel von Bodmann. Other composers also began to use their
poems, along with writings by contemporaries whom Strauss did not
draw on, such as Hart's brother Julius, M. G. Conrad, Wilhelm Wie-
gand, Karl Bleibtreu, Peter Altenburg, and Stefan George.

Strauss's selection of lieder texts has an even closer relationship to
the poems chosen by Reger and Pfitzner than it does to Brahms's choices.
All three set verses by Dehmel and Carl Busse. In addition to his settings
of fourteen of the same poems as Strauss, Reger used the same poets for
other lieder: Christian Morgenstern, Gustav Falke, Felix Dahn, Emanuel
Geibel, Hermann von Gilm, Bierbaum, Uhland, and Rückert.[8] Although
he strove to set poetry of high quality, Reger at the same time preferred
little known poems, especially if they had not yet been used in other
musical settings.[9] Reger admitted freely that he was often rebuked for his
choice of texts.[10]

Pfitzner and Strauss set four identical poems, and each also set
verses by Liliencron, Hermann von Lingg, C. F. Meyer, Uhland, and
Eichendorff. Toward the turn of the century some of these poets were
extremely popular among lieder composers. By 1903, for instance, it was
estimated that poems from Liliencron's many volumes had been used in
three thousand compositions. The long list of composers who used his
works includes Strauss, Reger, Pfitzner, Thuille, C. Ansorge, S.
Hausegger, O. Nodnagel, and many others less well known.[11]

The common poetic inclinations of Strauss and Ludwig Thuille were
strongest in their early years, when both set poems by Karl Theodor
Körner, Karl Stieler, Geibel, and Lingg. Some of Strauss's letters to
Thuille mentioned songs he was working on or had just completed.[12] On
22 July 1875 Strauss teased Thuille with the comment

> I recently found in a sort of supplement to Heine's *Buch der Lieder* a wonderfully
> beautiful sad poem. I won't tell you its name lest you grab it away from me.[13]

In the same letter he stated that he would next examine Lenau's works,
which he thought looked very promising.[14] It would be interesting to
know if either of the young composers set any of the same texts with the
knowledge of the other's work. I have found no index to Thuille's early
unpublished works, some manuscripts of which are apparently owned by

the Strauss Archive. Strauss and Thuille did not remain in close contact after about 1885, and it is possible that they did not know each other's settings of Gilm, Dehmel, Bierbaum, Liliencron (a personal friend of Thuille's), and other contemporary poets.

As an aspect of Strauss's selection of poems for lieder, it is worth noting that he never attempted to write his own texts, as did his contemporaries Mahler (*Lieder eines fahrenden Gesellen*), Pfitzner, and Theodor Streicher, or predecessors such as Peter Cornelius.[15] Since Strauss created his own libretti for *Guntram* and *Intermezzo* (each for a special reason—in the former because of its Wagnerian origins and in the latter because it was a very personal family statement) and with Clemens Krauss had a hand in creating the libretto for *Capriccio,* one might expect at least a few original song texts. But even for the occasional lieder, such as birthday, nameday, wedding, anniversary, and thank-you gifts, he searched for an appropriate pre-existent text. For the pointed and satirical *Krämerspiegel* (op. 66), Strauss found a poet, Alfred Kerr, who would incorporate into his verses the message he wished to communicate as well as the names he wanted to cite. The composer's own comments on the creation of his lieder will perhaps explain why he became inspired to write a lied and why he would not have attempted to create his own verses:

> I open a book of poems; I turn over the leaves casually; one of the poems arrests my attention, and in many cases, before I have read it over carefully, a musical idea comes to me. I sit down and in ten minutes the complete song is done.[16]

This may appear a gross exaggeration of his technical powers with the pen; Strauss continues, however, with an admission that a new work is not always ready for the public in such a short time. If the right poem for his mood is not to be found, he nevertheless pursues the composition, setting

> . . . any random poem that happens to be at all suitable for a musical setting—but the process is slow, the result is artificial, the melody has a viscid flow, and I have to draw on all my command of technical resources in order to achieve something that will stand the test of self-criticism.[17]

Anticipating that the reader would wonder why he did not create his own verses in such a situation, he continues

> That would be the right thing to do. But in my case the word-poet and the tone-poet are not in such immediate correspondence, the tone-poet being in technical skill and routine too far ahead of the word-poet.[18]

Some critics have suggested that Strauss never outgrew a youthful habit of indiscriminately choosing poems to set to music without much concern for their merit. His sister recalls an example of this: the boy once wanted to write a song for their Aunt Johanna for Christmas. Rather than search carefully for an appropriate text, he merely took whatever he found upon first looking in a book.[19] On the other hand, she—along with Oscar Bie

and others—claims that later he did become more selective, once remark-
ing of a poem "I can't set this to music; it doesn't interest me."[20] Strauss
made another statement of this sort in a letter to his father shortly after
completing op. 10. Having been pressed by his family for a group of songs
to be dedicated to Aunt Johanna, Strauss explained why they were not
forthcoming:

> Also, I cannot promise my Aunt the songs before I have found proper texts. For it
> no longer works for me—as it did before—to sit down and write a song without a
> feeling for it.[21]

These statements and others made later in his lifetime make it clear that
Strauss was guided in his selection of poets and poems not by his admiration of high literary values but by the desire to create a mood and to
express through his music the poetically conceived ideas. As he remarked
to Joseph Gregor, in the modern lied (presumably including his own)

> the poem gives birth to the melody—not, as so often happens even with Schubert,
> that the melody is poured forth over the verse without the cadence of the poem
> coming out quite right.[22]

Strauss's statements about his approach to lieder composition help
to explain why he did not devote himself to intensive study of a poet's
works, as Wolf did with Goethe, Mörike, and Eichendorff, or draw extensively on one source, as Schumann did on Heine's *Lyrisches Intermezzo*. Although Strauss read extensively and broadly throughout his life
(particularly poetry, literature, philosophy, and history), he did not try to
discover the deepest meanings of the poems he chose to set. Perhaps this
is why some of his word painting and musical descriptions of the text
sound to some so hackneyed and obvious rather than fresh and subtle.
Except for the four Dahn poems set as op. 22, the twelve Kerr verses in
op. 66, and Shakespeare's Ophelia lieder in op. 67, none of Strauss's
collections is based on a poetic cycle. Op. 66 is the only group of songs to
have musical continuity of the sort often expected in the song cycle. As a
result of Strauss's working method, songs of widely differing character are
found in many of his groups. In some (e.g., op. 33) the individual songs
are for voices of different ranges; in op. 68 and other groups, the poet
(and thus the singer) takes the part of a man for some songs and of a
woman for others. Even where a single poet's works form the basis of an
opus, the verses may come from different collections (Strauss, however,
may have found them together in an anthology) and encompass a variety
of subjects, moods, and styles of expression. Op. 68 in particular demands a versatile voice capable of both elaborate coloratura and broad
sustaining power. That the composer did not usually conceive of an opus
of songs as a sacred entity is reflected in his own lieder programing, his
desire that the songs be published separately rather than in opus groups,
and his selection of songs from different groups for orchestration.
    Oscar Bie expressed the opinion that as Strauss's stature as a musi-

cian grew his taste in lieder texts improved. He was, after all, quite young, not yet twenty-five, when setting the poetry of Gilm, Schack, and Dahn in opp. 10, 15, 17, 19, 21, and 22. By 1890 he had abandoned their precious, dilettantish verses in favor of contemporary poets whose works were more likely to endure (Liliencron, Bierbaum, Dehmel, Mackay, and others) and earlier poets whose writings had already proved themselves (Goethe, Uhland, Klopstock, Lenau, Rückert, the anonymous poets represented in *Des Knaben Wunderhorn*, etc.). Walter Thomas argues that Strauss consciously chose poets of quality for his opp. 67, 68, and 69 because—after his sometimes indiscriminate use of second-rate verses in the past—he felt the need to redeem himself in the eyes of Hofmannsthal and the world at large.[23] Although not all critics would agree with Bie that Strauss's text choices improved, there is evidence to support the view that his critical faculties were sharpened by his work in the operatic field and by his increasing concern over the relationship of words and music. If he did not always apply his knowledge and high standards to the lied, it is perhaps because of the purpose for which many of the later songs were written, occasions which required certain texts (or at least certain types of texts) which he may have found with an eye to their appropriateness rather than their quality.

In a statement that could well be applied to Strauss, the art critic and aesthetician Susanne Langer points out that the poem was for lied composers the means rather than the end, the raw material used to achieve the finished song:

> The poetic creation counts only in a song in exciting the composer to compose it. After that, the poem as a work of art is broken up. Its words, sounds and sense alike, its phrases, all become musical material . . . the words have been musically exploited, they have entered into a new composition and the poem as a poem has disappeared into the song.[24]

In choosing his verses for their expressive quality, Strauss was not concerned with their perfection as poetic statements. Bierbaum's *Traum durch die Dämmerung* for example, is a rather mediocre little poem. Yet, it provided the inspiration for one of Strauss's most successful works, a song that has remained popular from the time of its appearance in 1895 up to the present day. According to an oft-repeated anecdote, it is also one of the lieder which he wrote down spontaneously.[25] Once during an informal evening at the Villa Wahnfried, after Strauss had accompanied this song, Cosima Wagner remarked on how comical the phrase "das samtene Band" ("the velvet ribbon") was in its context of jasmine, stars, fields, and twilight. Strauss's reply was that he chose the poem for that very reference.[26] If this indeed was his reason for setting the poem, it appears that this phrase of the text was responsible for a principal vocal melody in the song. The simple stepwise line that includes these words describes them musically; it traverses a ninth and is richly harmonized.

Other examples in Strauss's works of less than the best poetry are the sickeningly sweet, drippingly sentimental "flower" verses of Felix [called by one of Strauss's biographers "Infelix"] Dahn. Although they are just too precious and dated when read, they achieve some merit in Strauss's setting of op. 22. (The decorative cover of the first edition of op. 22, included here as Illustration 1, is well matched to the verses within.) As Del Mar points out, here the poems ought not to be judged apart from the music: "The sole issue is whether or not Strauss's imagination was captured."[27] Although seldom performed and not available on commercial recordings until 1970, the songs in this opus have been considered a success by some. It is reported that Tilly Koenen sang the second in the group, *Mohnblumen,* "so charmingly that it always had to be repeated."[28] A French critic found the poem of no. 4 (*Wasserrose*) so foolish that he omitted the text from his music examples and expressed surprise that Strauss would have consented to waste his talent on such impoverished work. For him, this song and the others he singled out for their originality and expressiveness had musical interest that was not cheapened by their texts.[29]

Strauss's decision to set such poems as these verses by Bierbaum and Dahn might be questioned by those who recognize his excellent choice of librettists for the operas, the demands he made on these writers, and his concern for the relation of music and poetry in opera, especially as seen in *Capriccio* and the Prologue of *Ariadne auf Naxos.* A seeming inconsistency of values can be explained here by pointing out the difference of the textual-musical relationship in the lied and that in opera. In the former, an already existent poem is chosen to be set to music. In Strauss's own admission, it in fact inspires the music. His creative process is usually a relatively short one, with the musical material going through few large-scale changes from the first mental image to the final version (see below, pp. 124 ff.). The composer's approach to opera is entirely different since the libretto is designed from the start to be set to music. In *Der Rosenkavalier* in particular many changes in the libretto were made for musical reasons alone.[30] A further contrast between lied and opera is the importance of dramatic elements in the text of the opera; the lied, with its smaller dimension and duration, need not have any overtly dramatic content.

In spite of Strauss's claims to receiving his inspiration from the poetry, there often seems to be another influence on the musical success of his songs—one of more importance than the quality of the poetry or the appeal of the subject matter. This is the influence of the artist who would bring the written notes to life. Pauline, of course, was the inspiration behind many of the songs that remain the best known today, those between op. 27 and op. 56. The voices of the dedicatees of other songs certainly served as some impetus; a notable example is Elisabeth Schumann, for whom op. 68 was created and to whom op. 77 was dedicated. The strength of such influences is acknowledged by Ernst Krause:

His most beautiful songs were written for his young wife, or later for particular performers who were in close contact with his art.[31]

An example of the close connection between the poetry and the persons who served as his inspiration is found in op. 37. Written at various times between June 1896 and April 1898, the six songs in this set were dedicated to Pauline on the occasion of their son Franz's first birthday, 12 April 1898. Their texts—drawn from five poets of varying abilities—are cited by Gysi as examples of Strauss's unrefined literary taste. With the exception of *Herr Lenz* (no. 5, but the earliest song written, in 1896), all of the poems celebrate loyalty, love, marriage, and family. Strauss obviously searched for these poems with more concern for their subject matter than for other considerations. Although he has been accused of taking his texts where he found them, in his defense it must be said that the first three songs in op. 37 are far from neglected by performers, critics, and compilers of anthologies. Strauss returned more than once to this opus for material to orchestrate: nos. 2–4 were orchestrated in 1943, 1897, and 1933, respectively. No. 3, *Meinem Kinde,* was performed innumerable times by the Strausses as one of the three "Mutterlieder" (a term used early on by Schuh and others but not, I think, original with the composer) which Richard orchestrated especially for Pauline because of the appropriateness of their texts.

Strauss's attitude toward lieder and opera and the different ways in which he sought texts to compose in the two genres are to some extent echoed in the personal communication (or lack of it) between composer and librettist (poet). In contrast to the larger bodies of extant letters to and from his librettists Hofmannsthal, Gregor, and Zweig, the letters from Strauss to the poets of his lieder texts are few in number.[32] Even where there was communication between Strauss and those poets who were his contemporaries, he reveals almost no information about the composition of lieder; still fewer letters to Strauss from these poets are to be found.[33] Furthermore, what correspondence there is rarely relates to the compositional process or to the handling of the text; rather, it concerns projected larger works, commentaries on or reviews of completed compositions, or occasions for performance. One suspects that few other letters were written—the poet and composer did not really work together like librettist and composer, and Strauss rarely had time or energy for maintaining friendships through personal letter-writing.[34] The only occasion on which he wrote to poets before setting their verses was to solicit texts; he never asked for advice or interpretive help and never announced his intentions in advance. His approach to writing songs as referred to above would not have been consistent with such action, nor would it have allowed time for correspondence before the completion of a setting.

No letters to or from poets represented in Strauss's *Jugendlieder* are known; indeed, few of these poets were still alive at the time their poems occupied the young composer.[35] In these years, his interest in living poets rarely lasted beyond a single song. Two notable exceptions are Hoffmann von Fallersleben (1798–1874), two of whose poems Strauss set in 1873 and five of which attracted him after the poet's death; and Emanuel Geibel (1815–84), seven of whose poems Strauss drew on for lieder in a single year, 1879. The works of both Geibel and Fallersleben were perhaps introduced to him through the lieder of Schumann, Franz, Brahms, and other composers whose songs he heard and performed at Aunt Johanna Pschorr's musical afternoons.

There is in print a small selection of letters to or from poets represented in Strauss's mature songs, i.e., those songs published with opus numbers. There is little indication, however, of how many letters may have passed between them or of what personal contacts may have preceded or followed the extant letters. Whether or not Strauss knew Count Adolf von Schack, the poet of lieder in opp. 15, 17, and 19—and a fellow citizen of Munich—is not recorded in letters or biographies or by Strauss's contemporaries such as Steinitzer. The name of Felix Dahn, author of the texts of Strauss's opp. 21 and 22 (all of which settings were completed by 1890) appears only later, and then in connection with an entirely different subject.[36]

In the mid 1890's when Strauss turned to the writings of contemporary poets (some of whom were considered quite "modern" and even "revolutionary"), he became especially interested in a Berlin-based group that included the brothers Julius (1859–1930) and Heinrich (1855–1906) Hart, Carl Busse (1872–1918), Gustav Falke (1853–1916), Richard Dehmel (1863–1920), John Henry Mackay (1864–1933), Detlev von Liliencron (1884–1909), and Liliencron's cousin Karl Henckell (1864–1929). Some of these men, proclaiming themselves followers of the late Max Stirner (alias Kaspar Schmidt, 1806–56), an anarchistic Berlin writer of whom Mackay wrote a biography, had been trying since the late 1870's to establish a literary counter-movement. That Strauss met some of them on his trips to Berlin in 1890 (in February, as guest conductor of the Berlin Philharmonic) and in 1894 (in January, to visit Hans von Bülow) is quite possible, though undocumented. When he took over Bülow's post as director of the Philharmonic (upon the latter's death, 13 February 1894), Strauss was able to acquaint himself more with their works, ideas, goals, and personalities. Certainly by this date he knew some of these writers personally—along with Frank Wedekind and Graf von Sporck, members of the group whose poems he did not set.[37] The lieder in eleven of seventeen of the song groups Strauss composed between op. 27 (1894) and op. 56 (1906) draw on poems by one or more of the poets in this literary circle.

If the published correspondence is taken as an indication, Strauss was probably best acquainted with Henckell and Dehmel. A long letter to the composer from Henckell on 12 December 1895 thanks him for sending a copy of *Ruhe, meine Seele!* (op. 27, no. 1), Strauss's earliest Henckell setting, and praises the expressive musical rendering of the poem.[38] Henckell reports having asked his publisher to send Strauss other volumes of his works (unfortunately, neither works nor collections—several of which were then in print—are named in the letter), hoping that he might leaf through them and find other texts to arouse his creative powers. *Ruhe, meine Seele!* was followed by three more Henckell settings in op. 32, four in op. 48, and one each in opp. 49 and 56. The texts of these may well have come from the volumes Henckell sent. Later on, in March 1899, Henckell sent Strauss a copy of his *Gesammelte Gedichte. Grosse Ausgabe* (Leipzig, 1898) with a personal inscription.

Further correspondence between Strauss and Henckell concerned not the composition but rather the performance of lieder. On 16 March 1901, Henckell wrote to Strauss about the possibility of an evening program similar to one he had heard in Munich and of which he enclosed the program and review. The program consisted of a poet reading his words and a singer, accompanied by the composer, interpreting them in song.[39] At that time, Strauss's settings of eight of the poet's texts were in print. Henckell proposed a date for the following winter (perhaps with the hope that more of his poems could be set by that time), and suggested the possibility of including Pauline, "the most splendid interpreter of your lieder." Henckell appears quite humble in admitting that he is not a professional public speaker, but merely a poet reading his own works; a recent lecture tour to various cities, however, had been so successful that he wished to combine his good fortunes with those of the Strausses' popular *Liederabende*. Unfortunately, neither Strauss's reply nor any further plans for such an evening have been found to date. The closest event to it is recorded by Strauss in a letter to his parents on 16 March 1902, in which he reports a Sunday gathering of friends at the Strausses' Charlottenburg home. Among those present were Max Schillings, Baron A. von Stengel (to whom Strauss had dedicated *Junggesellenschwur*, op. 49, no. 6), Henckell and his wife, and the baritone Karl Scheidemantel. Scheidemantel, to whom Strauss had dedicated *Nächtlicher Gang* (op. 44, no. 2) and who frequently sang the composer's lieder, on this occasion performed his *Pilgers Morgenlied* (op. 33, no. 4) and had to repeat it because of uproarious applause.[40] At least one of Strauss's lieder on Henckell's texts (*Kling!*, op. 48, no. 3) was included in the collection of his poems entitled *Mein Lied* (Berlin, 1900); the publisher of Henckell's four-volume *Gesammelte Werke* (Munich, 1921) announced the inclusion of lieder by Strauss and others, but did not carry through with his intentions.[41] The Henckell volumes in the Strauss Archive reveal that Strauss not only leafed through them but also checked off certain poems, entering his ideas for tonalities next to particular lines or stanzas.[42]

Strauss composed settings for Dehmel's poems in opp. 31, 37, 39, 41, 44, and 49. According to Willi Schuh, Strauss's interest in Dehmel began shortly after 20 December 1895, the date on which Dehmel sent to the composer a copy of his as yet unpublished poem *Stiller Gang*. Ten days from the date of the letter, Strauss set it as his op. 31, no. 4.[43] Strauss's first meeting with Dehmel may not have been until 23 March 1899, the day on which he definitely met Hugo von Hofmannsthal for the first time.[44] The poet learned of Strauss's *Mein Auge* (op. 37, no. 4) almost immediately upon its completion; Strauss began the song on 13 April 1898 and signed the manuscript at the end 16 April 1898. Knowledge of the setting's existence prompted a letter from Dehmel (dated 22 April 1898) begging Strauss not to set any more texts of his such as this dreadful one. Vehemently rejecting his early poem as one that made him physically ill whenever he remembered it, the poet urged Strauss to throw the first edition of his *Erlösungen* (the source of *Mein Auge*) into the fire and to replace it with the second edition, which he enclosed with the letter.[45] Dehmel inscribed the book with a seven-line poem "An Richard Strauss"; in later editions it appeared under different titles ("Das Eine," "Sprachgeheimnis," "Dichtersprache").[46] He also requested in the letter that Strauss send him a copy of the lied so that he could try to patch up the text somewhat, but without requiring that the music be rewritten. The letter continues with a discussion of a proposed (but never completed) ballet, *Lucifer* (AV 226), based on Dehmel's *Lucifer. Ein Tanz- und Glanzspiel* (published in Berlin in the next year). Perhaps among the poems new to the second edition of *Erlösungen* were the four set by Strauss in op. 39 shortly thereafter, between 2 June and 8 July 1898. Upon their publication, Strauss always sent copies of his settings to Dehmel or had his publisher send them. One song, *Befreit* (op. 39, no. 4), caused Dehmel to express himself on Strauss's treatment of his poem and about the interpretation of it in general.[47] Since he knew that Strauss's song was frequently performed, and since people who had heard it often asked him about the meaning of his poem, Dehmel explained the various possible interpretations. Strauss's music, he felt was a bit weak for the text, even if it appealed to most people more than the composer's more complicated lieder. Strauss was apparently not pleased with Dehmel's slightly negative criticism; the last of his eleven Dehmel settings (op. 49, nos. 1 and 3) predate the article's appearance. Some personal contact, however, was maintained during the following decade.

Strauss was acquainted with Otto Julius Bierbaum while both were still living in Munich. The only published letter to Strauss from Bierbaum, written in response to a letter from Strauss that is not published, concerns ballet plans. No songs are mentioned.[48] The first of the composer's six Bierbaum settings was created in 1895, a year after his arrival in Berlin, where Bierbaum was then active. Among them are two of his best liked songs, *Traum durch die Dämmerung* (op. 29, no. 1) and *Freundliche Vision* (op. 48, no. 1). His last Bierbaum setting, *Freundliche Vision*, dates from 1900. After composing *Freundliche Vision* on 5 October 1900, Strauss wrote to the poet that he hoped his song would form a companion piece to the "already unbelievably popular" *Traum durch die Dämmerung.*[49] He probably intended to create other settings after this one, since he made marks beside several poems in his copy of Bierbaum's 1901 *Irrgarten der Liebe.*[50]

Bierbaum's negative review (in the 1903 *Allgemeine Zeitung*

[Munich]) of Strauss's *Taillefer* (op. 52), a setting for chorus and orchestra of an Uhland ballad, may be responsible for his abandoning the poet. In fact, where Strauss refers to "the dilettante" Bierbaum and his cutting, sarcastic review, he is careful not to mention his settings of the poet's verses or his earlier acquaintance with and admiration of Bierbaum.[51] The effect these reviews by Dehmel and Bierbaum had on Strauss may even have contributed to his gradual loss of interest in the lied from 1902 and finally his abandonment of it in 1906. From a few other statements by and about the composer, he appears to have taken a rather defensive attitude toward his songs.

No written communications between Strauss and Falke, Hart, Mackay, Busse or Liliencron survive in Grasberger's or other Strauss collections. Of these poets' correspondence, only Liliencron's is available in a modern edition.[52] Other "moderns" with whom Strauss became associated by setting their texts include Christian Morgenstern (1871–1914), Emanuel von Bodmann (1874–1946), Anton Lindner (1874–1929), Alfred Kerr (1867–1948), Anton Wildgans (1881–1932), Joseph Weinheber (1892–1945), and Hermann Hesse (1877–1962). The single letter to Strauss from Morgenstern available in print concerns a symphonic poem based on the poet's verses.[53] In this letter of 12 June 1895, Morgenstern claims that his poems are probably too complex and too weighed down by his mythological orientation to be set to music. He was surprised (but nevertheless pleased) that Strauss found inspiration in his writings.[54] Some four years later, Strauss found his *Leise Lieder* suitable for setting as a song (op. 41, no. 5); the same somewhat mystical but not overly difficult poem was also set by Max Reger and Hugo Kaun. The poet's evaluation of these settings would be interesting to discover.

The young poet Emanuel von Bodmann wrote to Strauss on 16 June 1896, after learning that the composer had set his poem *Herr Lenz* (op. 37, no. 5, composed on 9 June 1896). Having heard from one Herr Langen that Strauss was interested in setting to music his *Gesang der Priesterinnen des Apollo,* he sent along the manuscript of it and another poem, *Unterwegs,* which he thought suitable for composing.[55] Strauss set only one poem by the Viennese writer Lindner, his *Hochzeitlich Lied* (op. 37, no. 6), in 1898. Lindner later offered to prepare Oscar Wilde's *Salome* as a libretto for Strauss. Finding the subject of *Salome* more attractive as it stood than in Lindner's proposed re-working, Strauss decided to retain Wilde's original version.[56]

Strauss's association with Alfred Kerr (born Alfred Kempner) began when the composer sought texts for his *Krämerspiegel,* op. 66. The initial contacts between Kerr and Strauss may have been in person; they are, unfortunately, not documented. Only letters dating from the period after the texts' completion are available today. In a letter of 8 March 1918, with which he sent the finished texts to Strauss, Kerr stated that he wanted no fee for his work and that Strauss should not hesitate to indicate any alterations he required.[57] Kerr sent along a copy of his 1913 poetry collection *Die Harfe,* hoping that Strauss would set some of his more serious works to music, as well as the short satirical verses he had contrived especially for *Krämerspiegel.* Subsequent letters concern the publication and first private and public performances of op. 66, but do not hint at the possibility of further lieder. Another topic discussed at this time was the possibility of collaboration on a comic opera, *Peregrinus Proteus* (AV 257), to be based on Wieland's *Peregrinus.*[58] In 1921 Strauss met with Kerr in Garmisch to discuss the opera, then asked Hofmannsthal's advice about Kerr—rather cautiously, since Kerr had once attacked an article that praised Hofmannsthal's librettos. Although Hofmannsthal's reply indicated his willingness to be a collaborator (unknown to Kerr), all correspondence over the opera broke off in 1922. When Kerr had parts of the libretto published in 1927 (S. Fischer-Verlag, *Almanach,* XL, 135–41), he declared himself rather doubtful that anything might come of the plans.[59]

As with Bierbaum and Dehmel earlier, Strauss turned against Kerr after the appearance of Kerr's article "Richard Strauss, menschlich," *Die neue Weltbühne,* XXXIV (1938). In a letter to Willi Schuh, Strauss called his former collaborator a witless joker without journalistic taste who quarrels tactlessly.[60] Kerr did not cease to be fascinated with the composer's music or his personality: he wrote that the *Krämerspiegel* music was provocative, gracious, full of surprises, and very dramatic. Later, he modeled a character on Strauss (complete with Bavarian dialect and a reference to *Salome*) in his libretto *Chronoplan,* for which his wife, Julia Weismann Kerr, composed the music.[61]

Strauss's correspondence with Anton Wildgans offers a unique view of the composer's working methods, one that seems to contradict his statements to Hausegger and Gregor about how he received inspiration for a song. After having set Wildgans' *Austria* (op. 78) for male chorus and orchestra in 1929, Strauss solicited other poems from his Viennese colleague for the specific purpose of composing lieder for Lotte Lehmann to sing in a sound film.[62] Having looked through Wildgans' published works without finding anything ideal, he wondered if some other poems might be lying forgotten in the drawer. Two of the poems in the collection might, Strauss thought, be possibilities, but poems written to meet his needs as a composer would be even better:

> . . . "Akkord" (with its happy refrain) and also "Einsamkeiten" (with its simple line and musical high points). Create for me a few simple lieder [texts] in this manner: expressions of nature with "spiritual" emphasis in the manner of *Traum durch die Dämmerung, Freundliche Vision,* or *Du bist die Ruh,* etc., without many philosophical side-steps.[63]

Strauss would hardly have made such requests of a poet in the last decades of the nineteenth century. After the success of his operatic collaborations—and after becoming used to working with the authors of his texts—he was clearly more eager to have just the right text created for him, rather than spend his time leafing through volumes and awaiting inspiration. Of a setting of the first poem mentioned above, "Akkord," nothing is known. (It does merit a listing in Asow, as part of AV 266, but it has not yet turned up in a sketchbook.) The other verse Strauss was considering may have been the one he set as *Durch Einsamkeiten* (AV 124), an a cappella male chorus composed in 1938.[64]

Although no lieder appear to have resulted from his communications with Wildgans, Strauss did not give up on trying to find suitable poems by modern writers. In 1938 he asked Joseph Gregor for a list of Austrian poets whose works had not yet been given good musical settings. Gregor immediately returned a list, but Strauss did not set verses of any of the poets on it.[65] Shortly thereafter, the two artists became deeply involved in the issue of *primo la musica, poi le parole/primo le parole, poi la musica* which resulted in *Capriccio.* Thus occupied, Strauss did not set any more lieder until after completing the opera in 1941.

During preparations for the first performance of *Capriccio,* Strauss returned to the lied as he had done on many similar occasions, i.e., after the completion of a large composition. As in other instances, these lieder were created as occasional pieces: for the fiftieth birthday of the Viennese poet Josef Weinheber in 1942, he created two lieder on unrelated texts from Weinheber's collections *O Mensch, gib acht* and *Wien wörtlich.* In the following year, Weinheber sent the composer one of his latest poems in the hope that it might serve as the basis of a composition.[66] Neither Weinheber's letter nor other sources identify the poem he was sending; it may well have been his "Wie sing ich dich, du vielgeliebte Stadt?" which Strauss at one point considered using for the final chorus in his unfinished symphonic poem *Die Donau* (AV 291). As with the Morgenstern poem a half century earlier, here Strauss's inspiration from a poem resulted in a composition of greater scope than the lied. No other Weinheber settings by Strauss are extant. The poet honored Strauss with a dedicatory eightieth birthday poem which first appeared in the Vienna Philharmonic's program book on 11 June 1945.[67]

A few years later, Strauss got to know the works of Hermann Hesse, perhaps through their mutual friendship with Willi Schuh. I have found no documentation on whether or not Strauss ever corresponded with or met Hesse in person; none of Schuh's writings on Strauss suggest a personal acquaintance. The composer's interest in Hesse was great, as indicated by the number of poems he marked for possible setting in the copy of Hesse's *Die Gedichte,* second edition (Zurich, 1942), given to him by a friend. Of all the poets whose works Strauss set, Hesse lived the longest into the present century. In the *Four Last Songs,* the juxtaposition of his three poems with one by Eichendorff (almost a century older than Hesse) provides a fitting summary of the various generations of poets from whom Strauss drew his inspiration.

In addition to poems by his contemporaries and earlier nineteenth-century Germans, a few of Strauss's lieder are based upon texts from the following categories: Oriental and pseudo-Oriental writings, translations of Chinese, English, Italian, and Spanish poems; and folk ballads or "art" poems based on the folk idiom. His interest in Greek history and mythology, which resulted in five original operas as well as arrangements of Mozart's *Idomeneo* (1930) and Gluck's *Iphigénie en Tauride* (1889–90), did not extend into the realm of song. Historical and mythological subjects were obviously better suited to dramatic presentation than to the intimate and brief nature of the solo song. In his youth, Strauss made one attempt to excerpt a text from Sophocles' *Electra* and to set it for male chorus with small orchestra, perhaps for a performance at his school.[68]

Oriental poetry and exotic Eastern influences attracted German poets and composers during the nineteenth century. Zelter, Schubert, Schumann, Wolf, Strauss, and hosts of lesser figures set poems from Goethe's *West-östlicher Divan*. Brahms set some of G. F. Daumer's translations of the Persian poet Hafiz, while Strauss drew on Hans Bethge's renderings of the same for his op. 77, nos. 1, 2, 4, and 5. Daumer's translations date from 1846 and 1852 (Brahms's settings, op. 47, nos. 1 and 2, were issued in 1868), while Bethge published his in 1907. The third song in Strauss's op. 77 is based on Bethge's translation of verses from *Die chinesische Flöte*, the same source used by Mahler in *Das Lied von der Erde*. These works by Strauss and Mahler are rather late manifestations (1928 and 1908, respectively) of nineteenth-century German interest in Oriental literatures and Eastern themes.[69] Rückert, a specialist in Oriental philology and a translator of several Eastern languages, was a favorite of both composers. Some of the Rückert texts set by Strauss come from the poet's collections *Persische Vierzeiler* and *Östliche Rosen*, both of which were inspired by Goethe's *West-östlicher Divan*. Strauss's use of several of Rückert's poems in the "Persian ghasel" form will be discussed in the following chapter.

Strauss followed earlier composers—notably Schumann—in choosing to set several English poems in translation. Shakespearean settings had remained popular with German lied composers since the first translations of his works by A. W. von Schlegel and Ludwig Tieck in the 1820's. These translations were used by Mendelssohn, Schumann, Brahms, and Wolf. Brahms wrote his five *Ophelia Lieder* for a performance of *Hamlet* in Prague in 1873.[70] Strauss's *Ophelia Lieder* (op. 67, nos. 1–3), on the other hand, were not written for a performance, nor did he use the same translations. Instead, Strauss used a translation by Karl Simrock.[71] Schumann and Strauss both set texts by Robert Burns, but in different translations (by W. Gerhard and F. Freiligrath, respectively); Schumann, Wolf, and Strauss each used a different translation in setting texts by Byron.[72]

Aside from the above-mentioned translations, Strauss used very few poems translated from other languages, especially in comparison with Schumann or Wolf. At least half of Wolf's lieder have texts translated from other languages, primarily Italian and Spanish. Wolf, however, is the exception among lieder composers; Brahms's works with translated texts, comprising only some five per cent of his output, include mainly folk texts from Eastern European languages. Strauss limited himself not only in language but also in time: except for the fourteenth-century Hafiz poems, *Die chinesische Flöte,* and the Shakespeare settings, he used almost no poems that antedate the middle of the eighteenth century. His only text taken from the Italian is a poem by Michelangelo Buonarroti, which the composer called *Madrigal* (after the section of madrigals in the original Buonarroti manuscript collection in which the poem is found) and set as op. 15, no. 1 (ca. 1885–86, perhaps written after his spring 1886 trip to Italy). Wolf's four Michelangelo settings are in a different translation than that used by Strauss, but the coincidental choice is interesting.[73]

The only Spanish originals drawn on by Strauss were three poems of Calderón de la Barca (1600–81) from his play *El alcalde de Zalamea (Der Richter von Zalamea).* These songs, like Brahms's *Ophelia Lieder,* stand rather outside the lied tradition: they were written for a particular performance of the play and were meant to be accompanied not by piano but by guitar and harp (and an additional harp in one song). Whether these songs were performed in the context of the play is uncertain; one of them was never completed (see Appendix B of this study under [Chispa III]). Strauss totally ignored Geibel and Heyse's *Spanisches Liederbuch* translations (1852), which provided a wealth of lieder texts for many other composers. He did set some of Geibel's poems as a youth, but none with Spanish themes as, for example, Schumann's *Der Hidalgo.*

The final category of sources for Strauss's lieder texts is that of folk song and ballad. Certainly of a different temperament from Mahler or Brahms, both of whom relied heavily on folk-song sources, Strauss turned to traditional folk poetry only rarely. His settings of poems from Arnim and Brentano's collection *Des Knaben Wunderhorn* (Heidelberg, 1806–08) number only four; two other folk-song texts also appear in his lieder.[74] Other reminiscences of folk poetry and even a folkish musical suggestion or two are found in works such as his setting of a poem by Oskar Panizza, *Sie wissen's nicht* (op. 49, no. 5), which he followed with three real folk-poetry settings. On the whole, Strauss set folk poetry much in the manner he used for other poetic works, not altering his style significantly to adapt to their naïveté or simplicity.

Although he could hardly be considered nationalistic, Strauss did at times display an interest in the folk tradition. One need think only of the source of the *Feuersnot* story (a Flemish saga transferred to Munich and full of topical allusions) or the folk-song passages in *Arabella,* for which he studied Kuhač's South Slavic folk song and dance collection.

As with the folk song, Strauss showed his interest in the ballad—a primary source of texts for Reichardt, Zelter, Schumann, and Loewe before him—only occasionally. Perhaps as a mature composer he found the dramatic and narrative aspects of the ballad unsuitable for the type of lied he preferred. After setting a number of early songs with ballad or ballad-like texts (in an episodic form, rather like an operatic scena), Strauss returned to the ballad only a few times. Of significance here are not only the lieder but also the two melodramas, *Das Schloss am Meer* (AV 92, 1899), on a text by Ludwig Uhland, and *Enoch Arden,* (op. 38, 1897), with Alfred Lord Tennyson's text translated by A. Strodtmann. Strauss set another ballad by Uhland, a master of the genre, in *Taillefer,* for mixed chorus, soli, and orchestra, op. 52 (1902–03).[75] Among the lieder, *Von den sieben Zechbrüdern* (op. 47, no. 5)—also based on a ballad by Uhland—is a fine example that deserves to be better known.

Judging from the list of Strauss's songs that have remained the best known over the years, the quality of their poetry has little relevance to their critical and popular reception. Although Jack Stein laments the composer's choice of Gilm and Bierbaum texts in opp. 10 and 29, neither the poems nor their authors' lack of fame have hindered the acceptance of these songs into the repertoire of lieder singers. While Strauss's turning to Goethe and Rückert particularly in the years after World War I (and to Hesse after World War II) has been cited as evidence of his increasing literary discrimination,[76] among the later songs only the *Four Last Songs* are frequently performed.[77] Strauss's own attitude toward his texts as expressed in statements quoted in this chapter prove that the poem was first and foremost a source of inspiration to him as a composer. Many aspects of his handling of the texts he chose will be explored in the following chapter. He would no doubt have agreed with Susanne Langer that the poem is transformed as it becomes one element of expression in the lied. The effect of the poem as poetry is appreciated by the composer at work; once he has created his lied, his audience no longer perceives it apart from the setting. As the Countess declares in *Capriccio,* scene vii, "Alles verwirrt sich—Worte klingen, Töne sprechen." ("Everything becomes entangled: words make music and musical notes speak.")

III

ASPECTS OF TEXT SETTING AND VOCAL DECLAMATION

Poetic Types and Their Reflection in Strauss's Music

From Strauss's own comments about his selection of lieder texts, it would seem that the content of a poem was a more important stimulus to him than its form, meter, or rhyme scheme. Yet he was not unconcerned about these aspects of the poetry he set and probably consciously avoided poems in any strict set patterns. Aside from Rückert's ghasels (defined and discussed on pp. 66–68 of this chapter) and two unfinished sketches employing Italian sonnets by Hebbel and Goethe, Strauss chose texts not bound by complex formulaic structures that might either restrict his choice of musical form or be obscured or contradicted by it. For the most part his lieder have strophic texts, often with musical refrains as well as textual ones. Except for a few of the early songs, he never took the shortcuts of setting all stanzas to exactly the same music or using repeat signs; even the refrains usually have some modifications. Strauss usually set stanzaic poems in freely adapted strophic forms. Several songs are in ternary form, while a few others fall into rondo-like patterns. Through-composed songs make up the remaining category, but even in this large group there are songs with repetitions and variations of previously presented material.

Strauss set a number of narrative poems, including examples of folk poetry and art ballads. Although there are no real dialogues like Brahms's *Vergebliches Ständchen,* several of these lieder have at least one line spoken by a character other than the narrator.[1] Strauss and his editors were not consistently careful about enclosing such lines in quotation marks, and sometimes they are not distinguished musically from the surrounding narration. In one of his settings of poems from *Des Knaben Wunderhorn,* Strauss sets apart by means of rests and contrasting speech-like rhythms the line to be addressed to the narrator's beloved (Ex. 1). The first word of this line is preceded by repeated chords in the accompaniment which recall the "knocking" chords at a similar passage in *All mein Gedanken* (Ex. 2), another of his lieder with such a quotation. In *Himmelsboten* not only the style of declamation at this point but also the unique performance indication *gleichsam wie mit einer Verbeugung* ("almost as with a bow") suggest a separation of the line from the surrounding narration.[2]

Ex. 1, *Himmelsboten,* op. 32, no. 5 (mm. 32–37):

Ex. 2, *All mein Gedanken,* op. 21, no. 1 (mm. 16–22):

In other songs there are, for example, the night wind speaking (*Verführung*, op. 33, no. 1, mm. 32–34) and a nightingale singing (*Vom künftigen Alter*, AV 114, mm. 45–58). Strauss set four poems reminiscent of Schubert's *Heidenröslein* or Mozart's *Das Veilchen* texts in which a flower speaks. Two early Strauss songs, *In Vaters Garten heimlich steht* (AV 64, 1879) and *Ein Röslein zog ich mir im Garten* (AV 49, ca. 1878), have lines for the flower. In the former, Heine's child-narrator quotes both sides of his conversation with the flower, but Strauss does not give the characters distinctive music. Here he does set off the lines with quotation marks; he does not do so in *Ein Röslein*, nor does he differentiate the flower's music. In two later songs based on a similar poetic theme, *Gefunden* and *Ich wollt ein Sträusslein binden*, Strauss breaks the lyrical vocal lines for recitative-like statements by the flowers (Ex. 3a and b). In the latter example, the monotone recitation on "Ach tue mir nicht" gradually yields to lyrical movement, but the section spoken by the flower (mm. 45–68) has slower and more melodically confined declamation than does the surrounding text. An even clearer contrast of characterizations is found in Strauss's *Wer lieben will muss leiden*, op. 49, no. 7; here the two parts of an Alsatian folk poem are set to entirely different types of music. The lonely, weeping young girl's portion (mm. 1–27) is very chromatic and only vaguely anchored in its E minor tonality; when the deceased mother speaks to her from the grave (mm. 28–end), there is a sudden shift to a clear tonic F-sharp major. (The composer uses a similar contrast of dark sounding minor and bright major keys in *Rückleben*, op. 47, no. 3, as the poet, kneeling at the grave, imagines his beloved returned to life.)

In a few of Strauss's earliest lieder, the poetry determined the musical forms and styles. Four songs written between 1873 and 1878 are examples of multisectional dramatic lieder that approach the style of the operatic scena: *Der müde Wanderer* (AV 13), *Der Fischer* (AV 33), *Spielmann und Zither* (AV 40), and *Der Spielmann und sein Kind* (AV 46). In these settings Strauss attempted to capture the mood of each stanza in music (often including vivid musical descriptions of the scene or action) so that the poetic content was responsible for the musical form. The poems are dramatic narratives concerned with the romantic theme of nature and its power over man. Set in a background of pastoral meadows, haunted woodlands, and flowing streams, the themes of these poems and numerous others of their age are lonely daydreams, longing for youth and lost loves, and the tragedy of death. Appropriately for the poets represented—Hoffmann von Fallersleben (1798–1874), Theodor Körner (1791–1813), and Goethe (1749–1832)—the music is in an almost Schubertian idiom. Like others of Strauss's early songs, these four look back rather than forward; their phrase structures are clear-cut and balanced, and their harmonic vocabulary conservative. Their vocal styles range from classical sounding unaccompanied recitative (*Der Spielmann und sein Kind*, mm. 42–49) and dramatic arioso declamation to tuneful, lyrical lines which even include a few examples of Mozartian melodic ornamen-

Ex. 3a, *Gefunden,* op. 56, no. 1 (mm. 12–14):

Ex. 3b, *Ich wollt ein Sträusslein binden,* op. 68, no. 2 (mm. 43–58):

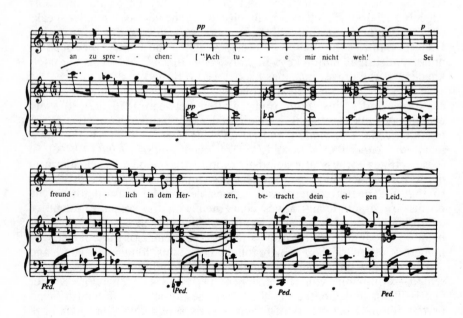

tation. The accompaniments realistically create the sounds of distant bells, turbulent waters, stormy winds, rolling waves, the blind man's fall into a ravine, and the minstrel's zither.

In contrast to these songs in which the style of the music changes dramatically as events are narrated in successive stanzas, there are among Strauss's mature songs pieces in which the piano and/or vocal parts do not reflect the same form or structural divisions as the poetry. Through constant reiteration of one or two ideas, the piano part may unify a song in which the vocal part is completely independent and frequently changing. In some songs, there is a lack of coincidence between vocal and piano phrases or sections, and in a few the voice sounds as if it had been added onto an instrumental composition as a separate layer.[3] *Morgen!*, op. 27, no. 4, is called by Roland Tenschert a song without words because of its formal structure.[4] Here a long instrumental introduction is interrupted just before its close by the voice, which slips in unobtrusively in the middle of the measure and in mid-sentence, ". . . Und morgen wird die Sonne wiederscheinen." (Mackay's poem both begins and ends with ellipsis points.) After a cadence in measure 15, the first fourteen measures are repeated literally with a vocal line now added contrapuntally. For the final two lines of text (mm. 30 ff.) the accompaniment merely supports the recitative-like vocal line with chords, then concludes with a five-measure recall of the introduction.

Although Tenschert claims *Morgen!* to be a unique example of Strauss's letting abstract music (instead of the text) determine form, there are other examples of similar structures among the composer's later songs. In parts of *Krämerspiegel* (op. 66), for example, the vocal line is almost incidental, being clearly subordinate to the development of instrumental motives. As in *Morgen!* there are long passages where the voice is silent.[5] The first two songs in op. 66 concentrate on the etude-like development of their common four-note motive, the fourth on the working out of a fugue. Sections of waltzes and polkas are inserted to contrast with the pseudo-learned contrapuntal style, the voice entering only so that the text can explain the musical references. Strauss was, of course, writing these songs in response to his obligation to the publishers Bote & Bock and had commissioned Kerr's verses as song texts. It is nevertheless tempting to speculate on what he might have created had he turned the same texts and instrumental music into a sort of melodrama instead.

In a few other songs besides *Morgen!* and those in op. 66 the textual and accompanimental sections and phrases do not coincide. The accompaniment of *Blauer Sommer* (op. 31, no. 1), for example, is constructed of five varied statements of a five-measure phrase, the last one extending into a postlude. The harmonic scheme moves down by minor thirds, with successive phrases in the major keys of B, A-flat (=G-sharp), F, D, and B. Five of the eight lines of the poem are divided into three-measure phrases, the others into two, four, and five measures. After the initial entrance by voice and piano simultaneously, none of their phrases ends or begins together. The piano and vocal phrases of other songs are also out of phase, as in *Morgenrot* (op. 46, no. 4), where stanzas two, five, and six begin during the middle of accompanimental phrases.

Strauss did not always plan his ternary songs so that the music of *A'* coincided with the reappearance of the text of *A*. In *Winternacht* (op. 15, no. 2) and *Stiller Gang* (op. 31, no. 4), there is no return of the first stanza as would be expected in the usual *da capo* structure. Instead, the music of the *A* section reappears with the final words of a later stanza. Thus in *Winternacht* a three-stanza text is spread out over a four-section musical form: *A*=stanza 1, *B*=2, *C* and *A'*=3. The recall of *A'* is justified by the sense of the text, but not reinforced by its structural divisions. The lack of formal agreement between voice and piano is of another sort in songs like *Traum durch die Dämmerung* (op. 29, no. 1), *Wiegenlied* (op. 41, no. 1), or *Freundliche Vision* (op. 48, no. 1). In these songs the accompaniment is based on one or two ideas repeated in the manner of a modulating ostinato throughout the lied. The unified accompanimental idea creates a constant musical mood or scene over which the voice independently articulates divisions of the poem.[6]

Many of the lieder Strauss composed in his first thirty years, or up to op. 27, fall into one of the forms—ternary, strophic, or through-composed—that were the common property of his predecessors and contemporaries. Even in some of these songs, however, the influence of his symphonic writing is obvious, especially in the area of motivic development. From his songs of the late 1890's through the *Four Last Songs* there are many examples—particularly in the orchestral lieder—where short, abstract motives (and occasionally pictorial or programmatic ones) rather than sectional contrasts provide the underlying structure. The motives are developed by both voice and accompaniment in op. 77, for example, while in songs such as *Sehnsucht* (op. 32, no. 2) and some of those from op. 46 the two are kept separate. Along with the influence of Strauss's symphonic writing on the piano parts, the effects of his operatic composition are felt in the dramatic vocal lines which often proceed quite independently of the accompaniment. He doubles the vocal line much less frequently than in his earlier songs and often sets up a rhythmic conflict between the voice and its accompaniment. The variety in both accompaniment and vocal line of the orchestral lieder is expanded far beyond that of earlier songs with piano; a single song may contain combinations of arioso, recitative, and lyrical or even coloratura writing. Especially in the orchestral lieder (but also in certain other songs) Strauss increases the length of instrumental passages where the voice is silent so that the total length of a song becomes much greater. The durations of the majority of Strauss's lieder fall between two and five minutes; a few songs in opp. 10 and 21 take even less than one minute. In contrast, the orchestral lieder of op. 44 last approximately sixteen and ten minutes, respectively.[7] *Das Thal* (op. 51, no. 1), all three songs of op. 71, and *Im Abendrot* are other orchestral songs of larger than usual dimensions.[8]

As Strauss absorbed elements of his symphonic and operatic styles into his song-writing technique, he sometimes used the designation "Gesänge" instead of "Lieder." Most of his published song groups with piano accompaniment he called "Lieder"; only three groups were labeled "Gesänge." In each of these three titles, Strauss directed attention to the sources of the poems: *Drei Gesänge älterer deutscher Dichter* (op. 43), *Krämerspiegel. Zwölf Gesänge von Alfred Kerr* (op. 66), and *Gesänge des Orients. Nachdichtungen aus dem Persischen und Chinesischen von Hans Bethge* (op. 77). Only op. 66 can be clearly set apart from his other songs in its treatment of both text and music.[9] Three groups of orchestral songs (opp. 33, 44, and 51) were also entitled "Gesänge." Strauss's designation "Hymnen" for the three orchestral songs in op. 71 probably derives from the title of the first song, *Hymne an die Liebe*. These are not hymns in the religious sense; nos. 2 and 3 are settings from Hölderlin's *Oden*, no. 1 from his very early collection *Gedichte 1788–1793*. Strauss's use of "Gedichte" in place of any of these musical designations for his opp. 10, 21, 22, and 46 appears to reflect only the fact that each of these groups is devoted to the works of a single poet, and not a difference in the importance of the poem or the type of setting it received.[10]

Construction and Style of the Vocal Lines

The styles of the vocal lines in Strauss's lieder can be divided into three categories, declamatory, dramatic, and lyrical. Each of them has parallels in his operatic writing. Regardless of whether they are called "Gedichte," "Lieder," "Hymnen," or "Gesänge," certain songs from various periods in his career contain a mixture of these styles, while others have one style predominantly or exclusively. In the first category, Strauss's declamatory style approaches recitative, with speech-like settings emphasizing the natural inflections of the words. In the early song *Der Spielmann und sein Kind*, the passage mentioned above is actually marked "Recitativo." Strauss has a few other later examples of brief unaccompanied recitative, some of which are given here in Ex. 4a–c. His songs that Max Steinitzer and others designated "Sprechlieder" (as opposed to "Melodielieder") contain examples both of monotone recitation or movement within a confined range and of wide, expressive, and unexpected leaps.[11] Some of the declamatory lines are made up of short, disjunct phrases punctuated by rests; interrogatory lines are especially likely to be set in a *parlando* style. Ophelia's *Wie erkenn' ich mein Treulieb?* and *Sie trugen ihn auf der Bahre bloss* (op. 67, nos. 1 and 3) are particularly good illustrations of this type of declamation. Edward Kravitt describes the disjointed and incoherent ejaculations of the twisted and irregular vocal part in the first song as a rare attempt on the part of a composer to paint a "truly realistic portrait of insanity."[12]

Examples of Strauss's recitative-like declamatory style are found in his operas as well as in lieder, most strikingly in sections of the

Ex. 4a, *Die Verschwiegenen,* op. 10, no. 6 (mm. 32–44):

bleib' mun - - ter nur und hei - ter; die es ge - wusst, sind al - le tot   und

sa- gens nicht mehr wei-ter.

Ex. 4b, *O, wärst du mein!,* op. 26, no. 2 (mm. 14–15):

Ich kann es mei-nem Schick-sal nicht ver-ge-ben.

Ex. 4c, *Heimliche Aufforderung,* op. 27, no. 3 (mm. 29–30):

(leichthin)

ver-ach- te sie nicht zu sehr

Marschallin's and Ariadne's parts. While at work on *Intermezzo*, the composer decided that a number of lines would be better spoken over accompaniment rather than sung. Accordingly, several vocal passages which he had set down in sketch form were replaced in the final version by spoken lines (see below, p. 136). A few years later, he wrote to Hofmannsthal that he had come to prefer spoken lines over monotone *recitativo secco,* which he now considered "not . . . a very fortunate art form."[13] Letters about *Die ägyptische Helena* passed between them with both agreeing that spoken dialogue was sometimes preferable to *Sprechgesang.* In the lieder written after *Die ägyptische Helena* (op. 79, composed in 1924–27)—and already in most of opp. 68 and 69—there are fewer examples of the declamatory style than in earlier songs. A variety of Strauss's other operatic styles are taken over into the later songs, with pure lyricism and broad, flowing lines dominating.

The second of the three categories, the dramatic style, includes arioso passages midway between declamation and lyricism, along with dramatic coloratura. In this style there are wide contrasts of vocal rhythms and ranges, unexpected shifts of style, and sometimes excited emotional outbursts. Strauss achieves an independence of voice and accompaniment—and sometimes rhythmic conflict between them—in his dramatic songs, most of which have accompaniments built around a few motives which he states and then transforms in the manner of his orchestral and stage writings. Del Mar uses the term *Schwung* ("energy," "ardor," or "springiness"), Günther Baum the word *Überschwung* to characterize the dramatic vocal quality of songs such as *Cäcilie* (op. 27, no. 2), *Heimliche Aufforderung* (op. 27, no. 3), *Anbetung* (op. 36, no. 4), and *Morgenrot* (op. 46, no. 4). Other writers have described these songs as effusive, having the qualities of ecstasy, fervor of expression, or even overblown, pompous enthusiasm. The *schwunglich,* "excited" character of such works is created by elaborate, soaring melodic arches, wide ranges, full accompaniments, and occasional melismatic flourishes. Particularly good examples of this style are Strauss's five drinking songs: *Bruder Liederlich* (op. 41, no. 4), *Von den sieben Zechbrüdern* (op. 47, no. 5), *Der Pokal* (op. 69, no. 2), *Schwung* (op. 77, no. 2), and *Erschaffen und Beleben* (AV 106).

Amor (op. 68, no. 5) is the most elaborate and stylized example of ornamental coloratura in all of Strauss's dramatic songs. Its melismatic coloratura is closely related to the operatic style of Zerbinetta's rondo "Als ein Gott kam jeder gegangen," Mizzi's yodeling in *Arabella,* the vocalises of the transformed Daphne, and the elaborate passagework of Aminta, Carlotta, and Henry in *Die schweigsame Frau. Amor* is unique among Strauss's lieder as a predominantly melismatic text setting. Melismas in the songs written both before and after *Amor* are limited to a few significant phrases or important words. In their occasional use of these dramatic flourishes within a smoothly flowing context, opp. 71 and 77, the Rückert lieder of 1929 and 1935, and the *Four Last Songs* stand midway between the second (dramatic) and third (lyrical) categories here under discussion.

By far the largest number of Strauss's lieder—from the simple, conservative songs of his youth to the retrospective *Four Last Songs*—fall into the category of lyrical songs, or "Melodielieder." Among them are *Freundliche Vision* (op. 48, no. 1), *Waldseligkeit* (op. 49, no. 1), and *Ich wollt ein Sträusslein binden* (op. 68, no. 2), which, with their long-lined, gently undulating phrases, have always ranked among his most accessible and popular lieder. Especially for listeners to whom the German lied suggests only Schubert, Schumann, Brahms, and perhaps Wolf, the unity and simplicity of Strauss's lyrical songs are more readily identified with that tradition than are the complexity and variety of his dramatic lieder. A song like *Traum durch die Dämmerung,* of which the melody is based on nothing more complex than scalewise movement and the mood is reminiscent of Schumann's nighttime songs, stands a great distance from the dramatic songs that Philip Radcliffe calls "ponderously turgid," and full of "fidgety and pointless" modulations, with accompaniments that are "rich to a fault."[14] The immediate popularity of op. 48 upon its first publication (see below, p. 170) is attributable to the fact that at least the first four of its five songs are in a simpler, quieter, more lyrical idiom than their predecessors in op. 46 and some of op. 47. Counterparts of these songs can also be found in Strauss's operatic writing: in the Sophie-Octavian duet "Ist ein Traum" at the end of *Der Rosenkavalier;* in the equally Schubertian nymphs' trio "Töne, töne, süsse Stimme" (*Ariadne auf Naxos*); and in Christine's reverie "Ein hübscher Mensch" (*Intermezzo,* close of Act I). The broad, hymn-like style of *An die Nacht* (op. 68, no. 1) or *Durch allen Schall und Klang* (AV 111) can also be found in Strauss's operas, for instance in Bacchus' three-stanza invocation of Circe (*Ariadne auf Naxos*).

In the lyrical songs Strauss varies his basically syllabic declamation with short melismas and other types of ornamentation. Usually he introduces these elaborations for textual reasons, either to illustrate by means of word painting or to emphasize important words more abstractly. His vocabulary of vocal ornaments in the songs includes (besides the melisma) the portamento, appoggiatura, turn, trill, and grace note. The first, portamento, is written with a wavy line into the scores of only three songs; it is probably implied in passages of certain others.[15] Vocal portamento tends to be overapplied in certain singers' performances of Strauss's lieder. Like the ubiquitous rolled chords of some accompanists (the composer himself included), excessive repetition of the device creates an undesirably mannered sound. Strauss writes strong-beat appoggiaturas as a means of emphasizing significant syllables in songs such as *Morgen!* (here the syllables change simultaneously with the resolution of the appoggiaturas). He indicates turns by the usual symbol only a few times, in other passages writing out the turns as part of larger melismas. Likewise, he rarely calls for a vocal trill, except in *Amor.* There are, however, numerous examples of trills in the accompaniment, usually illustrating the text. Except for the early lied *Im Walde,* which ends with a suggestion of a little vocal cadenza as the nightingale's song (Ex. 5), Strauss's lieder do not allow for any interpolations or added ornamentation.

Ex. 5, *Im Walde,* AV 43 (mm. 52–58):

Ge-sang, Ge-sang, Ge-sang,_____ Ge- sang,_____ Ge- sang_____ im Grü- nen.

The most common type of vocal ornament Strauss employs in his songs is the short grace note. He uses grace notes variously to stress important syllables, especially the final word(s) of a song; to illustrate the text; to give a mocking, humorous effect; and in pairs to create a lilting character in the music of two serenades (*Kling!* op. 48, no. 3, and *Liebesliedchen,* AV 96/I). Some of the words highlighted by grace notes (and by other ornaments) are recurrent favorites with Strauss, such as "Liebe," "mildes," "gold'nes," "Frühling," "Rosen," and "singen." Grace notes serve an onomatopoeic function in *Säusle, liebe Myrte,* op. 68, no. 3 (on the word "zirpt," for the chirping of a cricket); in op. 66, no. 1 ("schmatzt," "smacks"); and in *Der Arbeitsmann,* op. 39, no. 3 (at every appearance of "Vögel").[16] Some grace notes, like other ornaments, are part of a larger melisma. In a few songs, Strauss apparently had purely musical rather than textual reasons for the grace notes: in op. 66, no. 11 and in *Liebesgeschenke* the grace notes are on unimportant, non-pictorial syllables (see Ex. 6a and 6b). The stress on "mit" in the first example results from a musical parallel with the preceding line, without regard for its different textual accents.

Ex. 6a, op. 66, no. 11 (mm. 1–6):

Die Händ-ler und die_ Ma - - cher

sind mit Pro- fit_ und_ Scha - - cher des

Ex. 6b, *Liebesgeschenke,* op. 77, no. 3 (mm. 27–29, 52–53):

ein_ und brach - te   war ent- flohn

In addition to extended melismas and vocal ornaments, Strauss emphasized syllables or words by the use of high or low notes, wide skips, harmonic changes (just before or during the syllables), repetition, and a lengthening of note values. From his childhood songs to those of the 1940's, he created many works in which the end of the vocal part is signaled by one or more of the following devices: a broadening of textual rhythms (sometimes with hemiola), a melismatic flourish, or a repetition of or within the final line of text. Frequently he used two of these devices together; all three are combined in songs such as *Das Bächlein* (AV 118) and *Ein Obdach gegen Sturm und Regen* (op. 46, no. 1). As pointed out on pp. 110–11, Strauss broadened the final lines in the orchestrations of *Zueignung* (op. 10, no. 1) and *Ich liebe dich* (op. 37, no. 2).

The majority of the vocal lines in Strauss's lieder from op. 10 onward are characterized by a wide range: none encompasses less than a ninth, while the widest range is a minor seventeenth, from D to f[1], in the bass song *Erschaffen und Beleben* (AV 106).[17] From op. 10 to the late songs without opus numbers there is a slight and gradual expanding of the vocal range.[18] The vocal ranges of the orchestral songs do not vary significantly from those of the songs with piano, nor do the shorter songs necessarily have more confined ranges that the longer ones.

The ways in which Strauss uses the ranges in his lieder make some of them even more demanding than the width of the span would seem to indicate; some have a high tessitura within the range, like *Kling!* (range g^1–c^3, tessitura d^2–a^2) and *Amor* (d^1–d^3, d^2–c^3). Others remain in an especially high tessitura for an extended phrase, and many more have single phrases that stretch up or down from one end of the compass to the other in a fairly short time (see Ex. 7a–g).

Ex. 7a, *Zueignung,* op. 10, no. 1 (mm. 25–26):
(Range:)

hei- lig, hei- lig an's Herz dir sank

Ex. 7b, *Die Verschwiegenen,* op. 10, no. 6 (mm. 22–26):

und lau - ter der gross- äu- gi- gen Ka- mil-le,

Ex. 7c, *Aus den Liedern der Trauer,* op. 17, no. 4 (mm. 19–21):

[vor-] an- ge- gan- gen: was zö-   gerst du?

Ex. 7d, *Epheu*, op. 22, no. 3 (m. 29):

lie- bend

Ex. 7e, *Ich sehe wie in einem Spiegel*, op. 46, no. 5 (mm. 58–60):

dein leb'___ ich und ich ster- [be]

Ex. 7f, *Das Thal*, op. 51, no. 1 (mm. 136–47):

so öff- ne lei- se dei-nen Grund und nimm mich auf und schliess' ihn wie- der und

grü- ne fröh - - - - - lich und ge- sund._____

Ex. 7g, op. 66, no. 8 (mm. 74–77):

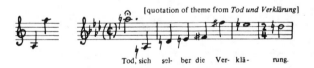

[quotation of theme from *Tod und Verklärung*]

Tod, sich sel- ber die Ver- klä- rung.

Strauss expects his singers to have agility and flexibility as well as the power to penetrate full orchestral sounds on low notes and to deliver the text clearly at sustained heights. A few songs have distinct ranges or tessituras in different sections, often reflecting contrasts in the text. *Leises Lied* (op. 39, no. 1) has a much lower tessitura for its first stanza (which sets the scene of a still garden at nightfall) than for subsequent ones. In *Ständchen* (op. 17, no. 2) there is a change of tessitura, harmony, and rhythmic rate to reflect the text at the third stanza "Sitz' nieder . . .": the vocal line here is lower, slower, and in fewer sharps (or more flats, in transposed versions). *Rückleben* (op. 47, no. 3) has one low tessitura for its first part (the poet kneeling at the grave of his beloved, a–f^1) and a higher one (a^1–f^2) during his daydream. Even Strauss's early song *Der Fischer* (AV 33) has a somewhat higher range for the stanzas sung by the mermaid than for those of the narrator.

In other songs extremely angular, disjunct vocal lines move rapidly from one end of the range to the other. In three of the songs of op. 41 the erratic melodies reflect the text: there are low points for words such as "versinkt," "tiefen," "Abgrund," and "Ebene." The phrase "der Flut entspringt ein Sternchen" ("a star arises from the stream") rises a thirteenth (see Ex. 30, p. 76). Other examples of extremely angular movement in op. 41 and throughout Strauss's songs are not textually related. Op. 66 has several examples of large, awkward leaps and generally wide ranges: besides the word painting and the self-quotations that are introduced with programmatic intent, some of the disjunct phrases reveal Strauss's musical humor and mockery. The portrayal of publishers in no. 10 as a collective Ochs von Lerchenau—nothing more than clumsy oafs trampling over artists' creations—has angular lines well matched to the message of the words. The *West-östlicher Divan* settings in op. 67 have some awkward but not particularly wide skips. Strauss's treatment of Goethe's texts as seen in this opus was carried to an extreme four years later in his *Erschaffen und Beleben* from the same Goethe collection. Besides having the widest range of any of Strauss's lieder, this drinking song is based on a combination of wide leaps and close chromatic melismas; some of these are included here in Ex. 8. Not surprisingly, it has not been recorded and is rarely performed; Asow cites only one performance (1957), while IRSGM lists the 1952 premiere.[19] In 1934–35 Strauss sketched two further drinking songs from the *West-östlicher Divan,* again using angular (but less awkward) vocal lines and in one of them even similar melismas (Ex. 9a and b).

Ex. 8, *Erschaffen und Beleben,* AV 106 [op. 87, no. 2] (mm. 1–2, 5–6, and 25–31):

Ex. 9a, *So lang man nüchtern ist,* unfinished sketch [see Appendix B], sketchbook 87, opening 3ʳ (mm. 1–4):

So-lang man nüch-tern ist   ge-fällt das Schlech- te.   wie man ge-

trun -   -   -   ken__   hat weiss

Ex. 9b, *Trunken müssen wir alle sein,* unfinished sketch [see Appendix B], sketchbook 87, openings 2ʳ and 3ᵛ (mm. 1–4, variant of 3–4, and beginning of 6th line of text):

Trun- ken müs-sen wir al- le sein Ju- gend ist Trun-ken-   heit oh- ne Wein

Ju- gend ist Trun -   ken -   heit oh- ne   Wein

Und Sor - - - - - - - - - - gen-brech-er sind die Re -   -   -   ben

Word and Mood Painting

The realistic portrayal of extra-musical ideas has always been considered an important trademark of ·Strauss as composer of tone poems and stage works. As suggested by the paragraphs above on vocal styles, ornamentation, and range, such literal representations or translations into music are not limited to his programmatic or dramatic works but can be found in many of his lieder as well. From the broadest level—the mood, scene or subject matter of the poem as a whole—to the tiniest detail of a phrase or word, the vocal and piano parts of numerous songs are full of examples of descriptive music. In many songs, Strauss combines an overall descriptive atmosphere (which will here be called mood painting) in the piano part with occasional representations of individual words (here word painting) by either piano or voice. Although some writers have claimed that as Strauss grew older he was drawn increasingly toward the more generalized and larger-scale mood painting, there can be found in his songs of all periods examples of word painting of such down-to-earth details as bird songs, hunting horns, depths and heights, and even bellowing, laughing, crying, and sneezing.

In his discussion of realistic pictorial effects in the lieder of Strauss and his contemporaries, Edward Kravitt divides their musical methods of portraying the text into analytic and synthetic description.[20] Analytic description (word painting) was a favorite compositional device of Renaissance madrigalists and of Baroque composers who subscribed to the aesthetic theory of *Affektenlehre*. To a greater or lesser extent it has survived in the techniques of later composers, with some writers of German lieder offering much vivid word painting. Kravitt's synthetic description, or the attempt to "paint" in music the character, scene, or mood of an entire poem, was also frequently employed by lieder composers. Strauss, Mahler, Pfitzner, and others used both types of description in their songs as well as in their programmatic instrumental music. Although in later years some of them (notably Mahler and Pfitzner) attacked program music or withdrew the previously written programs for their symphonic works (e.g., Mahler's for his First Symphony), nearly all of Strauss's contemporaries left examples of analytic description in their lieder.

Along with Mahler, Wolf, Pfitzner, and others of his lesser known contemporaries, Strauss used both word and mood painting, often in combination within a single lied. Even more than the others, he appears to have indulged in painting individual words throughout his life's work.[21] Karl Straube contrasts Strauss's approach with Reger's by the apt phrase "Während Richard Strauss darstellt—empfindet Reger!"[22] ("Whereas Richard Strauss portrays, Reger perceives!") Yet Strauss did not neglect generalized description, which is used especially in the accompaniments of the drinking songs referred to above, the lieder based on ostinato-like ideas, and those with storm scenes. He also created unified moods in his lullabies, walking and riding songs, working songs, and others. In the piano parts of *Waldesfahrt* and *Schlechtes Wetter* (op. 69, nos. 4 and 5), Strauss captures especially well Heine's ironic sense of humor.[23] *Waldesfahrt* begins and ends with the regular, flowing rhythms of the poet's carriage rolling through the woods; the central dream section is a musical

Ex. 10a and b, *Waldesfahrt*, op. 69, no. 4 (mm. 20–21 and 57–59):

description of the three ghosts surrounding the carriage, making faces, mocking and giggling, twirling about, and finally slipping away. Strauss uses contrasting tempos and meters (*Langsam* in 4/8 and *Sehr schnell* in 6/8), chromatic runs, a fragmentary voice part, and a "jumping" motive for the ghosts (Ex. 10a) which disintegrates into silence as they disappear (Ex. 10b).

Like others of Strauss's songs, this example combines mood and word description in its contrast of the real-life scenes and the poet's magical fantasies. Schumann's extremely different setting of the same text (which does not have the return of two lines of the first stanza, with which Strauss rounds out his ternary setting) is a much more abstract and monochromatic interpretation of the poem without changes of tempo, meter, or mood between the sections. Strauss's *Schlechtes Wetter,* certainly the best known song in op. 69, also uses different levels of description, from the persistent suggestions of the storm in the accompaniment to the melisma for the daughter's floating "goldenen Locken" and the stationary monotones at "Ich sitze am Fenster" and "Die liegt zu Haus im Lehnstuhl." Strauss uses similar repeated pitches in *Waldesfahrt* for "Ich sitze und sinne"; in later songs such static lines are written for words such as "Schlafenszeit" and "die Toten schlafen."

In contrast to these purposely motionless passages are the numerous literal descriptions in his lieder of words of direction, a type of vocal word painting to which Strauss was probably more addicted than any other lieder composer.[24] The use of low notes to paint words of descent, darkness, sadness, night, and death—along with high notes for floating, springing, height, sunlight, and the heavens—is found from his earliest lieder through *Frühling* and *September* in the *Four Last Songs.* Upon first reading a poem, Strauss often planned such details: in his edition of Heines' *Lyrisches Intermezzo* for poem no. 63 ("Wo bin ich . . .") he made the annotation "suddenly downward" by lines 2 and 7, which begin with the words "Finsternis" and "Abgrund." In addition, he placed an upward-pointing arrow by "Licht" at the end of line 4 and noted after "goldne Pracht" (line 6) "B-flat major, in the interlude as well."[25] His setting of this poem as *Der Einsame* for bass and orchestra incorporates all of these ideas, as shown here in Ex. 11. While the vocal ascent on "Licht" is hardly remarkable, the accompaniment supporting it and continuing in the next two measures is descriptive in its bright sounding D-flat major. This tonic major is heard here for only the second time; its first appearance was during line 3, anticipating the word "leuchtend." Both passages use solo strings; in the second one, the first violins sustain a high a^{b3}. The lowness of "Abgrund" is a shift of register in the accompaniment from full strings (*divisi*) to violoncellos and basses. The lowest vocal note is held in reserve for the final line (Ex. 12). It provides a great contrast to the highest pitch on "Liebes*sterne*" (mm. 32–33 in Ex. 11).[26] Woodwinds and brasses enter only for the final cadence (on the second measure of "Nacht"), the tuba contributing the bass note F_1.

Ex. 11, *Der Einsame,* op. 51, no. 2 [piano reduction by the composer] (mm. 5–8, 20–26, and 32–37):

Strauss's lieder sketches give evidence that word painting was part of his initial conception of a lied. Kravitt cites an unfinished sketch of Heine's *Nachts in der Kajüte* (not mentioned in Asow) in which "Himmel" and "Meer" (in the first two lines of the poem) are contrasted by high and low pitches.[27] Strauss's original setting of Rückert's *Die Göttin im Putzzimmer* provides another vivid example of high and low contrast (Ex. 13). In the second, choral version of this text, Strauss dramatizes the contrast even further. Here, six of the eight voices paint the text, the sopranos spanning nearly two octaves. "Plötzlich" is now described literally with sudden shifts of register (Ex. 14).

After vocal word painting of directions, the next most frequent text descriptions Strauss indulged in were those created by the use of melis-

Ex. 12, *Der Einsame,* op. 51, no. 2 [piano reduction by the composer] (mm. 45–51):

Ex. 13, *Die Göttin im Putzzimmer,* unfinished sketch for bass and piano [see Appendix B], sketchbook 87, opening 9^v (mm. 82–86):

Ex. 14, *Die Göttin im Putzzimmer,* AV 120 for mixed chorus a 8 (mm. 63–6⁹):

mas or chromaticism. A few examples have already been cited and a few more follow: the catalogue of such devices in Strauss's lieder is nearly endless. He rarely passed up the chance of portraying bird songs and other natural phenomena in any of his music. From the early lied *Die Drossel* (1877?), with its cadenza-like thrush's song as an introduction (Ex. 15a), and *Im Walde* (1878; see Ex. 5) to the *Four Last Songs* (Ex. 15b and c) there are numerous bird songs in both voice and accompaniment. Del Mar and others have pointed out similarities in some of these passages, citing especially the parallel thirds in the accompaniment before the mention of doves in *Heimkehr* (op. 15, no. 5) as a foreshadowing of the larks' song in *Im Abendrot*.[28] In *Liebesgeschenke* (op. 77, no. 3) bird songs are described by runs, trills, and parallel thirds in the accompaniment. Only one poem set by Strauss actually contains syllables of bird song, Brentano's *Lied der Frauen wenn die Männer im Kriege sind*, in which the exultant lark cries out "Tireli." In his op. 68, no. 6, Strauss gives the "Tireli" a distinctive vocal configuration and accompanies it by trills and runs (in the orchestral version the trills are played by flutes, piccolo, and clarinet, the runs by strings).

Der Arbeitsmann (op. 39, no. 3) has vocal melismas and piano trills (the latter added to a motive in parallel thirds that has already appeared throughout the accompaniment) at the mention of birds. In the orchestration of this song—which has not been authenticated as Strauss's own[29]— the trills are assigned to increasing numbers of woodwinds at each of their three appearances. The orchestral accompaniments, of course, increase the possibilities of word painting, a fact of which both Strauss and Mahler took advantage. (See, for example, from Mahler's *Des Knaben Wunderhorn* the songs *Revelge, Der Tamboursg'sell,* or *Wo die schönen Trompeten blasen.*) Strauss introduced many eerie effects into his setting for bass and orchestra of Rückert's Gothic horror tale *Nächtlicher Gang* (op. 44, no. 2). Particularly vivid descriptions are provided by the wind and percussion sections as well as by violoncello glissandos and harp harmonics.

In addition to portraying bird songs, high treetops, and low valleys, Strauss used both voice and accompaniment to imitate other aspects of nature. Goethe's mention of the artist-philosopher turning nature to his own advantage in *Hab' ich euch denn je geraten* (Strauss's op. 67, no. 5) caused the composer to quote two themes from his own *Alpensymphonie* (op. 64), a work he had completed only three years previously. Throughout op. 68 Strauss used melismas for flowers, roses, butterflies, garlands, flames, and fleecy clouds. Here the word painting is not so much literal description as it is aural imagery, i.e., beautiful sounds representing the beautiful aspects of nature.

In a more literal sense, *Säusle, liebe Myrte* (op. 68, no. 3) has picturesque descriptions of the flight of birds, the whisper of the myrtle trees, a chirping cricket, a bubbling fountain, a cooing turtledove, and a nightingale that laments chromatically. The wind is vividly described in passages of *Im Spätboot* (op. 56, no. 3), in measures 1–13 of *Wir beide*

Ex. 15a, *Die Drossel,* AV 30 (piano introduction):

Ex. 15b, *Frühling,* AV 150/I (mm. 16–21, voice and flute):

und Vo - - - - - - - - gel - sang.

Ex. 15c, *Im Abendrot,* AV 150/IV (mm. 39–44, voice and two flutes):

es dun- kelt schon die Luft.　　zwei Ler-chen nur noch stei- gen nach - träu- mend in den Duft

wollen springen (AV 90), and in the second verse of *Sankt Michael* (AV 129). Strauss portrays the rustling leaves in the accompaniments of *Einkehr* (op. 47, no. 4) and *Die Ulme zu Hirsau* (op. 43, no. 3) in a manner somewhat suggestive of the much later transformation scene in *Daphne*. In the particularly picturesque lied *Die Ulme zu Hirsau*, the full piano accompaniment later suggests the rushing wind (stanza 6) and the rays of the sun (stanzas 9–10).[30] The equally descriptive *Ruhe, meine Seele!* (op. 27, no. 1) begins with a static but harmonically unsettled chordal accompaniment that is broken as the soul's storms are dramatically compared to a raging fire. The poet, Karl Henckell, wrote to Strauss that his music matched the poetic mood handsomely.[31] Strauss's later orchestration, made in the midst of his work on the *Four Last Songs*, creates even more vivid images.

　　Die heiligen drei Könige aus Morgenland (op. 56, no. 6)—which Strauss conceived from the start as an orchestral song in spite of the fact that he published it with his own piano accompaniment in op. 56—uses brasses to imitate the ox's bellowing and violins with woodwind trills for the child's crying. These programmatic effects are introduced with the same realism that is found in Don Quixote's encounter with the sheep in *Don Quixote* or the sounds of the baby's bath in the *Symphonia domestica*. Additional painting of the text is provided by the abundance of thirds, triads, and triplets throughout—clearly referring to the three kings. Strauss uses trumpets and drums to describe the royal status of the kings; celesta and two harps add a "heavenly" atmosphere and recreate the star's light. Again, sketches prove that Strauss planned some of these effects from the beginning; see Chapter IV, p. 112. The bellowing ox and crying child are portrayed in the vocal line as well as in the accompaniment; the most striking vocal word painting in this song, however, comes at the end on the word "sangen," which is set to a triadic melisma (Ex. 16).

Ex. 16, *Die heiligen drei Könige aus Morgenland,* op. 56, no. 6 [version with piano by the composer] (mm. 64–67):

The description of songs or singing by lyrical singing is found in others of Strauss's lieder, for example in *Einkehr* (Ex. 17a) and *Wir beide wollen springen* (Ex. 17b). In op. 66, no. 9 (Ex. 17c), the effect is both mocking and overstated.[32] In *Frühlingsfeier* (op. 56, no. 5) Strauss portrays human sobbing, crying out, laughing, and lamenting through a combination of vocal and instrumental effects as well as the recurrent "Adonis," which serves as a song refrain. The ultimate example of Strauss's setting music to music is found not in his lieder but in the *Capriccio* fugue "Diskussion über das Thema: Wort oder Ton" (vocal score, pp. 140 ff.). The mention here of recitative (by the Count) and aria (by Clairon) invokes the appropriate vocal styles; La Roche's claim that the defect of opera is the deafening orchestra which forces singers to yell is fittingly accompanied by a loud orchestra which nearly submerges his very lines.[33] On a larger scale, the ensuing duet of the Italians, "Addio, mia vita," extends the idea of quoting music within an already musical context. Strauss uses other set pieces similarly, as the sonnet "Kein Andres, das mir so im Herzen loht" (also in *Capriccio*), the Composer's arietta "Du Venus' Sohn" in the *Ariadne auf Naxos* prologue, and the tenor aria "Di rigori armato" in *Der Rosenkavalier*, Act I.

Ex. 17a, *Einkehr*, op. 47, no. 4 (mm. 26–28):

Ex. 17b, *Wir beide wollen springen*, AV 90 (mm. 6–7):

Ex. 17c, op. 66, no. 9 (mm. 61–65):

Sources of and Alterations to the Poetry

As a lieder composer, Strauss usually exhibits a high degree of faithfulness to the poet's original text. Only rarely are there exceptions that conflict with the poet's intention, distort his meaning, or destroy his rhyme scheme. Since Strauss usually found his lieder texts in volumes which he himself owned, in several instances it is possible to compare every detail of orthography and punctuation in the original source and in its printed musical version. As mentioned here in Chapter IV, such comparison was made inconsistently in the preparation of the GL, and for many groups of songs no text variants at all are reported. Unless the exact edition that the composer used as the basis for his composition is known, the reporting of variants for certain poets' works becomes problematical. The works of Strauss's contemporaries such as Dehmel, Henckell, Mackay, and Martin Greif went through several editions and appeared in various anthologies, some of which contained revised readings of the poems. Others of their writings may have suffered minute changes or misreadings between one edition and another—or in Strauss's copying of the text—as did the works of earlier poets on which he also drew.

Trying to locate the source for a poem becomes difficult where several editions would have been available to the composer. Two of Henckell's poems, *Ruhe, meine Seele!* and *Das Lied des Steinklopfers*, for instance, were first published in his *Poetisches Skizzenbuch* (Minden in Westphalia, 1885); by the time Strauss used them (1894 and 1901, respectively), they had also appeared in several other collections of Henckell's verses. Del Mar, who identifies the sources of Strauss's lieder texts where they are known to him, cites Henckell's *Buch des Kampfes* as the source for both poems.[34] The *Buch des Kampfes,* however, was not assembled until much later, for publication as the second volume of Henckell's *Gesammelte Werke* (Munich, 1921). Del Mar's identification of *Das Lied des Steinklopfers* as the first poem in the "controversial" *Buch des Kampfes* and of the three Henckell texts used in Strauss's op. 32 as from his *Buch der Liebe* (volume III of the *Gesammelte Werke*) is inexact; these were not Strauss's sources for the poems.

In almost all his early songs for which an original poetic source has been located, it seems that Strauss introduced a few relatively insignificant departures from the poet's original diction. Some may have resulted from the composer's carelessness in copying or from slips of memory, while others may be his copyist's or a modern editor's misreading of the manuscripts. No autographs of certain of the early songs are extant; the copies in the manuscript collection "Jugendlieder (ungedruckte), Copien," upon which the GL and NL editions are based, contain some suspicious errors. The 1877 lied *Lass ruhn die Toten* (GL III, 242–43), for example, substitutes "steht" for Chamisso's original "ragt" (stanza 1, m. 5), "Frauen" for "Frommen" (stanza 2, m. 17), and "hervor" for "heraus" (stanza 3, m. 8). The only extant autograph for this song is a fragmentary pencil sketch; the GL and NL editions are based upon the copy in the "Jugendlieder" collection. Whether or not these are the thirteen-year-old Strauss's changes is difficult to determine. The first of the alterations replaces Chamisso's more poetic verb "hervorragen" with the common "hervorstellen" without changing the meaning of the line, which describes the ruins of a convent or monastery towering above the woods at nightfall. "Frauen" is probably a misreading. It establishes the dead as females, a detail which Chamisso's poem, in its use of the plural substantives "Toten," "Frommen," "Starken," and "Mächt'gen," leaves ambiguous. The use of "hervor" may be an attempt to improve upon the poet's redundant sounding "Und forderst her*aus aus* den Gräbern" (italics added). The final alteration in this text is Strauss's omission of "bei" before "nächtlicher Weile" in stanza 3. Grammatically, "bei" in this expression is optional; Strauss probably deleted it so that the syllables of this stanza would fit exactly the music of the first, although two measures later (and in several other places) this coincidence could not be maintained.

The few small changes Strauss made in his lieder texts can be summarized under the following headings: repetition of text, interchange of plural and singular or of different tenses, substitution of synonyms, change in word order, variation in number of syllables in a word, omission of unimportant words, and slight alteration in meaning. Almost all of his early songs have examples of text repetition, a practice common to many lieder composers. Strauss's longer texts, especially those of his later orchestral lieder, rarely have repeated words. The single repetition in the *Four Last Songs* (which do not have particularly long texts but are of greater duration than many of the lieder with piano) is of "deine selige [Gegenwart]" at the end of *Frühling*. Strauss usually repeated portions of the text for one of the following purposes: to create ternary forms, to provide further opportunity for musical development of the poet's refrain or other recurring text, or to emphasize the final and/or climactic lines of the vocal part. In the last instance, which occurs especially in the more lyrical, melodic songs from all periods of his creative life, the repetition may be reinforced by a broadening of vocal rhythms or a melisma on an important word.

Explanations for all of Strauss's alterations to his poetic sources are not always apparent in their musical settings or in their textual meanings. The occasional interchange of verb tenses or of singulars and plurals does not affect the flow of the music. Nor is there much lost or gained in his substitution of "Gold" for "Geld," "Nachtwind" for "Nachthauch," "Widerschein" for "Wiederschein," or "nun" for "jetzt." Some changes appear to be merely a result of Strauss's preference for certain words over the poet's diction, as is probably also the case with some of Schumann's alterations to his texts. In Strauss's *Nachtgang* (op. 29, no. 3), for example, Bierbaum's "dunkle" and "gütig" become "milde" and "heilig," words that already appear elsewhere in the poem. They are also words that Strauss sometimes repeats or gives melodic elaboration in other lieder of the same period. According to Max Steinitzer, a friend of Strauss's and his first biographer, the composer was not concerned about loyalty to his poet if he thought he could improve the poem's effect on the ear.[35] In this connection, melodic motives appear responsible for a few changes of word order and the addition or omission of syllables with short "i" or "e" ("habt" for the original "habet," "Kön'ge" for "Könige," "junger" for "jung'," etc.). The occasional deletion of relatively unimportant words ("so," "wohl," "es") may be a result of carelessness or inattention to detail: in most instances they could be slipped in unobtrusively on a short unaccented note without interrupting the basic outlines of the musical phrase. Like Schumann and other composers who altered their texts without always improving upon them, Strauss made a few changes that are aptly described by the German term "Verschlimmbesserungen" ("[things] made worse instead of better"). Willi Schuh (*Lebenschronik*, p. 470) suggests that some of these small alterations are a result of the composer's working method. The spontaneous way in which Strauss claims to have written down songs like *Traum durch die Dämmerung* and *Der Stern* would make small slips of memory seem quite likely explanations for these alterations.

Changes of the sort mentioned in the above paragraph are much less important to the meaning of the text than are Strauss's substitutions of "Lüfte" for "Lüste" in *An die Nacht* or of "ihn" for "mich" in *Amor* (op. 68, nos. 1 and 5). That "Lüfte" is the wrong word (". . . dips a rose into the depths of dark desires," not ". . . dark airs") was apparently never realized by Strauss or his editors. The change in *Amor* involves more than just the meaning of the word: in the original it was Amor (Cupid) himself who spoke "O how thoroughly the passion pains me!" (Brentano did not, however, use quotation marks either here or in similar lines of the poem.) In Strauss's version, the line becomes only the narrator's comment (". . . pains him," i.e., Cupid). While this may be an example of Strauss's unintentionally altering the poem, his change at the end of Eichendorff's *Im Abendrot* from "Ist *das* etwa der Tod?" to "Ist *dies* etwa der Tod?" is more probably an alteration intended to give the text a more personal meaning.

With very few exceptions, Strauss set all stanzas of the original poems in his early songs as well as in later ones. As noted above, he frequently added repetitions of words that were already in the poem, but did not interpolate words or phrases of his own.[36] His very first childish effort at song writing, *Weihnachtslied* (AV 2, December 1870), is an exception of the sort—fortunately for the poets' sake—that does not re-appear. Here Strauss set only the first of the original four stanzas of C. F. D. Schubart's poem. To the six rhyming iambic lines he added his own metrically unrelated ending, "Schlafe, Himmelskindlein, schlafe." Among the early songs, the only other significant omission occurs in Hoffmann von Fallersleben's two-strophe *Husarenlied* (AV 14, 1873?), where the refrain line of nonsense syllables "Trallerah vivallerallerah tra rah" is replaced by a simple "tra-la-la."

Among the songs published with opus numbers, only five are not settings of complete poems. The texts of two songs, *Gestern war ich Atlas* (op. 46, no. 2) and *Huldigung* (op. 77, no. 5), consist of short poems by Rückert (three separate poems) and Hafiz (five poems, in translations by Hans Bethge). For the orchestral song *Notturno* (op. 44, no. 1), Strauss omitted Dehmel's entire first stanza and the last line of his final stanza, passages which form the frame in which a dream is presented and which would have been inappropriate for his musical setting. The prosaic final line "und dankbar bin ich aufgewacht," for instance, would hardly be a suitable ending for the expansive, colorful tone and mood painting. Otherwise, Strauss was able to use this long poem literally, making only a few small changes (e.g., reversing the positions of "stumm" and "starr" in stanza 2, substituting "kühle" for "kalte" in stanza 4, and omitting "und zärter" in stanza 7). In setting Rückert's "Die Liebste steht mir vor den Gedanken" as *Anbetung* (op. 36, no. 4), the composer omitted the last four lines because they give the poem an undesirable topicality by naming (for the first time in the poem) the mourned beloved, the fair Freimund. From another Rückert poem in *Liebesfrühling* (the source of "Die Liebste"), "Dort, wo der Morgenstern hergeht," Strauss used only stanzas 1 to 8 for his *Morgenrot* (op. 46, no. 4). He did not continue with Rückert's next five stanzas since there is again a reference to Freimund (but only in the final line of the closing stanza).

Strauss's Settings of Rückert's Poetry

Of all the poets whose works Strauss set, Rückert seems to have been treated with somewhat more freedom than others. Aside from the alterations noted above, even his works suffered few changes involving more than the repetition of a few words or substitution of one or two related words for the original ones. The poet was undoubtedly a favorite of Strauss, who set his texts in twelve lieder and seven choral works— counting those he left unfinished—from the 1897 choral *Hymne* (op. 34, no. 2) to the incomplete eight-part chorus *Schlusslied* (ca. 1938; see Appendix B). In addition, Strauss suggested to Hofmannsthal his ideas for an opera based on Rückert's lengthy dramatic poem *Saul und David,* wondering if Hofmannsthal would read Rückert and write a libretto. Plans did not go beyond Hofmannsthal's promising to consider the project.[37] While the libretto of *Ariadne auf Naxos* was in progress, Strauss recalled the inspiration he always received from Rückert's poetry and pleaded with Hofmannsthal to spur his Pegasus

> so that the ring of the verses might excite me a bit. You probably know my preference for Schiller-like hymns and Rückert-like flourishes. Such things excite me to formal orgies . . . soaring oratory can drug me enough to let me continue composing when [the subject matter] is of no real interest.[38]

Throughout his years of interest in Rückert's works, Strauss used as his source his own twelve-volume set of the poet's *Gesammelte poetische Werke* (Frankfurt, 1868–69). Certain of the poems in this edition which he chose to set had not been included in the previous *Gesammelte Gedichte* (Erlangen, 1834 and 1836; Frankfurt, 1843) or other even earlier collections. One of the poems set by Strauss, *Vom künftigen Alter* (beginning "Der Frost hat mir bereifet des Hauses Dach"), had first appeared as an untitled sixteen-line poem in Rückert's *Östliche Rosen,* written in 1819–20. In this form it was set by Schubert with the title *Greisengesang* (D. 778). For the edition of *Östliche Rosen* in his 1836 *Gesammelte Gedichte,* II, Rückert added the title *Vom künftigen Alter* and four more lines at the end of the poem. This version, retained in later printings, was used by Strauss. His annotations of the keys E-flat and B-flat major next to lines 3 and 8 in his copy of Rückert's *Gesammelte poetische Werke,* V, 274, are typical of those markings he made either in printed copies of poems or in the margins of his own hand-copied versions in the sketchbooks. (For examples of the latter, see Illustration 5).

Vom künftigen Alter is of particular interest as one of Strauss's six settings of Rückert's poems in the form of a "Persian ghasel." The most rigidly structured poetic form set by Strauss in his lieder, the ghasel was adapted to German poetry by Goethe, Friedrich Schlegel, Rückert, August von Platen, and other romantics who shared an interest in Oriental literatures.[39] The principle of construction of the ghasel as adapted by the romantics is a rhyme in the first two lines and then in every subsequent

Illustration 5

Strauss's annotations to poems written into sketchbook 5, opening 1ᵛ, for *Befreit* (op. 39, no. 4), and opening 52ʳ, for *Notturno* (op. 44, no. 1), slightly reduced.

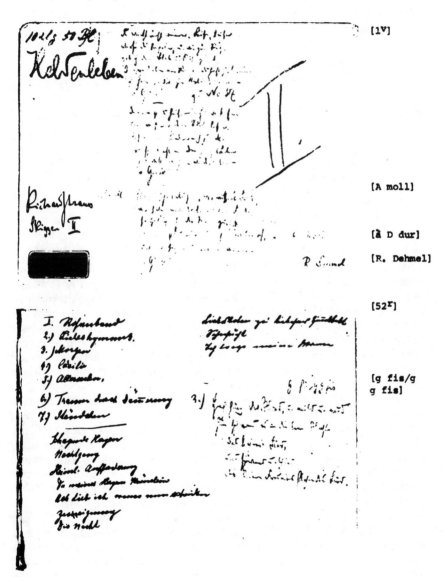

even-numbered line. If the rhyme does not occur at the end of the line, the rhyming word must always be followed by the same word or words, which form a refrain as in this example (italics are added to indicate rhyme and refrain):

> Ich sah sie nur ein einzig*mal, und dann nicht mehr;*
> da sah ich einen Himmelsstra*hl, und dann nicht mehr.*
> Ich sah umspielt vom Morgenhauch durchs Tal sie gehn;
> da war der Frühling im T*al, und dann nicht mehr,*
> Im Saal des Festes sah ich sie entschleiern sich,
> da war das Paradies im S*aal, und dann nicht mehr.*
> . . .

In ghasels such as *Vom künftigen Alter,* the rhyme does come at the end of the line:

> Der Frost hat mir bereifet des Hauses D*ach;*
> doch warm ist mir's geblieben im Wohngem*ach.*
> Der Winter hat mir die Scheitel weiss gedeckt;
> doch fliesst das Blut, das rote, durchs Herz gem*ach.*
> Der Jugendflor der Wangen, die Rosen sind gegangen,
> all gegangen einander n*ach.*
> . . .

Here the formal structure appears somewhat less restrictive since the only "refrain" is the rhyme itself, which is only part of a word. In this song Strauss stresses the rhyming syllable "-ach" by setting it to note values longer than those for the final syllables of most other lines. Although he usually places the rhyming syllables on a strong beat and sometimes follows them with a rest, the effect of the rhyme is not as obvious as a textual or musical refrain would be. Furthermore, if the only modern edition is correct, in the last line of the poem Strauss apparently altered the final word "Liebesach" to "Liebesweh," thus destroying the rhyme entirely.[40]

Each of Strauss's other five settings of Rückert's ghasels does have a textual refrain that is reinforced by a recurring musical phrase. In two of them, *Und dann nicht mehr* and *Im Sonnenschein* (AV 115 and 121), the poet's (and Strauss's) title calls attention to the refrain. In *Und dann nicht mehr,* Strauss adds three extra repetitions of the musical and textual refrain after lines 16, 18, and 20. (Rückert had already put in one extra repetition by using lines 1–2 as 19–20; thus the refrain appears fifteen times in Strauss's setting.) The other three ghasel settings are the lied *Anbetung* with the rhyme "-anken" and refrain "wie schön, o wie schön!"; the choral *Deutsche Motette,* op. 62 ("-angen" and "o wach in mir!"); and the unfinished choral piece *Schlusslied* ("-eiset" and "verlass mich nicht!"). Although he observes the refrains and repetitive rhymes, Strauss does not indicate in the manuscripts or printed versions that any of these poems is in the ghasel form.[41]

Nearly all of Strauss's remaining Rückert settings use strophic poems with regular rhymes and accentual meters. Even *Gestern war ich Atlas* (op. 46, no. 2), the text of which Strauss constructed himself, has its unity: the poems are consecutively printed "Persian quatrains" from the poet's *Liebesfrühling,* each with its own *aaba* rhyme scheme and a regular metrical pattern of five accents in each ten- or eleven-syllable line. Some of the poems, such as *Ein Obdach gegen Sturm und Regen* (op. 46, no. 1), are intricately worked out: of the four four-line stanzas, the first and third have the same iambic metric schemes (˘ ˘ ˘ ˘ ˘ ˘ ˘ ˘ / ˘ ˘ ˘ ˘ repeated), as do the second and fourth (˘ ˘ ˘ ˘ ˘ ˘ ˘ three times, then ˘ ˘ ˘ ˘ ˘). Furthermore, each stanza has an *abab* rhyme scheme. These are identical in stanzas 2 and 4, each of which begins with the exact same two lines of text and continues with slight variants. In Strauss's setting, the first halves of stanzas 2 and 4 are set to the same melodic lines (one step higher in stanza 4), the second halves to related melodies. The other two stanzas are much less closely connected, but the whole of the song is unified through a rhythmic motive that appears again and again in both voice and piano (Ex. 18). The rhythm of this motive (like that of the motive given here in Ex. 19) is not a musical representation of the poetic meter: the musical accents are trochaic (strong-weak), while the poetic ones are iambic (weak-strong). The accented syllables are, of course, placed on the accented notes of the motive.

Ex. 18, *Ein Obdach gegen Sturm und Regen,* op. 46, no. 1 (motives from mm. 1, 2, and 5 in the voice; mm. 4–9 in the piano, right hand):

Examples of recurrent rhythmic patterns pervading much of a text's setting and representing its original poetic accents are found in Strauss's two versions of Rückert's poem *Die Göttin im Putzzimmer.* Much of the dactylic meter in the incomplete sketch for bass and piano is represented by eighth notes in 6/8 meter or by quarter notes in 3/4. In the completed a cappella choral setting of this text, Strauss uses 3/4 as the basic meter, with triplet eighth notes abounding in the first half of the work; these patterns represent the dactylic units of the text. After a dramatic and homophonic pictorial representation of stanza 12 (see Ex. 14), eighth-note triplets are abandoned in favor of broader dactylic statements in quarter and half notes, the latter producing a hemiola effect.

Poetic Meter, Rhythm, and Accent Interpreted in Musical Meter, Rhythm, and Accent

In the majority of Strauss's text settings the rhythmic contours of the vocal lines are so varied that they obscure the original meter of the poem. Whether the composer intended to underscore the poetic meter or not, he was certainly concerned about proper accentuation of important syllables, accomplishing this not only through rhythmic emphasis but also through a variety of other musical means. Although the relative weight of syllables and words can be interpreted musically in many ways, preservation of a recognizable poetic meter with its prescribed number of regularly recurring accents is most readily discerned in the contrast of long and short, accented and unaccented notes. An informative study of Strauss's approach to meter and accent in the texts he set is provided by Roland Tenschert's "Das Sonett in Richard Strauss' Oper 'Capriccio.' Eine Studie zur Beziehung von Versmetrik und musikalischer Phrase," *Schweizerische Musikzeitung*, XCVIII (1958), 1–5.[42] There is great variety in Strauss's rhythmic setting of this iambic text, and no two lines are set to identical patterns. Where weak syllables appear on a strong beat, Strauss counteracts this rhythmic emphasis by placing the next strong syllable on a higher or longer note or by using a melisma or syncopation to stress its weight. Strauss echoes the pentametric scansion of the verses by five-measure phrases in ten of the fourteen lines, but never allows the rhythms to become too regular or to take on a singsong effect.[43]

In only a handful of Strauss's lieder are the rhythmic patterns so consistent as to suggest a conscious attempt to preserve the poetic meter. The vocal lines of the early songs *Winterreise* and *Einkehr* move predominantly in eighth notes and in patterns of dotted quarter and eighth notes, respectively. The even earlier *Weihnachtslied* flows in quarter notes (or subdivisions into two slurred eighth notes) with the stressed syllables of the iambic feet on the first and third beats in common time. Only at the last (added) line are both the poetic meter and musical patterns broken.

Among Strauss's mature lieder a few comparatively early songs such as *Geduld* (op. 10, no. 5), *Lob des Leidens* (op. 15, no. 3), *Wozu noch, Mädchen* (op. 19, no. 1), and *All mein Gedanken* (op. 21, no. 1) are constructed from one basic rhythmic idea. The trochaic meter is represented in *Geduld* by quarter-eighth combinations in 6/8 meter, in *Wozu noch, Mädchen* by long-short patterns on three levels in 3/4 meter: half-quarter, dotted quarter-eighth, and dotted eighth-sixteenth. In both examples the rhythms become progressively freer as the song proceeds. Over half the syllables in *All mein Gedanken* fall into a dactylic pattern of eighth and two sixteenth notes; these, along with other slightly varied figures, account for over two-thirds of the entire text. The repetitious vocal rhythms and the sparse texture of the accompaniment—offset here by variety in melodic and harmonic movement—are perhaps Strauss's attempt to create a folksong-like atmosphere for Dahn's poetry, which begins with a line of a real folk poem and continues in imitation of the folk idiom.

Repetitions of rhythmic patterns are less frequently found in the composer's later songs, and when present are usually part of a motive that pervades both the vocal line and its accompaniment. *Lied der Frauen,* op. 68, no. 6 (in 6/8 meter), has many two-syllable words set to ♩♪ or ♩ ♩ ♪ patterns and several other variations on long-short, strong-weak units such as ♪♪♪♪ ♩ . While the words remain correctly accented, the rhythmic variety of the musical setting does not facilitate scansion of the text.

In *Die Allmächtige,* the sequential principal motive includes a triple repetition of the ♩. ♪ (strong-weak) pattern (see Ex. 19). It appears six times in the vocal line and several more times in the accompaniment; in addition, its rhythms are used with other melodic progressions (Ex. 20). As in Ex. 18, the natural speech rhythms but not the poetic meter of the poem as a whole are represented by this motive.

Ex. 19, *Die Allmächtige,* op. 77, no. 4 (mm. 3–4):

Die höch-ste Macht der Er- de sitzt___

Ex. 20, *Die Allmächtige,* op. 77, no. 4 (mm. 9–10 and 31–33):

An- ge- sicht, du Herr-   und auch die dun-kle Macht des To- des

Ex. 21, *Liebesgeschenke,* op. 77, no. 3 (mm. 7–10 and 55–60):

und brach-te sie der schö-nen jun- gen Frau,___

ent -flohn___ in je- ne fer- nen_ blau - - - en_ Ber- [ge]

In *Liebesgeschenke,* Strauss sets many two- and four-syllable words in 2/4 meter to ♩. ♪ or ♩. ♪ patterns; these also form part of the song's recurring motives. That musical expansion of the motive was more important to the composer than preservation of the poetic meter is shown in passages where these rhythms are not strictly syllabic (Ex. 21).

Vocal Rhythms: Variations and Patterns

Of more importance than Strauss's adherence to regular musical rhythmic patterns are the changes of pace that reflect the poetic sense rather than the meter of the text and the departures from already established patterns in repetitions of strophic material. In his study of *Ich trage meine Minne* (op. 32, no. 1), Tenschert calls attention to the number of lines that begin with eighth-note movement and slow to quarters (halves in the final line of A^1), thus emphasizing the words near the end of the line.[44] In other songs the opposite of this fast-slow movement is used to give the text a forward-moving urgency without always pausing on its end-of-line rhymes. In *Junggesellenschwur* (op. 49, no. 6), each stanza ends with the fast rhythms of the curse ("Schwur"), which abruptly breaks the mood set up in the previous lines. Strauss uses contrasting vocal rhythms as characterizations in *Für funfzehn Pfennige*[45] (op. 36, no. 2). The narrator (stanzas 1–5) speaks mainly in eighth notes. The clerk (stanzas 6–7) speaks in 2/4 ♪ ♪ ♪ ♩ patterns over a simpler accompaniment, while the girl's stanza 8 is short and snappy. Rejected—and thus reduced to the state of an observer—the clerk takes over the narrator's opening rhythms and part of the melodic material for his concluding stanzas 9–10.

Nearly all of the musical means by which Strauss emphasized both the important words and the stressed syllables of the poems he set are found in his perhaps overly popular *Ständchen* (op. 17, no. 2). Count Adolph Friedrich von Schack's poem, as Strauss set it, reads as follows:

1. Mach' auf, mach' auf, doch leise mein Kind
   um Keinen vom Schlummer zu wecken.
   Kaum murmelt der Bach, kaum zittert im Wind
   ein Blatt an den Büschen und Hecken.
   D'rum leise mein Mädchen, dass nichts sich regt,
   Nur leise die Hand auf die Klinke gelegt.

2. Mit Tritten, wie Tritte der Elfen so sacht,
   um über die Blumen zu hüpfen.
   Flieg' leicht hinaus in die Mondscheinnacht
   zu mir in den Garten zu schlüpfen.
   Rings schlummern die Blüthen am rieselnden Bach
   und duften im Schlaf, nur die Liebe ist wach.

3. Sitz' nieder, hier, dämmerts geheimnisvoll
   unter den Lindenbaumen,
   die Nachtigall uns zu Häupten soll
   von uns'ren Küssen träumen

und die Rose, wenn sie am Morgen erwacht,
hoch glühn [hoch glühn] von den Wonneschauern der Nacht.

Strauss himself supposedly admitted that not all of his solutions to the problems of text accentuation were effectively worked out in his lied.[46] In fact, if accentuation of the text is considered only a matter of rhythm, musical meter, and relative lengths of note values, *Ständchen* provides some poor examples of text setting. In his 1905 article on techniques of musical declamation, Edmund von Freyhold cites passages from Strauss's op. 17 (and a few of his other songs) to illustrate both good and bad examples of his three rules of declamation.[47] Freyhold's rules take into account only rhythm and meter: 1) short [i.e., unaccented] syllables should be set to short notes, 2) long [accented] ones to long notes, and 3) metrical stresses in the music should be limited to long [accented] syllables. He cites Strauss's setting in *Ständchen* of "Nachtigall" as wrongly emphasizing the third syllable over the first (Ex. 22a).[48] (Nearly the same accentuation occurs earlier on the word "geheimnissvoll"; see Ex. 22b.)

Ex. 22a and b, *Ständchen*, op. 17, no. 2 (mm. 60–63 and 53–55):

die Nach-   ti-   gall___

ge-   heim-   niss-   voll___

Freyhold does not point out that although the final syllable is in both cases on the longest note in the word, its rhythmic stress is counterbalanced by its being on the same pitch as the previous stronger syllable. The chromatic alteration to $c\natural^2$ during "geheimnissvoll" further draws attention to the syllable "heim." Furthermore, the final notes of the lines are not heard as long notes in the same way as the tied notes of "Nach" and "heim" are. The latter, because they occur in the middle of the phrase, do affect the rate of declamation. Since both words are followed by eighth-note rests, a diminuendo also seems appropriate in each passage, though not indicated by the composer. Freyhold gives another example of what he calls incorrect stress from Strauss's *Barkarole:* the weak syllable of "süsser," he asserts, is given too much emphasis (Ex. 23).[49] In making this claim, Freyhold has neglected the pitches and total lengths of the two syllables. Furthermore, in these measures Strauss is repeating the last line of text and naturally broadens the rhythms of its first appearance. The first statements of "süsser" in the song provide two examples of correct declamation, even by Freyhold's pedantically strict standards (Ex. 24).

In setting *Ständchen,* Strauss uses a modified strophic setting for Schack's first two stanzas and new music for the third, which has a slightly different structure and a very different tone and mood. His slight changes in the vocal line between the first two stanzas reveal a sensitivity to the text and concern for the differences in rhythms and meaning. For

Ex. 23, *Barkarole,* op. 17, no. 6 (mm. 50–54):

a- ber süs- - - ser.___ an__ ih - - - rer Brust.

Ex. 24, *Barkarole,* op. 17, no. 6 (mm. 42–45):

a- ber süs- ser, süs- ser an ih- rer Brust.

Ex. 25, *Ständchen,* op. 17, no. 2 (mm. 7–8 and 29–30):

um Kei-nen von Schlum-mer zu wec-ken,

um ü- ber die Blu - men zu hüp- fen.

example, his settings of the second line in each of the first two stanzas
(Ex. 25) are slightly different, although both have the same strongest
musical stress (on *"Blu*men" and *"Schlum*mer") and both end identically.
In order not to overemphasize the first syllable of "über" (which is strong
but not so important as "Kein"), Strauss moves it from the first beat and
adds a slur from the previous note so that the highest pitch will not be too
prominent in the line.[50] For the final two lines of stanzas 1 and 2, Strauss
changes his 6/8 meter to 9/8, ostensibly for the accompanimental figurations which at this point change from two-beat to three-beat patterns.
This change does not help one weakness of the text setting, that many
important syllables fall on the second instead of the first beat in the
measure; in stanza 1 alone, this occurs on *"Schlum*mer," *"we*cken,"
"Bach," "Wind," "Blatt," *"Busch*en," and *"Heck*en." In the 9/8 section
of this stanza, the following words are relegated to the third beat:
*"Mäd*chen," "regt," "Hand," *"ge*legt" (and *"Klin*ke" to the second).
Had Strauss retained his 6/8 meter, at least some of these words would
have fared better (Ex. 27). Melodic direction does help to counteract the
metric accents in this line, but not for all of the words mentioned above.
Strauss began to set Schack's *Barkarole* in a pattern of alternating 9/8 and
6/8 (mm. 1–20), but abandoned this combination in favor of straight 9/8
(mm. 21–29) and then 6/8 (mm. 30–56). Again in the first section of this
song some of the more important words (especially nouns) could be better accented if they were to fall on the first beat of the measure.

Steinitzer points out other examples of Strauss's misapplication of Schack's accents in *Ständchen,* for instance his stress on "*Mor*gen" instead of "er*wacht*" in the penultimate line. ("Erwacht" parallels "Nacht" of the final line.) Although Strauss may have violated the poet's intentions, it is clear that he chose to emphasize "Morgen" for musical reasons: in these last two lines there are four descending figures, one on "Morgen" (Ex. 28). This motive is similar to the motive continued in the piano postlude, one which originally derives from the 9/8 sections of the first two stanzas and occurs here as a musical refrain to unify the entire lied (Ex. 29).

The combination of poetic rhythms and meters with musical ones in the setting of texts is handled differently by various lied composers. Although a personal style is sometimes evident, a variety of approaches is found among the works of Strauss and many other composers. Wehmeyer (*Max Reger,* p. 58 et passim) contrasts this aspect of text treatment in

Ex. 27, *Ständchen,* op. 17, no. 2 (mm. 19–22 in Strauss's version and rewritten in 6/8):

Ex. 28, *Ständchen,* op. 17, no. 2 (mm. 76–87):

Ex. 29, *Ständchen,* op. 17, no. 2 (mm. 87–88):

er by Reger and Wolf, pointing out Reger's preference for repeated rhythmic sequences and the rarity of such sequences in Wolf's lieder. In strophic songs or in passages with repeated text, Reger usually repeats his rhythmic patterns literally or with only slight variants while changing the melody; Wolf, on the other hand, is more likely to retain his melodic outlines and set the text to new rhythms. Strauss's technique is on the whole closer to Reger's, although many of his modified or varied strophic lieder contain variations in both melody and rhythm, and the final lines of songs are more often than not given broader note values upon repetition. In certain songs both Strauss and Reger establish characteristic rhythmic units that are closely tied to the textual rhythms. Even in basically through-composed songs like *Am Ufer* Strauss creates remarkably parallel rhythmic structures for the first two sections of text. The rhythms of the third section bear some slight relation to the other two; none of the melodic contours, however, suggests any of the others. The vocal lines of the three sections of the song are shown one under the other in Ex. 30; the few adjustments in numbers of measures result from the different numbers and accentual patterns of syllables in each phrase.

The close parallels in rhythm among the phrases of Strauss's *Ich trage meine Minne* are discussed by Tenschert in his *Zeitschrift für Musik* article cited above. Here Strauss reuses rhythms on two levels: the first

Ex. 30, *Am Ufer*, op. 41, no. 3 (mm. 1–52):

two phrases have nearly identical rhythms but quite different melodies (Ex. 31); the composer's repetition of the first stanza after the second uses the music of its first statement with only a slight broadening at the end. Although Tenschert describes stanza 2 as the *B* section of an *ABA¹* form, it too bears a rhythmic and melodic similarity to the first stanza (at least at the outset of its first and third lines, Ex. 32), again with adjustments to accommodate the different texts.

Rhythmic Motives and Other Musical Details Derived from Word Sounds

In a number of songs Strauss uses rhythmic repetition on an even smaller scale than in *Ich trage meine Minne* or *Am Ufer,* that is, as a motive within the phrase unit. In this type of repetition he exploits the sound of certain words, syllables, and single consonants even more than poetic meters or end-of-line rhymes. Rhythmic motives derived from important words can be found throughout certain songs, sometimes becoming a principal element of the structure. These motives are closely tied to the text in the manner of the rhythmically distinctive "Agamemnon" motive in *Elektra.* Table 2 on the following pages includes several examples of such motives from Strauss's lieder. Since many of them fall on words within refrains they are repeated—most often to the same melody as well—and sometimes developed in the course of a song. Some are repeated to different words later in the song, while others are reserved for only one word or phrase. The "Einerlei" motive—one of three main ideas pervading op. 69, no. 3—is stated first by the piano (m. 17); only in

Ex. 31, *Ich trage meine Minne,* op. 32, no. 1 (mm. 1–4 and 5–8):

Ex. 32, *Ich trage meine Minne,* op. 32, no. 1 (mm. 19–22 and 28–31):

measure 57 does its textual significance become clear. In op. 66, no. 5, the pattern occurs in the voice, beginning at measure 24. It is heard three times each on "Reinecke" and the similar sounding "Deinige." The rhythm of the name "Reinecke" (one of the publishers Strauss was singling out for criticism) together with its broader meaning (the German equivalent of Reynard the Fox) determined the character of the hunting-horn-like accompaniment, which reiterates this characteristic rhythm in almost every measure. The "heilige Nacht" motive of *An die Nacht* appears with other words, in an augmented form, and in various forms in the accompaniment. As shown in Chapter V, pp. 132–33, Strauss originally planned to use even more versions of the motive. In arriving at this motive, he altered Brentano's original two-syllable "heil'ge" to three, later in the poem expanding "zücht'ge" and "brünst'ge" as well.[51]

The above examples suggest that Strauss may have selected some of his lieder texts at least in part for the rhythmic character of their words and for the sound of their consonants. Since he felt that an audience should always be able to understand the words being sung, clear enunciation of the consonants is essential in the interpretation of his lieder. In the foreword to *Intermezzo*, he remarked that singers would do well to consider consonants as weapons with which to break through even the loudest accompaniment, where vowels could never compete.[52] While the chances of the text being covered by the accompaniment are fewer in the lied than in opera, in some of the songs consonants reassure strong attacks in extreme ranges or after wide skips or rests.[53] Certain of his settings emphasize the explosive initial consonants of refrain words such as "rack schack" in *Junghexenlied,* "Kling Klang!" in *Schlagende Herzen,* "Kling!" and "Sing!" in *Kling!,* and "Pfennige" in *Hat gesagt—bleibt's nicht dabei.* In *Das Lied des Steinklopfers* the hard consonant sounds (especially "k," "b," "t," and "g"), along with the ostinato figures of the *sempre staccato* accompaniment, characterize both the task and the attitude of the stone cutter. The poet's regular repetition of "kein" in seven of the eight lines is echoed by Strauss, who sets it as an afterbeat eighth, usually followed by a leap. Beginning at measure 45, he continues with a partial repetition of Henckell's verses, extracting from these eight lines "kein" and its appropriate following noun. These fragments are sung to variants of the earlier music; they occupy the same position in the measure as before, but with rests now on the preceding first (strong) beat. Strauss continues his extraction through the remainder of the text, ending the song with a gradual disintegration of the piano figuration as well.

The smoothness created by an abundance of liquid "l"s in Strauss's songs like *Traum durch die Dämmerung* and *Ich schwebe* provides a great contrast to the rough-edged effect created in *Das Lied des Steinklopfers.* In *Traum durch die Dämmerung* the stepwise melodic lines and the flowing sound of words such as "mildes, blaues Licht," "eile," "liebe Land," and "schnell" contribute to the dream-like atmosphere. A similar effect is created in *Die Nacht* by alliterative verses, numerous repetitions of "alle"

Table 2

Text-Derived Rhythmic Motives in Strauss's Lieder

Title, op., no.	Text and Motive
Nichts, op. 10, no. 2	nen - nen soll ich
Die Georgine, op. 10, no. 4	Ge - or - gi - ne
Cäcilie, op. 27, no. 2	wenn du es wüsst - est
Schlagende Herzen, op. 29, no. 2	Kling Klang
Hat gesagt–bleibt's nicht dabei, op. 36, no. 2	Pfen - ni - ge
Bruder Liederlich, op. 41, no. 4	Hal - li Hal - li und Hal - lo / Hal - lo
Ein Obdach gegen Sturm und Regen, op. 46, no. 1	Ob - dach / Re - gen (etc.)
In goldener Fülle, op. 49, no. 2	wir schrei - ten in gol - de - ner Fül - le
Frühlingsfeier, op. 56, no. 5	A - do - nis

The Lieder of Richard Strauss

Table 2 (continued)

Title, op., no.	Text and Motive
op. 66, no. 5	 Rei - ne - cke Dei - ni - ge
An die Nacht, op. 68, no. 1	 hei - li - ge Nacht züch - ti - ge Braut
Säusle, liebe Myrte, op. 68, no. 3	 Säu - sle lie - be
Amor, op. 68, no. 5	 A - mor
Einerlei, op. 69, no. 3	 Ei - ner - lei man -cher- lei
Liebesgeschenke, op. 77, no. 3	 schö - ner jun - gen Frau (etc.)
Die Allmächtige, op. 77, no. 4	 die Höch - ste Macht der Er - de (etc.)
Und dann nicht mehr, AV 115	 und dann nicht mehr
Im Sonnenschein, AV 114	 im Son - nen - schein

and "aus," and frequent stepwise movements. It is achieved also in *Weisser Jasmin* through the use of many alliterative lines. In op. 68, no. 5, Strauss exploits words containing the letters "f" and "l" and combinations thereof in Brentano's poem *Amor*—as well as the meaning of the words themselves—to produce an ornate but flowing vocal line.

The Treatment of Identical Texts by Strauss and Reger

Certain aspects of Strauss's text setting in his lieder can be summarized in the comparison of a few of his songs with those on the same texts by Max Reger. Their lieder on two poems from Felix Dahn's forty-poem collection *Schlichte Weisen* show that at least in these examples the two composers created similar types of settings, yet each varied the details according to his usual style. Strauss used the poems, *All mein Gedanken* and *Du meines Herzens Krönelein*, as nos. 1 and 2 of op. 21, a group of five lieder on *Schlichte Weisen* texts which he composed between February 1889 and January 1890 and which were published within a year by Joseph Aibl. Reger's acquaintance with Strauss's settings resulted in his transcriptions of these two songs for solo piano. Issued in 1899 by Aibl, these transcriptions may have been made at the request of the publisher rather than upon Reger's own initiative (see Chapter II, n. 5, pp. 211–12). In any case, Reger composed his own setting of *All mein Gedanken* in the fall of 1903 and had it published as no. 9 of the eighteen songs in op. 75 (Leipzig: Lauterbach & Kuhn, 1904). His *Du meines Herzens Krönelein* was written shortly thereafter (winter 1903–04); it forms the opening lied of his six-volume *Schlichte Weisen,* op. 76 (also published by Lauterbach & Kuhn, volume I in 1904). In spite of its title, Reger's sixty-song *Schlichte Weisen* uses no other texts from Dahn's collection. As a reflection of the poems, which begin with folk-song incipits and continue in Dahn's imitation of the folk style, both composers' settings are short, without preludes, interludes, or long postludes.[54] The predominantly syllabic vocal lines are less complex that those of many songs by either composer, and doubling of the voice by the accompaniment is more frequent than usual. On the other hand, Reger's accompaniments in particular hardly suggest the simplicity of folksong. In all four songs the voice and piano begin simultaneously; text repetitions and alterations are few indeed. The extent to which Strauss's settings may have affected Reger's conception of the lieder is difficult to determine. There are in these and other pairs—of which Strauss's are, with one exception,[55] earlier—certain similarities, especially superficially. Such features are found in their other lieder as well, however, and are more properly described as aspects of their individual styles that happen to coincide than as attempted imitations on the part of Reger. For example, in each pair of Dahn songs the vocal ranges are similar: Strauss's *All mein Gedanken* (in E major) has a range of $c^{\sharp 1}$ to $g^{\sharp 2}$, Reger's (F major) of c^1 to $f^{\sharp 2}$. Strauss's *Du meines Herzens Krönelein* (G-flat major) encompasses $d^{\flat 1}$

to g♭², Reger's (F major) d¹ to f². In all instances the ranges are of a typical compass for each composer.

Both Strauss and Reger preserve the dactylic poetic meter of *All mein Gedanken* in their music, although within different musical meters. As pointed out above on p. 70, Strauss uses a preponderance of ♪♫♫ figures (and variants thereof) in 2/4 meter. The dactylic feet are thus limited to the quarter-note unit; Reger's 6/8 meter allows for greater variety, with the foot taking up either half or whole measures. The regularity with which Strauss returns to his basic unit and the sparseness of his accompaniment result in a much simpler, more folkish setting than Reger's. Diatonic stepwise and triadic movement pervades Strauss's version, while Reger's vocal line moves about less predictably. The profusion of tempo, dynamic, and expression indications and changes in Reger's setting also creates a more complex lied. The notation of such details (or lack thereof) throughout their lieder reveals yet another difference between the two composers. It is probably coincidence rather than intent to imitate that both composers inserted a single triple bar into their duple structures. Strauss has a measure of 3/4 in part of the second line, "da, wo die Liebste ist," to further emphasize the high note on "Lieb." Reger's 9/8 measure occurs in lines 3–4, on "Mauer und Tor,/da hält kein."

The differences in their conceptions of the poem *All mein Gedanken* are obvious on a larger scale as well. Strauss's rhythmic regularity provides a series of two-measure phrases for each of the first eight lines of text. For the next two (final) lines he expands the phrases to four measures and repeats the tenth line, then the second half of the ninth. Thus the last two lines make up nearly half of his song—13 (and 2 of postlude) of a total of 31 measures—while in Reger's setting there is no text repetition, and these final lines take up only 7 (plus 1 of postlude) of the song's 29 measures. As in many of their other lieder, both composers create musical descriptions of certain text details. Here and in other examples Strauss's word painting is more frequent and explicit, almost to the point of being naive. They both precede and accompany "und klopfen und rufen" by staccato chords in imitation of knocking sounds, and both use similar vocal lines (see Ex. 2 on p. 40 and Ex. 33). Both set "hoch" in line 5

Ex. 33, Reger: *All mein Gedanken*, op. 75, no. 9 (mm. 21–23):

to high notes and "mach auf" (line 9) to rising intervals (Strauss on the repeat only). There is a hint of the bird's flight (after "Vögelein hoch durch die Luft" in line 5) in the accompaniments, but neither example is as unmistakable as most of Strauss's usual bird imitations. As a final pictorial emphasis, Strauss sets "grüssen" (line 10) to a nine-note melisma and echoes it literally in the final two-measure postlude.

Along with *All mein Gedanken, Du meines Herzens Krönelein* contains features that illustrate both the differences and the similarities between the lied styles of Strauss and Reger. Again, each uses a different meter (Strauss 2/4, Reger 6/8), key, formal structure, and accompaniment. As in *All mein Gedanken,* each composer varies the basic meter for one triple measure (again in different lines), and Strauss's structure is more clear-cut, with two-measure units for each line of text. On important words Strauss uses a unifying motive: a descending G-flat major triad appears four times and a three-note slurred figure three times. He unifies lines 3, 5, and 9, where the beloved is acclaimed as superior to all others ("andere" or "andern"), by reducing the texture in the accompaniment. Reger's phrase lengths, while less regular, can be divided into a musical repetition pattern of a b b^1 c b^2 d e a^1, with each section taking up two lines of text. Each of the b sectons begins with the lines containing "andere" or "andern," thus revealing a formal similarity with Strauss's lied. In most other lines, the two composers emphasize different words, and Reger's recurrent motives fall on words other than those stressed by Strauss; Reger uses formal structures—the a and a^1 sections—to unite the beginning and end of the song; Strauss achieves his unity by using the triadic motive and similar accompaniments at the beginning and end.

Neither Strauss nor Reger indulges in word painting in his setting of *Du meines Herzens Krönelein,* in *Glückes genug* (Strauss's op. 37, no. 1; Reger's op. 37, no. 3), or in certain other songs.[56] The mood established by both voice and piano in such songs is sustained throughout, not broken up by a succession of textual descriptions. Karl Straube claimed that in *Glückes genug* Strauss painted a picture of a nighttime scene, or the outward aspects of the poem, while Reger described only the inner mood, the overflowing emotional expression of a loving heart.[57] Certain similarities, particularly in textual rhythms and overall structure of the song, suggest here—more strongly than in other settings of identical texts—that Reger was influenced by Strauss's version, either consciously or unconsciously. Composed on 8 February 1898, Strauss's *Glückes genug* was published before the end of 1898. Reger composed his setting in the summer of 1899, certainly before 22 August, the day on which he completed his op. 37. In this same year his first set of Strauss transcriptions for Aibl was printed; *Glückes genug* was among the songs transcribed. Reger later returned to his own song for a harmonium transcription (published by Aibl in 1903) and again in 1916 for an orchestral version for voice and small orchestra (published by Universal-Edition in 1916).

The poem of *Glückes genug* comes from Detlev von Liliencron's

Der Haidegänger (1890). It consists of two rhyming four-line stanzas, each followed with the refrain "Glückes genug." The metric pattern of each stanza is 89894, the rhyme scheme *ababc dedec*, alternating feminine and masculine endings. Both composers set the iambic lines in 4/8 meter and separate the refrain from the body of the stanza. Strauss uses a musical as well as textual refrain, surrounding it with full measures of rests for the voice and broadening the declamation considerably. Reger typically sets his textual refrain to different melodic ideas. While Strauss expands the second refrain as a characteristic slowing down at the end of the song, Reger compresses it from three to two measures. The two settings are approximately the same length: Strauss's is longer by nine measures, eight of which are in the accompaniment only. Although Reger's second "Glückes genug" makes his text setting appear one and a half measures shorter, the approximate rate of declamation is similar in each song, except where Strauss moves more quickly in line 3. Both composers use an abundance of ♪.♪ and ♪♪ patterns (and subdivisions thereof) for the iambic feet of the poem; on many syllables the rhythms chosen by each coincide: line 6, for instance, is set entirely to the same note values. Ex. 34 provides a comparison of the rhythmic patterns of the two settings, showing how in the second stanza some of the values coincide even where barlines do not. This song is typical of other settings of identical texts by the two composers in that Strauss maintains regular two-measure phrases up to line 9, while in the second stanza Reger begins and/or ends lines 6–9 in the middle of the measure. The similarities of text declamation are of course obscured by the totally different melodic lines and accompaniments of these settings. In his piano part Reger has the right hand moving in undulating sixteenth-note triplet chords throughout; Strauss uses a variety of rhythmic configurations, among them his favorite parallel thirds in sixteenth notes. Just before Strauss's second stanza there is a sudden change in texture, dropping down to a single pitch in the accompaniment. In a manner reminiscent of Schumann's *Mondnacht*, he then builds up this single note into chords by the addition of adjacent pitches. This is an example of a dramatic device he also used in *All mein Gedanken, Die Nacht,* and other songs.

　　Several other texts set by both Strauss and Reger reveal the basic differences in their use of word painting or textual description and in their representation of poetic meter and rhythms by musical meter and rhythms. Strauss's word painting in his *Morgen!* is much more obvious than Reger's in his setting of the same poem. Strauss describes in music the phrase "langsam nieder steigen" by slowly descending intervals (Ex. 35a).[58] Reger's more gradual descent is—except for a ritardando—not in slower notes than the surrounding phrases (Ex. 35b). In the subsequent line, "stumm werden wir uns in die Augen schauen," Reger barely hints at the painting of "stumm" with a brief first-beat rest, while Strauss has a much longer rest followed by repeated-note declamation over slowly moving piano chords (also shown in Ex. 35a and b). In contrast to the

Ex. 34, *Glückes genug* (Detlev von Liliencron), rhythms of settings by Strauss (op. 37, no. 1) and Reger (op. 37, no. 3):

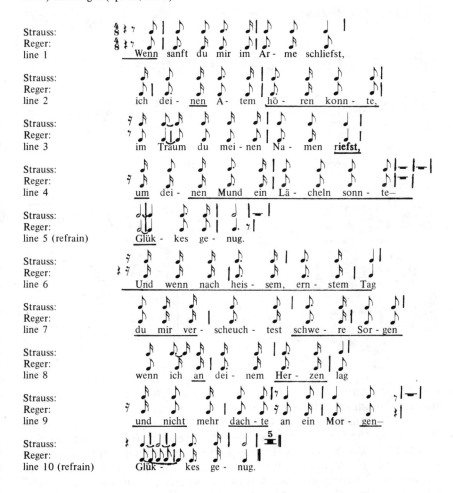

Note: Underlined syllables are those set to identical rhythms. Eleven instances of ♪♪ in the original are here represented as ♪ because the rate of declamation is the same as for ♪. In line 3, the phrase "im Traum du meinen" has the same rhythmic configuration in both settings, only Strauss's version moves twice as fast. In line 9, the sixth note of Reger's setting has here been corrected to ♪; it is wrongly engraved as ♪ in *Max Reger. Sämtliche Werke*, XXXI, 119.

Ex. 35a, Strauss: *Morgen!*, op. 27, no. 4 (mm. 27–32):

Ex. 35b, Reger: *Morgen!*, op. 66, no. 10 (mm. 12–13):

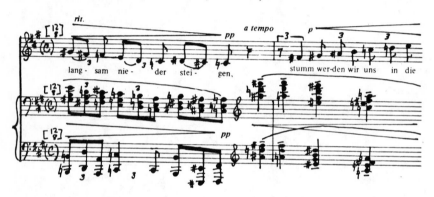

first 29 measures of his lied, Strauss completes the remaining text, through "stummes Schweigen," in this character.[59]

Both composers begin the first line of text in *Morgen!* with similar rhythms; as the songs progress, however, Reger restricts himself to note values from a sixteenth to dotted quarter, with triplet eighth notes predominating. His signature of common time could just as well have been written as 12/8 from measure 6 onward, where he indicates "quasi 12/8" for both voice and piano. As in his setting of *Freundliche Vision* (no. 2 in the same opus), the too frequent long-short triplet patterns are in danger of becoming sing-songy.[60] Strauss's vocal rhythms, on the other hand, range from sixteenth notes to whole notes, with duplet eighths and dotted quarter-eighth combinations used most frequently. The whole note is used dramatically on the final word "Schweigen." Both composers reflect another aspect of the text, the fact that Mackay's poem both begins and ends with ellipsis points.[61] These are translated into music by both composers: they both begin the text on a chromatically altered upbeat, end the text on a note other than the tonic, and conclude the postlude without settling on the root of the tonic chord. Strauss ends on a tonic six-four chord (cadencing vi-I$_4^6$ in G major), Reger on a I$_4^6$-iii cadence in the tonic (A major).

In their settings of Henckell's *Ich schwebe*, Strauss and Reger capture in their opening vocal phrases (Ex. 36) not only the literal description of the first line but also the essence of the entire poem. In both examples almost the entire vocal range of the song is covered in this single phrase. Later in the song, Strauss emphasizes "Melodien," which Reger passes over quickly.[62] Strauss's interpretation of the text of Bierbaum's *Traum durch die Dämmerung* also emphasizes details with unmistakably graphic descriptions of the words in music. Both composers use

Ex. 36, Strauss: *Ich schwebe,* op. 48, no. 2 (mm. 8–12), and Reger: *Ich schwebe,* op. 62, no. 14 (mm. 1–2):   (Range:)

ostinato figures throughout the accompaniment to give their lieder a dream-like character and continuity of mood. Strauss also describes in the repeated piano rhythms the poet walking through the meadows at twilight, as he does in another lied, *Des Dichters Abendgang*. He begins *Traum durch die Dämmerung* with the accompaniment in a low range, providing further atmosphere and imagery. In the vocal line he returns several times to the lowest pitch of the range (c$\sharp^1$). Certain of his favorite words ("schönsten," "mildes," and "blaues") are given slurred figures of two or three notes to a syllable. Rather than be too obvious about placing "tief" on a low note, he sets line 5 ("tief . . . Jasmin") to a descending line. Although it may not have been intentional description, line 7 ("ich gehe nicht schnell, ich eile nicht") could even be said to contain word painting, since it does not move in faster rhythms than the surrounding lines. Word description in the following phrase is certainly intended, as the voice (doubled at the lower octave by the piano) ascends in a continuous line to describe the velvet ribbon drawing the dreamer through the twilight to the "land of love."[63] Strauss repeats this ascent, without the final d^2, to words drawn from various textual phrases at the end of the lied (see Ex. 37a). Reger also uses ascending scales in his lied for both statements of the line "durch Dämmergrau in der liebe Land" (lines 6 and 9; see Ex. 37b). Like the rest of his setting of this text, Reger's chromatically rising vocal lines are more abstract and do not attempt to paint the text as graphically as Strauss's. At least one critic claimed that Reger's lied could easily

Ex. 37a, Strauss: *Traum durch die Dämmerung*, op. 29, no. 1 (mm. 17–22 and 28–33):

ich ge- he nicht schnell, ich ei- le nicht; mich zieht ein wei-ches, sam- te- nes Band durch Däm- mer- grau in der

Lie- be Land, durch Däm-mer-grau in der Lie- be Land, in ein mil- des, blau- es Licht.___

Ex. 37b, Reger: *Traum durch die Dämmerung*, op. 35, no. 3 (mm. 11–14 and 18–21):

Durch Däm- mer grau in der Lie- be Land ich ge- he nicht schnell,

durch Däm- mer- grau in der Lie- be Land, in ein blau- es, mil- des Licht.

stand up to Strauss's—if not surpass it—in the illustration of the text through its musical setting.[64] What Strauss accomplishes through the description of details overlaid on the mood painting of the piano part Reger achieves through a more abstract rendering of the text as a whole. This lied and several others illustrate Straube's claim that Strauss is more concerned with the sense of individual stanzas and with providing a musical translation for single words, while Reger enwraps the poem in a "gentle, idealized aura that gradually and peacefully unfolds."[65]

In a very different kind of song, *Hat gesagt—bleibt's nicht dabei*, Strauss's word painting is extremely obvious and perhaps intentionally naive because he is using a folk poem. In the first stanza he uses short descriptive melismas for "wiegen," and in the second stanza for "Vögelein"; Reger does similarly in his setting (op. 75, no. 12). Strauss's unmistakable descriptions of "seiden" ("to boil"), of "drei Küsslein," and of other words are not echoed by Reger (see Ex. 38 for motives from Strauss's illustrative accompaniment). Both *Hat gesagt—bleibt nichts dabei* and *Traum durch die Dämmerung* are typical of the two composers' lieder in other respects. For instance, in both Strauss repeats the text of much of the final stanza; Reger uses no text repetition in *Traum durch die Dämmerung* and only a little (nine words) in *Hat gesagt—bleibt's nicht dabei*.

As these comparisons of Strauss's and Reger's lieder show, some features of Strauss's text setting can be found in the songs of other composers. His closest affinity is definitely with such contemporaries as Reger, but there are clear precedents for several aspects of his text setting in the songs of early nineteenth-century composers as well. Certain features stand out as characteristic of Strauss, although they are not his exclusive

Ex. 38, Strauss: *Hat gesagt—bleibt's nicht dabei,* op. 36, no. 3 (motives from mm. 5–6, 16–18, and 25–26):

property. The aspects of his lieder that one could call most clearly "Straussian" are often found in his larger works too. There are, for example, the wide ranges, extreme tessituras, and sudden changes of register in the vocal lines of not only the songs but also the choral works and, more importantly, the operas. The descriptive word painting in certain of the songs appears just as clearly (and often just as naively) in the tone poems and in passages of most of the operas. Text-related rhythmic motives are also found in a variety of his large and small compositions. Other Straussian musical characteristics are found in a small dimension in the songs as well as on a grander scale in the major works. This is true particularly of harmonic language, a topic which is outside the scope and aim of this study. In several ways, the songs of the 1880's and 1890's can be viewed as studies for later and larger compositions.

IV

MANUSCRIPT AND PRINTED SOURCES OF THE LIEDER

The manuscript and printed sources of Strauss's lieder fall into four categories: autograph sketches and fragments; manuscripts of complete songs or groups of songs (autographs and a very few copyists' copies); printed editions including the *Gesamtausgabe der Lieder;* and manuscripts and prints containing new versions, primarily orchestrations of lieder originally written with piano accompaniment. Within all of these divisions there are subdivisions, each of which will be taken up in turn. The lack of preliminary sketches, intermediate drafts, and final autographs for many songs makes a thorough study of the creation of Strauss's lieder very difficult. At best, we are able to reconstruct the stages of composition and to suggest how many sketches and manuscript versions may have preceded the first edition. The *Sechs Lieder nach Gedichten von Clemens Brentano* of op. 68, dating from 1918, are exceptional in being the only group of songs for which there are nearly complete sources in each of the categories. This opus will be discussed in some detail in Chapter V as an attempt to understand the composer at work. The steps taken in the creation of op. 68 cannot, however, be assumed to have been Strauss's invariable method of working. A number of factors stand in the way of such a generalization; most important among them are his age and professional occupations of the moment, the length of time spent on the composition, opportunities for performance, other compositions in progress at the same time, and other personal matters.

Autograph Sketches and Fragments

The surviving sketches for Strauss's lieder fall into two types: single sheets or leaves of various sizes and the sketchbooks, most of which are in a small oblong format ca. 12 by 16.5 cm, with six to twelve staves per page. Rather few of the former are known to be extant, catalogued, and available to the scholar today; the handful of lieder sketches now in European libraries date from various periods of Strauss's life and show songs at different stages in their conception. There are also a few loose sheets of sketches for songs in the Strauss family's private collection, the Richard Strauss-Archiv (listed throughout Asow as "Sammlung Strauss"), at their home in Garmisch-Partenkirchen. As a sample of these, there is a group of sketches for three early songs (AV 5, 6, and 7, dating from ca. 1871) transcribed by Willi Schuh and published in NL, pp. 101–08. The first song, *Waldkonzert,* survives in two versions: a sketch of the entire song and a more fully worked out autograph ink copy of the first forty-five measures. (Both versions are printed by Schuh.) Of the other two, *Der weisse Hirsch* is an autograph ink copy, possibly representing a version of the entire song (but not in polished, final form), while *Der böhmische Musikant* is a fragment in pencil.

Most of Strauss's sketches were made in small bound volumes, some 160 of which are known to be in existence today. Like Beethoven, he is reported to have carried these books with him, always prepared to jot down ideas, and to have done much of his sketching out of doors. The rather tattered appearance of many of the books—along with their nearly indecipherable pencil markings, especially for those works in the earliest stages of composition—would seem to bear this out. Writing about Strauss's sketches, Ernst Roth described some of them as nearly unreadable. At the same time, he found that the basic ideas present in even the earliest sketches were often retained in the finished compositions.[1] Around 1890 Strauss explained to a friend the importance of his initial ideas for a composition:

> It is of the utmost importance to put them on paper immediately lest they quickly fade away. Once [they are] fixed, I often look at them again and this conjures up the same frame of mind that gave them birth; thus the ideas grow and expand. I am a firm believer in the germination of the idea.[2]

The contents of 139 of these sketchbooks (numbered 1–143 but lacking 14, 55, 119, and 132) are summarized in a supplement of Asow, pp. 1485–88 and 1663. This listing, by opus or AV number in chronological order, includes several lieder and most of the major works. The numerous books devoted to operas (e.g., nineteen for *Die Liebe der Danae,* ten for *Die Frau ohne Schatten*) indicate the extent to which Strauss first put down his ideas in sketch form. The editors of Asow have not cross-listed the books themselves in numerical order, and nowhere is the numbering system explained. No reference is made to these books in the first two volumes of Asow; in the third volume, a few works without opus numbers have sketchbooks listed among the sources, but the books are not identified with the numbers used in this list. A glance at the listing of the contents of the sketchbooks in Asow as well as on or inside the covers of some of the books themselves informs the scholar not to expect extensive sketches for shorter works in these books, since several compositions may appear in a single volume. Sketchbook no. 1, for example, includes sketches for at least one song in each of opp. 15, 17, 19, 21, and 22—as well as for the first four tone poems (*Aus Italien, Don Juan, Macbeth,* and *Tod und Verklärung*), the opera *Guntram,* and two choral works.[3]

The length of the individual sketchbooks varies considerably; some of the longer ones run to over one hundred pages, while others have only five or six pages filled (and filmed). The average sketchbook has between fifty and sixty fully or partially filled pages. There is no consistent pagination. In certain sections of some books—particularly in sketches or rough drafts for larger works—Strauss numbered either pages or openings, while in other books he used no numbering at all. No modern pagination for the books has been established to date, nor have the sketches been discussed enough in the Strauss literature for any definitive numbering system to have been adopted. When first working with the sketchbook films, I found it most convenient to refer to opening numbers; to avoid error and confusion, I have retained this system in the present study. It should be usable with both the Bayerische Staatsbibliothek films and the original sketchbooks (if completely blank openings are disregarded), should they again be made available for study. Since a consistent procedure was not used for the filming, some books begin on film with the outside cover (linen or heavy unlined paper, if present), some with the first opening (inside cover verso, unlined page recto), and others with the second opening (unlined page verso, first page of staff paper recto). Blank openings and unfilled sections of the books were apparently omitted from the films; this is the case with at least four of the books containing lieder (nos. 39, 42, 139, and 143).[4] Since very few outside covers were filmed, I begin my numbering with the first opening (whether actually filmed or not) because it often lists contents or contains texts and annotations by the composer. Thus the second opening always has the first page of staff paper on its recto side.

The location of these sketchbooks is not indicated in Asow, nor is their existence acknowledged in the GL critical commentary. When Asow compiled the first two volumes of his thematic catalogue, the sketchbooks were probably not yet indexed; only a few single sketches are even mentioned for the entries in these volumes (all works with opus numbers), and nothing is said concerning the possibility that more loose sketches or any sketchbooks might be extant. For the AV works in volume III, more sketches are accounted for, especially those in the large collection "Kindermanuscripte" at the Strauss Archive and those for lost works where only sketches are extant. In some instances, sketchbooks referred to in one part of volume III as belonging to the Archive do not turn up in the numbered listing on pp. 1485–88 and 1663. Unlike certain other manuscripts to be discussed below, the sketchbooks listed on these pages are actually present in a safe within the Strausses' Garmisch home.

As an expansion of his listing of sketchbooks in Asow, Franz Trenner has recently published a catalogue, *Die Skizzenbücher von Richard Strauss aus dem Richard-Strauss-Archiv in Garmisch* (Tutzing, 1977), the first volume in the series *Veröffentlichungen der Richard-Strauss-Gesellschaft München,* of which he is also general editor. Trenner's particular advantage in the preparation of this volume was access to the original sketchbooks in the Strauss Archive. Since the collection is not open to the public, most interested scholars have to rely on the filmed copies of the sketchbooks in the Bayerische Staatsbibliothek. There are variants in sequence between the films and Trenner's book, requiring that any user of the films work out his own equivalencies from the *Textteil* (pp. 1–143) and from the facsimiles (*Bildteil*, pp. 147–276) of the first page of music in each book.[5] To the 139 books enumerated in Asow, Trenner has added 5 more.

The contents of each sketchbook are described in considerably more detail in Trenner's monograph than in Asow. The listings in the *Textteil* follow this sequence: approximate date(s) of origin, number of pages, writing medium, number of blank or missing pages, binding, annotations (if any) on the cover, size and format. Next, under a section headed *Inhalt*, appear the names of works for which Trenner has found sketches in the book (these are limited to completed works). In italics, denoting Strauss's own entries in the books, appear a mixture of titles, tempo markings, dates (extremely rarely), movement headings, first lines of texts, and other textual material that aids in identification of the books' contents. The final entry for each book indicates any text on the back cover.

Approximately twenty other surviving sketchbooks are owned by other individuals or institutions; these are not included in the numerical listing of sketchbooks in Asow, but some do appear in the source citations for individual AV works. How many sketchbooks beyond these Strauss may have filled is not known. Considering the number of pages devoted to certain of the larger works, it seems likely that there were once many more books or loose sheets—or that there are even now numerous privately owned sketches, not accounted for in the thematic catalogue or in critical commentaries of the GL volumes, which may eventually come to light.

The discovery, identification, and cataloguing of the works in the sketchbooks reveal an important aspect of Strauss as song composer, one which has hitherto been almost completely neglected. If the works included in Asow's section V ("Fragmente . . . Pläne und Anregungen," AV 193–306) are taken to include all works planned and/or begun by Strauss but not surviving in complete form, one would assume that the lied was not a genre in which he abandoned compositions before completion. Only three unfinished songs are listed in this section: AV 193, 221A, and 244. A few songs which did not reach final form are indexed in other parts of Asow (II, "Werke ohne Opuszahlen"—see AV 5, 6, and 7 mentioned above—and III, "Verschollene Kompositionen"). Still others are omitted entirely from Asow. Certain sketches, fragments which Strauss apparently abandoned, are the only surviving sources of several songs. Besides the three songs appearing in NL, the only other sketches for unfinished songs discussed in the Strauss literature are *Nachts in der Kajüte*, mentioned by Kravitt as an "unpublished song (maybe never completed),"[6] and two incomplete late songs included in Schuh's 1950 study of Strauss's last compositions. These two songs are *Nacht* (AV 303), of which only some fifteen measures were sketched (sketchbook 141, opening 10; see Illustration 6) and *Malven* (AV 304), which apparently survives in a complete draft version.[7] Although the complete lied is at present unavailable, sketchbook 142 contains a copy of the complete poem in Strauss's hand, with rough drafts for most of the music.

In addition to sketches for songs that eventually reached publication, there are in the sketchbooks I have examined fragments of at least twenty-one songs, three choruses on texts similar to the texts used for lieder, and three texts copied out for eventual use in composition, probably intended for lieder. Appendix B of the present study lists these works, none of which is mentioned in any section of Asow or, to my knowledge, in any other source besides those few cited in the righthand column of the Appendix, "Description of sketch." Schuh indexed seven of the unpublished Goethe settings in his *Goethe-Vertonungen,* but has not mentioned them in any of his numerous writings on Strauss to date.[8] The sketches for these songs and choruses range from a mere two-measure introductory piano figuration—as for *Sonnensegen*—to nearly complete statements of text and melody with partial accompaniment—as for *Freundliches Begegnen* and *Blumenglöckchen.* Most of these sketches date from a period in Strauss's life—the first few years of the twentieth century—when he was turning away from lieder composition. Their incomplete state further attests to his dwindling interest in the lied, which came as a result of his arguments with and promises to his publishers, the end of his wife's performing career, and his growing preoccupation with larger dramatic compositions. Most of the poets whose works inspired these sketches are the same poets whose verses Strauss set in the completed and published songs of this period, the six groups between op. 46 and op. 56. Among the incomplete song sketches, only two are dated in the sketchbooks. These are *Freundliches Begegnen* and *Blumenglöckchen,* composed in the two days following the completion of *Gefunden,* op. 56, no. 1. *Gefunden,* like the other two a setting of a Goethe poem, appears in the sketchbook on the two pages immediately preceding the sketches of the other two songs and is dated "Marquartstein, 31. Juli." In a letter to his parents on 3 August 1903, the day after the last of these three songs was sketched, Strauss mentions that he has just set a couple ("ein Paar") of Goethe poems.[9] Since the other newly identified sketches do not bear dates, their place in the chronology of Strauss's lieder can be determined only by the works surrounding them in the books (few books have any dates at all in Strauss's hand) and by bits of evidence such as the above-mentioned letter.

It is noteworthy that of the twenty-seven items in Appendix B eleven have texts by Goethe; these nearly double the number of Strauss's Goethe settings. Five of the eleven poems come from the *West-östlicher Divan,* a favorite source of the composer's, especially in the years between 1918 and 1942. From the sketch of *Lesebuch* (1903–04), it now appears that Strauss's interest in this collection of verse dates from an

Illustration 6

Sketches of *Nacht* (AV 303) in sketchbook 141, opening 10 (bottom half), and *Beim Schlafengehn* (AV 150/III), opening 10ᵛ (top half), slightly reduced.

[10ᵛ]

[mm. 65–70]

[10ʳ]

[2. Strophe]

[die Schwalben sind müde, später als Geigenmotiv u. in der 3. Strophe dissonierend]

earlier period than hitherto suggested. *Bleiben, Gehen, Gehen, Bleiben* and *Wanderlied*, from *Wilhelm Meisters Wanderjahre*, Book III, indicate for the first time that Strauss may not have completely overlooked the *Wilhelm Meister* stories. Although he was well read and seems to have spent much of his time with poetry volumes in his search for suitable lieder texts, Strauss may not have been aware of the original source of these two poems. At the top of the *Wanderlied* sketch (book 17, opening 47ʳ), he indicated the source of the poem in this way: "zu Gôthes Wanderlied/Vermischte Gedichte/Gedichte I." (This poem appears only in the *Wilhelm Meister* book, not among the miscellaneous poems in any of the complete editions I have examined, nor is it excerpted in the other collections of Goethe's poetry I have checked.)

In light of Strauss's own comments on how he was inspired by the poetry and his manner of composing lieder, it might be suggested that he decided that certain of the texts begun in the sketchbooks were not sufficiently inspiring to pursue to completion. Perhaps this, rather than the larger reasons cited above for the sketches that were abandoned shortly after 1900, is the case with the Brentano (?) song *Abendständchen*, found in sketchbook 39 (which dates from early 1918). *Abendständchen* occupies seven pages in the middle of a long sketchbook otherwise devoted exclusively to the six songs published as op. 68. While only some twenty measures of instrumental ideas centering on two motives are given for *Abendständchen*, sketches for each of the other songs include substantial portions of the accompaniment as well as most of the vocal line and its text.[10]

An entirely different reason can be suggested for Strauss's abandoning the third song for Calderón's play *Der Richter von Zalamea*. This sketch follows its two companions, *Liebeslied* and *Lied der Chispa* (AV 96, nos. I and II) in sketchbook 11, which dates from 1903–04. The songs are sung by the soldier Rebolledo (*Liebesliedchen*); by Chispa, a canteen proprietress, with a refrain by the soldiers (*Lied der Chispa*); and by Chispa alternating in a duet with Rebolledo (untitled sketch, here designated by the title *[Chispa III]*, since Strauss originally entitled the preceding song *Chispa II*). The sketches for all three songs show the outlines of a guitar-like accompaniment on two staves; in the final version no. I is for guitar and harp, no. II for guitar and two harps. In the sketchbook, no. I is most nearly complete; it contains all of the vocal line, which is identical to that of the ink copy and GL version, but a whole step higher throughout. The sketch of no. II lacks the soldiers' three refrains but includes all of Chispa's lines and music. In no. III, the existence of which is hinted at in Asow, p. 1230, the accompaniment is outlined in only thirteen of the first thirty-four measures, and then breaks off completely. Next follows an alternation of fifteen more measures of textless melody for Chispa and twenty-five for Rebolledo.

Strauss was originally to have composed a group of three songs for Otto Brahm's new German production of the play on 7 September 1904 at the Berlin Lessingtheater.[11] The theater program makes no mention of the music or its composer, and it is not clear whether any of Strauss's music was actually used. The play is well suited to music; it contains references to songs or short outbursts of song in places besides the ones where these three songs would fit. On 16 August 1904 Strauss prepared clean ink copies of the two completed songs; no other source for the third one is known. Perhaps it had already been decided at this time that his music would not be used in the production, and he saw no point in continuing with the composition. Strauss, it seems, made no effort in his lifetime to have these songs published—although the two ink copies were gathered together in a manuscript collection which he labeled "Gedruckte Lieder." (All of the other songs in this collection at the Strauss Archive, now divided up by opus number, were indeed published in Strauss's lifetime.) The Calderón songs were probably forgotten, along with some of his earlier attempts at writing incidental music for plays and arias for singspiels.

Manuscripts of Complete Songs or Groups of Songs

The autograph manuscript sources for Strauss's completed songs can be brought under better bibliographic control than can the sketches. Of the eighty-six opus numbers used by the composer, a full thirty are devoted to songs. Of these, approximately half are known to exist in final manuscript versions containing the complete opus. The Garmisch archive holds complete manuscripts for opp. 43, 46, 47, 67, and 68 (all for voice and piano, once part of the collection "Gedruckte Lieder") and for opp. 33, 44, and 71 (for voice and orchestra). A second important source is the archive of Universal-Edition, which took over the Munich firm of Joseph Aibl in 1904. The manuscripts owned by Universal include opp. 19, 21, 29, 32, and 36; these served as the engraver's copies (*Stichvorlagen*) for Aibl's first editions. Since 1961, the manuscripts have been on loan at the British Library (Loan 49, nos. 8–12), where it is believed they will remain. A second publisher, Adolph Fürstner, owns *Stichvorlagen* of opp. 22 and 31.[12] Library collections are another source for Strauss's song manuscripts, but of these autographs only a few are devoted to a complete opus. The *Stichvorlage* of op. 10, for example, was sold by Universal shortly before World War II; it is now in the Mary Flagler Cary Collection at the Pierpont Morgan Library in New York. It and other *Stichvorlagen* show that Strauss was the ideal composer in the eyes of his publishers and engravers. Rarely did he change his mind after submitting a manuscript for publication—even in instances where he submitted early scenes of an opera while still orchestrating the final ones. The song manuscripts contain the editor's and engraver's markings and an occasional note to Strauss, but almost no additions or alterations in the composer's hand. These markings are for the most part limited to numbers designating systems and pages; translations of German tempo and expression indications into Italian; the crossing out or addition of dates, poets' names, and opus numbers; the addition of copyright and other notices; and English versions of the texts. The *Stichvorlage* of op. 10 is unique in that it includes a ninth song, *Wer hat's gethan?*, which remained unpublished and forgotten until the 1970's. Both pages of the manuscript on which this song occurs are marked out with a large "x." The addition of the composer's name and opus number as well as the crossing out of the date of completion (which Strauss systematically recorded) at the end of this song—as for the other eight—suggest that an editor began to prepare the manuscript for the engraver before the deletion was decided upon. There are no engraver's indications of system divisions on these two pages, as there are on all other pages of the manuscript, nor are the pages themselves numbered. Schuh suggests certain musical reasons why this particular song may have been eliminated from the opus.[13] A purely practical reason can be added: Aibl published op. 10 in two *Hefte* of four songs each, preferring this format to the issue of single songs. As printed, the music of the two groups takes up ten and eleven pages, respectively. To add a fifth song to either would create a sixteen- rather than a twelve-page publication; this would unbalance the two parts of the opus and cost more to produce. (The cost of publishing Strauss's lieder was a topic about which Spitzweg complained to the composer.)

All of the *Stichvorlagen* bear witness to Strauss's attention to correctness of detail in matters of placement, stemming, and accidentals. Throughout his life he wrote out his manuscripts (but not his sketches) in a clear and consistent, if miniscule, hand. The manuscripts of the *Four Last Songs* are penned as carefully as the earlier works. Capitalizing upon his neat manuscript, during and after World War II Strauss recopied the manuscripts of some of the tone poems and other compositions (some writers claim from memory!) to sell in order to ease his financial straits. Some of these scores and new copies were provided as security in Swiss hotels where it was known that the Strausses might be unable to pay their bills. The Strauss Archive now holds such copies of *Don Juan, Till Eulenspiegel,* and *Tod und Verklärung* made ,in 1944; presumably others exist because both the composer and other writers refer a number of times to this copying.[14] Few lieder appear to have been copied at this time, doubtless because their value would have been less than that of the orchestral compositions. A single song manuscript, that of *Breit über mein Haupt* (op. 19, no. 2), is known to have been made then (the copy, now in the Strauss Archive, is dated 31 March 1944). Several decades earlier, Strauss prepared a fair copy of *Morgen!* for the Paris Exposition of 1900 on their special Exposition paper.[15]

Besides the *Stichvorlagen,* manuscripts of individual songs are scattered about in various German, Austrian, British, and American libraries as well as in a few other collections. Taken together, all of these sources cover approximately ninety percent of Strauss's more than two hundred lieder. Of the groups published with opus numbers, the only complete group without any extant manuscripts is op. 77; all that appears to survive of it is the sketch of one song. Of the early songs—those written before op. 10—at least seventeen are totally lost. Their manuscripts may have disappeared just before or during World War I; certainly they did not survive World War II.[16] When writing his *Richard Strauss*, first edition (Berlin, 1911), Max Steinitzer had access to these works. The thematic incipits he provides are, for a few of the songs, their only known music.[17] Steinitzer also indicates the owners of the manuscripts (including himself). The now lost works belonged primarily to Strauss's Aunt Johanna Pschorr, and their subsequent fate is not known. Some of them are, however, extant at the Strauss Archive in an undated collection of sixteen early songs copied in two hands, both unidentified. The title "Jugendlieder (ungedruckte), Copien" is added in Strauss's own hand (mature rather than childish, suggesting a date well after their original composition in the 1870's). Only a few early authenticated autographs are in existence at the Garmisch Strauss Archive and in other locations.

It appears that Strauss did not preserve manuscript copies of his songs in an intermediate version between the sketches and the final *Stichvorlage,* though it is hard to imagine that he did not make such copies. Few single autograph songs exist today, and these are mostly transposed versions or copies made for specific singers and performances rather than versions that might have preceded the *Stichvorlagen* or other fair copies. If the unique preserved manuscript was entrusted to the publisher and retained by him, this would certainly explain the neglect of *Wer hat's gethan?.* Aibl was in the habit of retaining the composer's manuscripts; Fürstner did so at first, but with the songs after 1900 sometimes returned the *Stichvorlage* to Strauss. The manuscripts themselves show that the engraver actually worked from the autograph, and the annotations on a few manuscripts seem to indicate that Strauss read proofs against these originals. Only in relation to the later operas is there evidence that a copyist prepared a new working copy for the engraver.[18] If any such copies are extant, they are not catalogued in Asow. For transposed editions of the songs, the engraver did not require a separate manuscript, but effected the proper transpositions from the original manuscript or printed copy. English translations were entered in ink directly on the original manuscript.

A few additional manuscripts created as gifts, some of which might more properly be called fragments, also survive. These are rather like the manuscripts copied for profit in the 1940's in that they are not authoritative in helping to establish authentic readings (in the rare cases where this is necessary). Strauss sometimes copied out the voice part or only a few measures of it for his friends. The vocal line of *Mohnblumen* (op. 22, no. 2), for example, he wrote out with a dedication to Marie Fleisch-Prell on 16 January 1889.[19] Originally composed on 29 March 1888 but not published until early 1891, this song has a voice part that remains unchanged in the different manuscripts and prints. Other examples of copies include the complete voice part and text of *Gefunden* (op. 56, no. 1), which Strauss wrote in a letter and inscribed to his friend Anton Kippenberg on the latter's seventieth birthday (22 May 1944).[20] In a letter to Stefan Zweig on 24 January 1933, in which he expressed his pleasure at working with Zweig on *Die schweigsame Frau,* Strauss wrote out eight measures of the vocal line with its text from *Ich trage meine Minne* (op. 32, no. 1). The slightly varied rhythms may indicate that Strauss wrote the melody from memory; the song was originally composed thirty-seven years earlier.[21] In a thank-you letter to Eugen Antosch on 29 February 1945, the composer quoted a fragment of the voice part and text of *Zueignung* (op. 10, no. 1), again because of its suitable text.[22] Such self-quotations may be looked upon as an extension of the composer's penchant for quoting himself in tone poem, opera, and song.

A dedicatory manuscript of more musical interest than the above fragments is the version of *Notturno* (op. 44, no. 1) that Strauss prepared for Ernestine Schumann-Heink in 1902. The song, for low voice and orchestra, was originally written between January and 16 September 1899. Before the year was out, the score was published by Robert Forberg (Leipzig), who also issued in that year a version for voice with solo violin and piano reduction by Otto Singer.[23] Frau Schumann-Heink's copy provides an opportunity for comparison of the two piano reductions, one made by the composer after the first performance and publication of the song, and the earlier one by Singer, who prepared several other reductions for Strauss's operas and songs—as well as piano arrangements for two and four hands of orchestral works—with the composer's complete approval. Strauss's version is on the whole scored less fully and contains less of the thematic material than Singer's. The sparseness of the accompaniment, the empty staves in place of a postlude, and a few indications of orchestral instruments show that this is probably a study copy to be used by the singer in preparing for an orchestral performance of the song or a reduction for her rehearsal pianist.[24] It is certainly not a final pianistic rendering of the accompaniment, but it is of interest if taken as an example of the sort of reduction that Strauss himself might have used in coaching a singer before orchestral performances. Why he prepared such a manuscript instead of supplying the soloist with a printed copy is unclear, since the song remains in its original key and there are almost no changes in the voice part. The only details at variance with the voice part of the orchestral score are missing dynamics in measures 27 and 149, a missing tempo indication in measure 47, and one half note replacing a whole note in measure 220. Added in this manuscript but not in either orchestral or piano printed versions are several dynamic markings (mm. 70, 72, 81, 88, 92, 95, 101, and 179), a single expression mark (m. 94), and two tempo changes (mm. 114 and 235). Perhaps Strauss felt these additional interpretative indications would be helpful for the singer, particularly if he himself was not preparing her for the performance. The manuscript may also have been written out as a personal gesture toward a favorite singer, who in 1909 was to be his first Klytemnestra and to whom he had recently (in 1899) dedicated the three songs in op. 43—without, however, giving her a manuscript of them.

It appears that Strauss did not ordinarily give the manuscripts of his songs to their dedicatees until his last years. Even when he created works for particular artists who would perform them (as op. 68 for Elisabeth Schumann) or dedicated works to singers who had served him well in the past (Schumann, Hans Giessen, Eugen Gura, and others) or would in the future (Heinrich Vogl of the Munich Opera, to whom op. 10 was dedicated some months before Strauss returned to Munich), he did not provide dedicatory manuscripts. Later on, it became his custom to give away sketchbooks of already completed works. References in his correspondence mention such gifts to Willi Schuh and Joseph Keilberth.[25] This tradition is being continued by Strauss's heirs, who, unlike him, are at least retaining photocopies for their own collection. The gifts, like some of the dedications of songs, do not always bear a direct relationship to the person or event; they are given mainly as gestures of gratitude. Sketches of songs, for instance, were given to Keilberth (*Ruhe, meine Seele!*) and Rudolph Hartmann (*Die Ulme zu Hirsau*) for their work in the fall 1963 performances of *Die Frau ohne Schatten* in Munich. Since the Strauss Archive has sketchbooks containing material for this opera, one wonders why more appropriate gifts were not made. Perhaps (as with the copying of the larger works in the 1940's) the greater value of the tone poems and operas was recognized, and the family was less willing to part with whole sketchbooks than with single sheets for smaller compositions. Further song sketches were given to Willi Schuh as a Strauss centenary gift in 1964 (*Waldseligkeit*) and—most appropriately—in 1969 Hans Hotter received sketches of *Vom künftigen Alter*. The last of these songs was dedicated to Hotter, who gave the first public performance of it in 1964 (also the year of its initial publication).

While the spirit of giving these gifts is consistent with Strauss's concern for and interest in his fellow musicians and family friends, it is making worse an already confused situation regarding the manuscript sources of his music. Both Asow and GL list all sources owned by the Strauss family as being in the Garmisch home (Asow's "Sammlung Strauss"). Sketchbooks and a few other items are kept (at least as of 1971) in a safe in the family house itself. Certain complete manuscripts, such as the piano version of op. 68, which I was able to examine in person, are kept in a Garmisch bank vault. Still others, among them some of the orchestral lieder, are unavailable today for study purposes (again because of the greater value of Strauss's orchestral music?). Not wishing to reveal the location of these works, the family prefers to list them as in the Archive. Although I have no conclusive evidence, I suspect that these manuscripts may remain on deposit in Switzerland, either in a bank or elsewhere. It seems likely that Strauss took with him many of his works when he left for Switzerland in 1945, leaving them there when he returned to Garmisch in May 1949.[26] In the 1950's the first (Berlin) Internationale Richard Strauss-Gesellschaft made an appeal for original manuscripts—or at least photocopies of them—for the Garmisch collection.[27] Some copies were obtained, but the project was short lived and has not been continued by the present Viennese Gesellschaft. The family does not appear to have persisted in assembling copies or cataloguing all of the manuscript sources now in existence elsewhere. The Strauss Archive did for a time (in the 1950's or 60's) receive funds and staff from the German government; ever since this aid was discontinued at the family's request, access to the collection has not been encouraged.[28] The Strausses appear to view the archive as a personal monument to their ancestor—a private collection to be admired by those who make a pilgrimage to Garmisch to honor his memory.

Printed Editions

The various editions of Strauss's lieder show rather few changes of substance from the first edition (and its *Stichvorlage*) to the recent versions of the GL. Most of the latter, in fact, are reprints. Besides the exact reprints, the editions after the first include transpositions and translations, as shown here in Chapter I with the example of op. 10. The transpositions were prepared from the original manuscript (as in the case of opp. 27 and 32, where two or three versions of the songs appeared simultaneously) or from the first edition (as in most of the earlier song groups, of which transpositions were made some years after the initial release, often at the time of reprinting). Translations could easily be added to or deleted from existing plates. Except for the addition of an occasional tie or slur or the subdivision of a note to accommodate the new text, the translations did not require new engraving. In some cases plate numbers confirm the use of the same originals (whether plates or printed copies made from them) for reprints with added translations. In other cases, as in Universal's substitution of its own plate numbers for Aibl's and as in most of the GL, new sets of plate numbers do not indicate new engraving, since the main part of the engraved page remains the same. Certain sloppily made corrections are easy to spot in such reprints, as are new titles, names, and copyright notices.

The most complete and standard text for Strauss's songs today is, of course, the *Gesamtausgabe der Lieder,* which was designed as a deluxe and limited folio edition for the centenary celebration of the composer's birth. An earlier complete edition of the songs had been planned during Strauss's lifetime, but had to be abandoned during World War II. Except for most of the early songs, a few without opus numbers (both of which groups are in GL III), and five of the orchestrated songs in GL IV, this edition consists of reprints. The appearance—overall format, staff and notehead size, and type style—varies from group to group.[29] On some pages the staves and text are quite worn and broken, presenting a disappointing contrast to the fine gold-stamped red bindings and quality paper.[30] The texts of all songs are in German only; in a few passages syllables of the translation or stems for extra syllables were not removed. A few errors in GL IV, which is not the only volume to contain misprints, may be cited as examples requiring corrections in future printings. In several songs phrasing and expression marks as well as dynamics are omitted from the voice part of the orchestral versions. As the Schumann-Heink manuscript discussed above shows, these matters were of importance to the composer and should certainly be reflected in both versions of the songs. At the climax of the vocal line in *Muttertändelei* (GL IV, 195), the vocal dynamic is wrongly indicated as *mf;* surely the *ff* of the piano version should be retained, particularly against a full orchestral chord marked *ff.* There are pitch errors in the vocal lines of *Ruhe, meine Seele!* and *Lied der Frauen* (five discrepancies between the piano and orchestral versions of the latter!). These and other errors in op. 68 should certainly have been corrected, since the full scores had already been printed in 1941. Nor are other errors confined to the songs newly printed in GL. Norman Del Mar, in a 1958 article "Confusion and Error," called attention to four errors in the 1950 printing of the *Four Last Songs.*[31] Three of these were corrected for the GL reprint (somewhat carelessly, for a deluxe edition), but the fourth, a missing rest in the timpani part, which could easily have been inserted, was not.

Both publisher and editor worked hurriedly on the GL, hoping to issue the collection before 1964 was out. (The first three volumes were copyrighted in 1964, the fourth in 1965.) As a result, Trenner was not given proofs for his *Revisionsbericht* and had to settle for having "someone in London" read them. Trenner himself explained the matter of deadlines to me, acknowledging the countless errors and recommending use of the NL *Revisionsbericht* for the *Jugendlieder.* It is inexcusable that, upon reprinting the four volumes of the GL during 1972 (in an octavo size), the publishers did not make any corrections. The critical commentary should have been completely redone. As it stands, the German version must be used with caution; the French and English translations of it must be avoided entirely. Unfortunately, all the faults cannot be blamed on a proofreader or lack of one. The musical and textual variants are presented with no degree of consistency, and there seems to be no effort toward establishing an authoritative version. Given the incomplete state of manuscript sources, a search for variants must sometimes be confined to the printed versions. Because of missing manuscripts (and supposed but not documented manuscripts that may have existed), the preparation of a more nearly authoritative edition for all of the songs would be a tremendous task, and any report of variants would still remain incomplete.

For many songs, even those for which more than one source is known, Trenner gives no information about alternate readings. When there are musical variants, it is not clear from which version the readings come—autograph manuscript, copy, first printing, or subsequent edition.

The textual variants given in the critical report are even more difficult to work with. For a few songs the editor cites the collection of poetry used by Strauss, and we assume that the alternate readings come from that source. But when no textual source is given, we have no idea from where the other readings derive. An even more sticky situation occurs at least a dozen times where a "variant" is listed and, upon comparison with the word or note in the song itself, is revealed not to be different at all. On the basis of the information given in the critical report, it appears that the entire matter of variants in Strauss's lieder is not extensive or of tremendous significance. (This is reconfirmed by my investigations in the preparation of Chapter III, section 4, "Sources of and Alterations to the Poetry.") In the preface of the GL, Trenner refers to five bound volumes of first editions of the lieder, corrected in Strauss's hand, which are now in the Strauss Archive. The corrections must be few indeed—as must be those of Walter Seifert who (as acknowledged in Trenner's preface) attended to the "revision of the musical texts"—for there are very few variants tabulated. Musical variants are confined mainly to the correction of accidentals, the reading of a note one step too high or too low (an understandable mistake in dealing with noteheads in Strauss's hand), and other minutiae. Most of the textual alterations are likewise small (see Chapter III, pp. 61–65). For songs where a large number of variants are reported, as for *Lied der Frauen,* it would be helpful to know if the variants are from a volume of poetry Strauss owned and perhaps even annotated. Trenner makes a general statement about the existence of such volumes in the Strauss Archive, but cites no source for the op. 68 Brentano poems. Many different editions of his poetry would have been available to Strauss by 1918, the date of his op. 68 lieder.

Manuscripts and Prints Containing New Versions and Orchestrations

The final category of sources to be considered here includes only a few new versions, in contrast to the many reworkings of songs or resettings of texts found in the lieder of Schubert and Liszt. In this respect, Strauss is closer to Brahms and Wolf, neither of whom made a practice of recomposing a text. The only poem that Strauss left in two complete lied versions is Uhland's *Einkehr,* a poem which also attracted other lied composers. Strauss's first *Einkehr* setting (AV 3) dates from August 1871; it was engraved and published as a supplement to the *Richard Strauss Heft* of *Die Musik,* IV, no. 8 (January 1905). This version is a straightforward modified strophic setting with the piano doubling and supporting the voice and echoing it in the interludes. The harmonies are simple, modulations move only to and from the dominant, and the vocal range is limited to an octave. This setting is a good representative of the type of lied Strauss created in his early years—derivative works clearly stemming from the early nineteenth-century repertoire which he heard, played, and studied. Whether he remembered the earlier setting when returning to

the same text in 1900 for his op. 47, no. 4, cannot be stated with certainty. Quite possibly he did not recall it, since he seems to have forgotten about the unpublished *Wer hat's gethan?* and once in a list of his own
songs included *Du bist die Ruh,* by which he probably meant *Ruhe, meine
Seele!* (see quote, p. 34). Both settings of *Einkehr* happen to be in the
same key (A major), have the tempo indication "Andante," and are
clearly divided into musical sections that correspond to the five stanzas.
Beyond these superficial similarities, there are no significant relationships
to be found. Like the earlier setting, the *Einkehr* of 1900 is typical of the
composer's lied style at the time of its writing: now the piano is more of a
partner in expression than a supporting accompaniment, the modulations
are more varied and are effected in Strauss's "side-slipping" fashion so
well known from the tone poems, important motives are divided equally
between voice and piano, and the range is a thirteenth. The poetic structure is reinforced musically by the return of motives (stanzas 1, 2, and 4
could be represented as A, A^1, A^2) as well as by the use of vocal rests
and the shape of the lines, but not by the harmonic plan. Different
portions of the text are stressed here than in the early setting, and three-
fold textual repetition appears at the end of the last stanza. There is a
single variant in the poem: stanza 1, line 4, has "grünen Äste" in the
earlier setting and "langen Äste" in the later one. According to Trenner
in GL III, 283, Strauss's father corrected "grünen" to "langen" for him,
but both editions (GL III, 222, and NL, p. 4) print "grünen." Two other
corrections attributed by Trenner to the elder Strauss are adopted in both
editions of the 1871 song and correspond to the text of the 1900 setting.[32]

There is evidence that Strauss set three of his early songs in two
versions each, although only a single version of one of them has survived.
In a letter of 8 May 1879 to Ludwig Thuille, Strauss wrote that he had
just composed three lieder anew—this time without strange modulations
and thus to his conservative, anti-Wagnerite father's satisfaction. From
the date, the three songs appear to be *Die Lilien glühn in Düften* (AV
160), *O schneller, mein Ross* (AV 159), and *Waldesgesang* (AV 55), only
the last of which survives.[33] The extant manuscript version, dated 9 April
1879, is probably the second one; it contains several brief modulatory
excursions to A and D minor and C major, but all are effected by common chords and remain fairly close to the tonic key of F major. One of
Strauss's best early songs, it exhibits a good variety of piano figurations,
clear expressive declamation, and more interesting harmonies than most
of his other lieder from the same period. Presumably the second versions
of the three songs were the ones performed by the dedicatee, Cornelie
Meysenheym, in a Munich concert on 16 March 1881, the occasion which
marked the first public performance of any of Strauss's lieder.

Another text of which Strauss made two settings is Rückert's *Die
Göttin im Putzzimmer.* As mentioned above in Chapter III, he first
planned to create a song for bass voice. Perhaps he intended it as a
companion piece to his two Rückert songs for bass written in 1929. The

sketches in book 87 for the solo version probably date from late 1934 or early 1935. Before he finished drafting the song, Strauss changed his mind about the medium and on 6 February 1935 sketched the choral version in book 88. Another Rückert text, *Im Sonnenschein*, replaced *Die Göttin im Putzzimmer* as a bass lied; completion of this lied followed on 24 February 1935.

Strauss may possibly have created two different versions of another song, *Weihnachtsgefühl* (AV 94). Steinitzer lists a manuscript in the possession of Georg Pschorr, Strauss's uncle, and gives a two-and-a-half measure incipit of the piano part in D-flat major.[34] No date is suggested, but the work appears as no. 20 in Steinitzer's chronological list of *Jugendwerke*, between two other works from the spring of 1879. Steinitzer does not account for the facsimile published in the Berlin journal *Die Woche*, I, no. 41 (23 December 1899), of a manuscript in E-flat which is clearly dated "Charlottenburg, 8. Dezember 1899."[35] Although Pschorr's manuscript is now lost, none of the editors of Asow, NL, or GL denies Steinitzer's suggestion of an original 1879 date. They do agree that on stylistic grounds the published facsimile is probably a transposed reworking of an earlier song, not an original composition from 1899, the winter in which Strauss composed his op. 46. In NL the Christmas song does not appear with the early works, but follows after *Wir beide wollen springen* (AV 90), which dates from 1896 and was also first published in facsimile in a periodical. In GL, it is included with the early songs, yet the critical report (GL III, 283) omits mention of the original (?) 1879 date, referring to the 1899 manuscript vaguely as "probably a transposed copy." (Both modern editions are of the 1899 E-flat version.) Although there are no other examples of Strauss's going back to rework a much earlier song, it may be that in this instance he found it easier to hunt up an old song with a Christmas text and copy it over rather than search for a new text to set. Since Martin Greif's poem *Weihnachtsgefühl* was first printed in the first edition of his *Gedichte* (Stuttgart, 1868), it is possible that in 1879 Strauss used the poem from this collection. On the other hand, the existence of a choral sketch based on another Christmas text by Greif, *Der fromme Hirtenknabe* (see Appendix B), dating from ca. 1903, could make the later date of composition seem more likely. The publication of Greif's complete works in 1895–96 and the issue of numerous editions of his *Buch der Lyrik*, in which both poems appear, toward the turn of the century suggest that Greif's poetry enjoyed a certain popularity at this time.

The twenty-seven songs that Strauss orchestrated are listed here in Table 3 in chronological order of their orchestration. The changes he made in them are too slight to qualify the orchestrations as resettings. Beyond the increased density of texture and width of range, the instrumental ideas remain much as in the original, while the vocal lines are kept intact. Particularly in the songs orchestrated soon after their original composition with piano accompaniment there are almost no changes. Eight

Table 3

Strauss's Orchestrations of his Lieder

Title, op., no.	Date of Orchestration	Date of Composition
Cäcilie, op. 27, no. 2	20 September 1897	9 September 1894
Morgen!, op. 27, no. 4	20 September 1897	21 May 1894
Das Rosenband, op. 36, no. 1	22 September 1897	10–20 September 1897*
Liebeshymnus, op. 32, no. 3	27 September 1897	25 February 1896
Meinem Kinde, op. 37, no. 3	1897? (no later than 8 July 1900)	7–8 February 1897
Wiegenlied, op. 41, no. 1	1897? (no later than 8 July 1900)	22 August 1899
Muttertändelei, op. 43, no. 2	21 February 1900	15 August 1899
Die heiligen drei Könige, op. 56, no. 6	7 October 1906	ca. 1904–06
Des Dichters Abendgang, op. 47, no. 2	15 June 1918	8 May 1900
Waldseligkeit, op. 49, no. 1	24 June 1918	21 September 1901
Winterweihe, op. 48, no. 4	28 June 1918	23 September 1900
Winterliebe, op. 48, no. 5	29 June 1918	2 October 1900
Freundliche Vision, op. 48, no. 1	1 July 1918	5 October 1900
Der Arbeitsmann, op. 39, no. 3	12 December 1918	12 June 1898
Frühlingsfeier, op. 56, no. 5	3 September 1933	ca. 1904–06
Mein Auge, op. 37, no. 4	5 September 1933	16 April 1898
Befreit, op. 39, no. 4	10 September 1933*	2 June 1898
Lied der Frauen, op. 68, no. 6	22 September 1933	4 May 1918
Das Bächlein, AV 118	6 April 1935	3 December 1933
Zueignung, op. 10, no. 1	19 June 1940	13 August 1885
Amor, op. 68, no. 5	3 July 1940	21 February 1918
Ich wollt ein Sträusslein binden, op. 68, no. 2	6 July 1940	6 February 1918
Als mir dein Lied erklang, op. 68, no. 4	22 July 1940	4 February 1918
An die Nacht, op. 68, no. 1	27 July 1940	18 February 1918
Säusle, liebe Myrte, op. 68, no. 3	2 August 1940	9 February 1918
Ich liebe dich, op. 37, no. 2	30 August 1943	7 February 1898
Ruhe, meine Seele!, op. 27, no. 1	9 June 1948	17 May 1894

* 10 September was the day of Strauss's wedding anniversary; note the large number of compositions and orchestrations created on and near this day in various years.

songs have slight modifications—additions of between one and four measures in the instrumental prelude, interlude, or postlude—but no changes in the vocal part. Three purposes are served by these expansions. The first is further emphasis of a main motive (*Zueignung, Ruhe, meine Seele!,* and *Frühlingsfeier*). The second is the sustaining of a chord that would have died out if held so long in the piano (*Als mir dein Lied erklang*). Finally, there is the provision of an introduction where the voice previously entered without benefit of accompaniment (*Ich liebe dich, Winterliebe,* and *Amor*). In a single song, *Cäcilie,* the orchestral postlude is compressed by one measure from the piano version. Aside from omitted dynamics, phrasings, and other such discrepancies or outright errors in the editions, actual changes in the vocal lines are rare. Four songs have tiny alterations of note values (e.g., dotted versus undotted half notes at the ends of phrases) and two have octave transpositions for a few pitches so that the voice is not lost in the orchestral sound.

The most interesting examples of modification are found in the lieder *Ich liebe dich* and *Zueignung*. Both of these orchestrations were prepared decades after the original composition and publication of the song. Both are among Strauss's best known lieder, and he would have had ample opportunity to perform, listen to, and think of improvements for them.

When orchestrating *Ich liebe dich*, Strauss designated the vocal line for tenor instead of the original soprano, but retained the original key of E-flat major. Besides adding a two-measure orchestral introduction, he evened out two dotted rhythms (Ex. 1a) and changed an even pattern to a dotted one (Ex. 1b). Like the other changes noted below, these appear to have been made with attention to the rhythms and to communication of the text. The first of the dotted patterns actually detracts from the even duplet-triplet flow of the remainder of the line. In order to make the text

Ex. 1a, *Ich liebe dich,* op. 37, no. 2 (mm. 3 and 37–38 in piano version, 5 and 39–40 in orchestral version):

vo- ran un- serm Wa-gen,   vo- ran un-serm Wa- gen,

und fern auf der Hai- de   und fern auf der Hai-de

Ex. 1b, *Ich liebe dich,* op. 37, no. 2 (m. 34 in piano version, 36 in orchestral version):

tra- gen zu   tra- gen zu

more intelligible over the orchestra, four notes are moved up a sixth, while three notes are transposed up an octave (Ex. 2a and 2b). The altered rhythms in the final measures of the vocal part (Ex. 3) dramatize the text by leaving the voice unaccompanied on "in den," while placing "Tod!" in the same part of the measure as "nach" and accompanying the former with somber trombones. The timpani motive in the following measure further suggests word painting of "Tod!" The broadening of the final vocal phrase in this song is very characteristic of Strauss. Even the original version with piano accompaniment is an expanded reworking of his original sketch, which is shown here in Ex. 4.

Ex. 2a, *Ich liebe dich,* op. 37, no. 2 (mm. 35–36 in piano version, 37–38 in orchestral version):

Ex. 2b, *Ich liebe dich,* op. 37, no. 2 (m. 24 in piano version, 26 in orchestral version):

Ex. 3, *Ich liebe dich,* op. 37, no. 2 (mm. 42–45 in piano version, 44–47 in orchestral version [my reduction]):

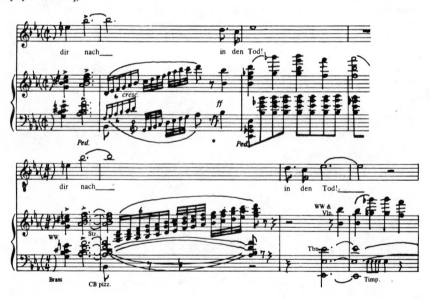

Ex. 4, *Ich liebe dich,* op. 37, no. 2 (mm. 42–43, pencil sketch, Bayerische Staatsbibliothek, Mus. Mss. 9048):

dir nach in den   Tod

In the orchestration of *Zueignung,* Strauss also expands upon the rhythms of the final climactic line, while retaining all but one of its original pitches. Measures 25–26 of the piano version are expanded into three measures, the last of which is in 3/2 meter, the only change from common time in the entire song. This drawing out of the text further emphasizes "heilig," which Strauss had already admitted to be an important word by repeating it and by placing it on the highest pitch in the song (see Ex. 5).[36] The effect of this improvement—and the whole issue of Strauss's seriousness when concerned with the text—is somewhat spoiled by the following two measures, of which the added vocal part is best left unperformed today. This consists of a dedicatory message to Viorica Ursuleac, for whom the orchestration was prepared and who had sung the title role in the first performance of the revised *Die ägyptische Helena* in 1933 (Ex. 6).[37] In this song also, Strauss indulges in a bit of new word painting by raising the pitch of the word "hoch" a sixth (Ex. 7).

Ex. 5, *Zueignung,* op. 10, no. 1 (mm. 25–26 in piano version, 25–27 in orchestral version):

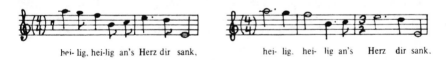

hei- lig, hei-lig an's Herz dir sank,   hei- lig, hei- lig an's   Herz   dir sank.

Ex. 6, *Zueignung,* op. 10, no. 1 (mm. 27–30 in piano version, 28–33 in orchestral version):

ha- be   Dank!   du wun-der-ba- re He- le- na, ha- be   Dank!

Ex. 7, *Zueignung,* op. 10, no. 1 (mm. 14–15 in both versions):

hoch den A- me- thy- sten Be- cher   hoch den A- me- thy- sten Be- cher

It is doubtful that Strauss required sketches for his orchestrations of lieder; the sketchbooks appear to contain none. There may, however, exist a group of loose sketches for the five songs that he orchestrated in 1918.[38] An examination of these sketches might prove very useful in this matter. It is quite conceivable that as a master of orchestration Strauss did not require sketches when filling out an accompaniment, just as he did not need an intermediate version between the *Particell* and the full score of an opera or tone poem. By an almost mechanical process and on a regular schedule of work (which Pauline is credited with imposing upon him), he transferred ideas from his head and from the shorthand *Particell* version to the complete score. The sketches in sketchbook 2 for the orchestral song *Der Einsame* (op. 51, no. 2) show that he first wrote down the accompaniment for even an orchestral song on two staves, with the vocal line on a third. The same evidence is provided by the sketches in books 14 and 17 for *Die heiligen drei Könige aus Morgenland*, which is counted here as an orchestrated (as opposed to orchestral) song because it was originally published in op. 56 with piano accompaniment. Occasionally Strauss required a third instrumental staff, as for the trumpet part of *Die heiligen drei Könige* (sketchbook 14, opening 51^v). That the sketches for these two songs were conceived with the orchestra in mind is clear from such indications of instruments, from lists of instruments in books 17 (opening 13^r) and 2 (opening 20^r), and from the beginning of a celesta part in book 17 (opening 13^r). These sketches, along with the numerous sketchbooks of operas and orchestral compositions, show that Strauss usually worked on two or three staves (but not at the piano) and probably expanded from there directly onto the full score. Among the song sketches, *Frühling* of the *Four Last Songs* is exceptional in being sketched on four staves (sketchbook 142, openings 3^v–9^r). A section of the sketches for *Frühling* is given here in Illustration 7. Most of the sketches for the other three songs in this group use three-staff systems.

In his diary and correspondence, Strauss distinguished between the original sketches, the final composition, and the writing out of the full score. The first work on a song was usually annotated with "begonnen" or "skizzierte," the next by "componiert" or "Composition vollendet," and the orchestration as "instrumentiert" or "Instrumentation vollendet." The final copying out of either the piano or orchestral manuscript was sometimes designated in his writings by the term "fertig ausgeschrieben." For some works, he was very explicit in his diary annotations.

Pilgers Morgenlied, op. 33, no. 4:

21–22 December 1896 composed, 11:00 PM completed
6–25 January 1897 orchestration
(The manuscripts confirm these dates; no sketches are known.)

Illustration 7

Sketch of *Frühling* (AV 150/I) in sketchbook 142, opening 4, slightly reduced.

Illustration 8

Text and sketch of *Das Rosenband* (op. 36, no. 1) in sketchbook 5, opening 2, slightly
reduced.

[2ᵛ]

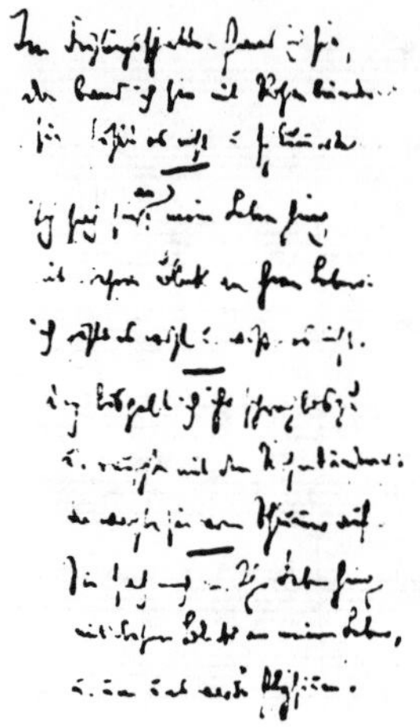

[Marquartstein]

[2ᴿ]

[10 September 1897 Marquartstein]

Das Rosenband, op. 36, no. 1:

> 10 September 1897, composed on third wedding anniversary
> 20 September 1897, written out and orchestration begun
> (The substantially complete sketch in book 5—reproduced here as Illustration 8—
>   is dated 10 September, the manuscript for voice and piano 22 September. The
>   orchestral manuscript is unknown.)

Für funfzehn Pfennige, op. 36, no. 2:

> 20 August 1897 at 2:30 composed a joyous little song from *Des Knaben Wunder-
>   horn*
> 2 September writing out finished[39]
> (The dated sketch and manuscript confirm these dates.)

When Strauss's diaries are made available, it will be possible to suggest
dates for works not surviving in dated manuscripts and to establish more
precisely a chronology showing what works were in progress at the same
time. Presumably the diaries will also give a further glimpse into his
working method.

V

STRAUSS'S OP. 68:
FROM SKETCHES (1918) TO ORCHESTRATION (1940)

The *Sechs Lieder nach Gedichten von Clemens Brentano . . .* , op. 68, belong to the four groups of songs (the others are opp. 66, 67, and 69) that mark Strauss's sudden return to the composition of lieder after a hiatus of twelve years. Although no single but totally convincing explanation has been put forth for this resurgence of his interest in song and no statement from Strauss himself has been discovered, the following facts and circumstances should all be considered to have had some influence. It is most likely that both his ceasing to write lieder around 1906 and this renewal of interest in 1918 are attributable to a combination of factors rather than to a single reason.

Background to the Songs of 1918

During the years of World War I, Strauss was worrying over the revisions and new versions of *Ariadne auf Naxos* and *Der Bürger als Edelmann,* completing them by 1917. After finishing these works and *Die Frau ohne Schatten,* he may well have been ready to try his hand at a shorter and less problematic genre of composition. A number of writers have pointed out that the years in which Strauss created large numbers of songs were the years following the completion of larger works. It is in some of these same years (notably 1897, 1900, and 1918) that he looked back to his earlier songs and prepared orchestrations of them, perhaps as a release from the work at hand. The majority of the orchestrations were undertaken during the summer months in Garmisch or at vacation retreats, when the pressures of his heavy conducting and touring schedule of the winter season were behind him. It has been claimed that in turning to his past compositions, and to a genre many thought dead in the new century, Strauss was also withdrawing from the realities of the troubled external world. Although in 1918 the ideas for his next opera were already taking shape, he was in no hurry to create a new work for the stage. Even if not interested in politics or world events, he could not help being aware enough of the turmoil in Europe to realize that the royal patronage to which he had been accustomed was at an end and that the immediate prospect of having operas produced was not an encouraging one. In 1918 the Berlin Court Opera and Orchestra were re-organized into the Berlin State Opera and Staatskapelle. Coincidentally, this year marked the expiration of Strauss's twenty-year contract there. He had repeatedly had disagreements with the Intendant Count Georg von Hülsen-Haeseler ever since the latter's attempts to have much of the text of *Der Rosenkavalier* altered before its Berlin performance in 1911. By May 1918 these disagreements had reached a high point. Nevertheless, Strauss might have been content to remain in Berlin if he had not received a tempting offer from the Vienna State Opera. As it turned out, the Intendant resigned in the fall of 1918, and Strauss remained with his Berlin musical establishments until October 1919. By the time he departed for Vienna, the four groups of new songs had been completed and were in the hands of the publishers.

With the end of the war, Strauss resumed his concert tours, actually writing some of the new songs while in Zurich and Amsterdam. A revitalization of concert life probably further encouraged him to orchestrate some of his earlier lieder at this time. Certainly the songs—even those with orchestral accompaniment—had better chances of being performed than did the operas.[1] Another impetus toward the composition of songs in this period was Strauss's meeting Elisabeth Schumann for the first time in 1917. As the creation of op. 68 for her indicates, he was newly inspired by her lyrical voice. It has often been suggested that Strauss hoped to find in Schumann the ideal interpreter of his lieder that Pauline had been in earlier years. In addition to creating op. 68 for her, he once offered to rewrite the part of Salome in a more lyrical vein for her (but never carried out his intention). He convinced her to go to the Vienna Opera to work with him and toured the U.S. with her in 1921. Schumann sang op. 68 at the Salzburg Festival in 1922,[2] and performed at least one of the songs during the American tour with the composer himself at the piano.[3] The five orchestrations from the summer of 1918 were probably intended for Schumann's voice, just as the five orchestrations of 1897 were created for Pauline's, and those of 1933 and the 1940's for Viorica Ursuleac's. The five new orchestrations were published by Fürstner in 1919, and some of them were sung on Schumann's American recitals.

The single explanation offered by Norman Del Mar for Strauss's return to lieder writing in 1918 is that he was threatened with a lawsuit by the publishers Bote & Bock, to whom he had promised a dozen songs when negotiating for the publication of the *Symphonia domestica*, op. 53, which they brought out in 1904.[4] In 1906 the firm issued the six songs of op. 56, which half filled the composer's obligation. The creation of op. 66 was his response to Bote & Bock's renewed threats; they naturally refused to publish these songs, of which the specially written texts were designed to mock numerous publishers, actually naming them in the text and describing them in the music. Looking at the chronology for the year 1918 as presented here in Table 4, one may well ask why Strauss did not meet their demands for another half dozen lieder with the six songs of op. 68. This opus was completed before op. 66, while op. 69 (which would

Table 4

Strauss's Compositions of 1918

Date*	Place	Work
26 January	?	*Ich wollt ein Sträusslein binden* ended in sketchbook 39
4 February	Munich	*Als mir dein Lied erklang* MS completed
6 February	Munich	*Ich wollt ein Sträusslein binden* MS completed
9 February	Munich	*Säusle, liebe Myrte* MS completed
18 February	Zurich	*An die Nacht* MS completed
21 February	Zurich	*Amor* MS completed
(8 March)	?	Strauss received Alfred Kerr's poems for op. 66 (DM III, 358)
15 March	Amsterdam	op. 66, no. 1 composed
16 March	Amsterdam	op. 66, nos. 3 and 5 composed
17 March	Amsterdam	op. 66, no. 7 composed
(9 April)	Berlin	first performance of *Der Bürger als Edelmann*
4 May	Munich	*Lied der Frauen* MS completed (end of op. 68; op. 68 published in 1919)
19 May	Garmisch	op. 66, no. 2 composed
20 May	Garmisch	op. 66, no. 8 composed
21 May	Garmisch	op. 66, nos. 9 and 10 composed
23 May	Garmisch	op. 66, nos. 11 and 12 composed
24 May	Garmisch	op. 66, no. 4 composed
25 May	Garmisch	op. 66, no. 6 composed (end of op. 66; published in 1921)
15 June	Garmisch	*Des Dichters Abendgang* (op. 47, no. 2) orchestrated
21 June	Garmisch	*Schlechtes Wetter* (op. 69, no. 5) composed
24 June	Garmisch	*Waldseligkeit* (op. 49, no. 1) orchestrated
24 or 25 June	Garmisch	*Einerlei* (op. 69, no. 3) composed (2 dated MSS)
26 June	Garmisch	*Waldesfahrt* (op. 69, no. 4) composed
28 June	Garmisch	*Winterweihe* (op. 48, no. 4) orchestrated
29 June	Garmisch	*Winterliebe* (op. 48, no. 5) orchestrated
1 July	Garmisch	*Freundliche Vision* (op. 48, no. 1) orchestrated
(June or July)	Bad Ischl	*Der Stern* (op. 69, no. 1) composed
(summer)	?	*Der Pokal* (op. 69, no. 2) composed (perhaps the last song in op. 69 to be composed; op. 69 was published in 1919)
3 August	Altausee	autograph page of op. 66, no. 12, mm. 33–48, dedicated to Frau Irene Hellmann, also the dedicatee of *Schlechtes Wetter,* op. 69, no. 5
(summer?)	?	op. 67, nos. 1–6 composed (probably between the completion of op. 66 and beginning of op. 69; op. 67 was published in 1919; Library of Congress copy indicates copyright date as 1 January 1919)
(12 December)	?	*Der Arbeitsmann* (op. 39, no. 3) orchestrated (Schuh, *Lebenschronik,* p. 467)

* Unless given in parentheses, all dates are from manuscripts.

have required a sixth song to meet the terms of the publisher) was nearly finished.⁵ Perhaps Strauss recognized the greater artistic merit as well as possibilities for performance of these groups and preferred to save them for his principal publisher, Fürstner, who was one of the publishers not criticized in op. 66. With op. 67, which was ultimately offered as a substitute for op. 66, he may still have been trying to make a pointed statement to Bote & Bock, though couched in less obvious terms. The choice of the three Ophelia fragments (which he marked to be sung "in Wahnsinn") is particularly suggestive of his attitude at the time.⁶

While Bote & Bock may have been responsible for the subject matter of op. 67 as well as op. 66, their threats cannot be claimed as reasons for the writing of opp. 68 and 69 or for the orchestrating of the five other songs in 1918. From the order in which the songs of this year were written, it appears that the inner needs of expression were more responsible for Strauss's return to the lied than were any external demands placed upon him. Having resumed the composition of lieder with op. 68, he knew he would have to satisfy Bote & Bock before he dared turn over more songs to another publisher.

The songs of opp. 66 and 67 are certainly not lacking in musical interest or clever motivic working; they are, however, stylistically quite different from the majority of Strauss's lieder. Harmonically, op. 67 is more dissonant; its tonalities are less solidly rooted than are those in either his earlier lieder or the surrounding groups of songs. The vocal line, aptly reflecting the poetry, is rarely lyrical. It is more often abrupt or contorted, moving syllabically in rapid note values.⁷ In op. 66 there is far greater emphasis on the piano, with its musical jokes, quotations, and descriptions of the publishers named in the text, than on the singer, whose main function is to announce who or what is about to be quoted.⁸ There are also concentrated developments of a few main motives in the rich and varied piano part, along with some extended fugal sections. Contrasting with these are fragments of waltzes, ländler, polkas, mazurkas, and hunting songs. Op. 66 might almost be considered a programmatic piano cycle and a successor to Strauss's *Stimmungsbilder*, op. 9. The poet Kerr was well pleased with the musical rendering of his verses, calling the composer's creation "enchanting music, witty and delightful, funny and even solemn."⁹

Various writers have called the songs of op. 67 "sketches" or referred to their being "sketched" (rather than "composed"), implying a careless and hasty approach on the part of the composer. Yet they have also been said to represent the work of a fluent craftsman who knew well how to interpret the verses in music.¹⁰ Although op. 67 may have been written in a short time, it was not hurriedly dashed off without revision or concern for good text setting. Sketches for op. 67 are found in sketchbooks 18 (nos. 4–6) and 41 (nos. 1–3). The former group is fairly complete, showing that for the final version Strauss made only a few changes in the vocal line and meter of no. 5 (see Ex. 19b in this chapter) and further filled in the accompaniment. The songs in sketchbook 41 are less complete: these sketches cover only the first halves of nos. 2 and 3, with the vocal line of no. 3 more widely at variance with the final version than is usual in Strauss's lieder sketches. The first song in the group is fairly complete even in its sketched version.

The number of songs Strauss created in 1918 exceeds that of any other single year, including the years from 1898 to 1901, which mark the heaviest concentration of lieder writing in his entire life. Given these figures, it is not surprising that no new large works appeared in this year. (A few ideas for operatic projects passed between Strauss and Hofmannsthal as well as between Strauss and Alfred Kerr during the summer, but these came to nought.) Since the *Stichvorlagen* for op. 67 (now in the Strauss Archive) lack dates, these items cannot be assigned positions in the chronology of Table 4 with any certainty. It is unusual for Strauss to have omitted dates from his final manuscripts; this omission may indicate his hurry to get the works off to the publisher and rid his mind of the whole affair. Op. 67 bears no dedication, is rarely performed or recorded, and, so far as I know, was never given with the composer at the piano.

The Sources for Op. 68

Strauss's best efforts of 1918 were clearly the *Sechs Lieder nach Gedichten von Clemens Brentano*, op. 68. The sketches and manuscript sources for this opus include the following: an entire sketchbook (no. 39)[11] filled in with one or more version(s) of substantial parts of each song, along with sketches of the accompaniment for a seventh song; a second sketchbook (no. 42)[12] containing a section of *Lied der Frauen* (op. 68, no. 6) that does not appear in the other book; *Stichvorlagen* for the first edition of all six songs; and *Stichvorlagen* for the orchestral versions of all six. No sketches for the orchestral versions, which date from 1933 (no. 6) and 1940 (nos. 1–5) have been located. Both sketchbooks for the original version of op. 68, with piano accompaniment, date from early 1918. A single date—26 January 1918—appears in no. 39, at the top righthand corner of opening 40ᵛ, concluding the second set of sketches for *Ich wollt ein Sträusslein binden*. Although Strauss indicated no dates in sketchbook 42, on the basis of its contents it can also be assigned to early 1918. Besides a continuation of *Lied der Frauen* on its first thirteen pages, this book contains early sketches for *Intermezzo*, Act I, scene ii.

The surviving manuscripts of op. 68 in its original version (now in the Strauss Archive) were used as the basis of the first edition, with which they agree in almost all details. Op. 68 was published by Fürstner in 1919 in versions for both high and low voice with German text only. In all probability no transposed manuscript was prepared by either Strauss or a copyist. Each song was issued separately with one of Fürstner's typically decorative covers (see Illustration 4 for one example).

Whatever the initial reasons he had for determining to compose lieder, Strauss drew his inspiration from the poems themselves. He is known to have been reading both the prose and poetical works of Clemens Brentano and Achim von Arnim in 1918.[13] Op. 68 and the first three songs in op. 69 are the results of this reading. Although years earlier Strauss had been interested in the combined work of these author-compilers and had created lieder on texts from *Des Knaben Wunderhorn,* the 1918 songs are his only settings of their original poetry. He is unlikely to have known of any other settings of these particular poems and might not have been interested in creating his own lieder if he had.[14]

Description of the Sketches for Op. 68

In his sketches for op. 68 Strauss did not consistently indicate time or key signatures, rests, dots, ties, or slurs for the vocal line. As a result, certain measures appear to be incorrect or incomplete; yet to the composer the absence of these symbols would have created no problem because the ideas were clear in his mind. In some instances it might be suggested that these symbols were left out to allow flexibility or reconception. Strauss's song sketches on the whole lack such details, even where melodic, harmonic, and rhythmic ideas are fairly close to or the same as the final version. The fuller song sketches are comparable to the *Particell* (short score) for the operas and orchestral works. Some of these short scores, in fact, appear in the sketchbooks. Scene iv of *Salome* (pp. 241–341 in the full score) is found in sketchbook 13. This *Particell* version is in turn derived from other preliminary sketches, many of which are found in sketchbook 15. Both the preliminary sketches and the fuller versions of op. 68 are found in sketchbook 39 (with no. 6 continuing in book 42). The arrangement of the songs in sketchbook 39 is the following:

2^r–3^v	*Als mir dein Lied erklang*
3^r–4^r	*Ich wollt ein Sträusslein binden*
5$^{v \cdot r}$	*Säusle, liebe Myrte*
6$^{v \cdot r}$	*Lied der Frauen*
7^v–9^r	*Als mir dein Lied erklang*
10^v–16^r	*Säusle, liebe Myrte*
17^v–20^v	*Abendständchen*
20^r–26^v	*Amor*
26^r–34^r	*An die Nacht*
35^v–40^v	*Ich wollt ein Sträusslein binden*
40^r–53^v	*Lied der Frauen*

Strauss's song sketches usually cover three staves with the top staff for the voice; the text is written above or below that line. The text has little punctuation and may be abbreviated or missing a few syllables. The horizontal placement of the text is often a more reliable guide in the melismatic passages than are slurs or ties, which Strauss seldom bothered with at this stage of composition. Sketchbooks 39 and 42 measure 8 by 12.5 cm and are slightly smaller than most of the books he used. These two oblong books are conveniently laid out with six staves per page, thus allowing him two systems of music on each page. (In other books with eight-staff pages, he often compressed the voice and right-hand accompaniment onto a single staff at the bottom of the page, thus making the individual parts harder to decipher. This happens in books 141, 142, and others. On ten-staff pages, he sometimes used only two staves throughout a song sketch; see Illustration 8). The titles in book 39 are more clearly marked than usual; in book 42, the title for *Lied der Frauen* does not appear until the third page of music for that song. It is not unusual for the sketches for a particular song to be spread out within one book; several of the other sketchbooks have more erratic arrangements than book 39. The blank pages following the final sketch of *Lied der Frauen* (which ends on opening 53ᵛ) are rare in Strauss's sketchbooks. Several of the lieder sketches are found near the backs of books otherwise devoted to larger works. Book 41, for example, has its seven final pages and the inside back cover filled with op. 67, nos. 1–3; the remainder of the book contains sketches for *Intermezzo*. *Intermezzo* sketches also follow those for *Lied der Frauen* in book 42. While these works all date from the same period, in other instances Strauss went back' to partially filled books (sometimes as much as a decade later, it appears) and entered new, unrelated works on the empty pages. Since his sketches are rarely dated, this economical practice makes dating of the sketches even more of a problem.

A comparison of the sketches and the final manuscripts for op. 68 shows that intermediate manuscript versions or drafts of at least some of the six songs must once have existed. The sketches appear in varying stages of completion. Except for *Abendständchen*, which did not become part of the finished opus, *Als mir dein Lied erklang* is the least developed.[15] Almost all measures of the final version are accounted for in the sketches of *An die Nacht, Ich wollt ein Sträusslein binden,* and *Säusle, liebe Myrte,* but neither the vocal lines nor the accompaniments are in final form. Although the main melodic ideas and outlines of the harmonies are well established for most of the six songs, it is hard to imagine Strauss proceeding directly to the *Stichvorlage*—except, perhaps, from the most complete sketch. The presence in the earliest sketches for *An die Nacht* and *Ich wollt ein Sträusslein binden* of some melodic and harmonic ideas that do not appear at all in the final versions suggests that Strauss reworked parts of these songs. The differences between successive versions of certain measures in the sketches of *Amor* seem to indicate a gradual working toward the final version. This suggestion of Strauss's working method contradicts the oft-repeated tales of how *Traum durch die Dämmerung* was created in twenty minutes, how Strauss dashed off songs between the acts of an opera he was conducting, or his own statements of how the music for *Der Stern* came to him instantly upon his reading of the poem. Perhaps some of the shorter songs were indeed "born" in this way, but the present sketches prove that the more substantial lieder were not merely the facile creations of a "note-spinner."[16]

The various stages of the op. 68 sketches show that Strauss's initial and major concern was the vocal line—its rate of declamation, the shapes of its phrases, and its exact rhythms and pitches. When planning his vocal melodies, Strauss seems often to have had in mind the general outline of the whole song, or at least the lengths of the texted sections. In some of the preliminary sketches, there are passages where the text but no vocal melody is written in. This stage of planning is more frequent in other sketches than in this group; it can be seen particularly in the sketches for songs that never reached completion. (Illustration 7, a sketch from the *Four Last Songs,* contains some measures with the text laid out without vocal notes.) In op. 68 and elsewhere there are also a few passages where measures are marked off but neither music nor text is entered. Where both text and vocal line do exist in an early sketch, the note values at the ends of phrases and the lengths of interludes between lines of text may not be indicated; such details are usually solidified in later, more complete sketches or drafts. The sketches for op. 68, particularly for the most elaborate song of the group, *Amor,* along with the sketches for the *Four Last Songs,* contain slightly simpler versions of the melismatic passages than do the final printed scores.

Strauss often notated the accompaniment sparingly in his sketches, putting only a bass note or chord in the left hand for each measure or at major changes of harmony. He placed somewhat more melodic (and occasionally harmonic) material in the right hand. The rhythms of the accompaniment were not so soon fixed as were those of the vocal lines; the left hand often has its chord or note indiscriminately as half, quarter, or whole note without regard to the meter. Repetitive figurations in the accompaniment which may seem quite important in the final version are not always written out at first; whether Strauss had a clear idea of them but kept them in his head or whether they were not yet decided upon is difficult to determine. For most songs, he filled in the preludes, interludes, and postludes less thoroughly than the sections with text; some of these passages have only a single melodic line ending with a cadence at the same place as the final version of the song. In the extended instrumental passages toward the end of *Lied der Frauen* (sketchbook 42), nearly every measure is accounted for, although very meagerly filled in.

Als mir dein Lied erklang, op. 68, no. 4

Als mir dein Lied erklang, the earliest song of op. 68 to reach completion, is also the first song to appear in sketchbook 39. There are eight pages of sketches for it. Like *An die Nacht,* this song has in some of its sketches music not incorporated into the final version. The first two-page entry for *Als mir dein Lied erklang* is in F minor instead of the later F-sharp major, with 6/8 meter instead of 2/4. On these pages two main (but simple) motivic ideas which survive in the accompaniment of the final version are already present; the second of these also appears with the first two vocal notes, though with different rhythmic emphasis than in the final version (see Ex. 1). This sketch probably represents the composer's very first attempt at setting down music for this poem. His second attempt a few pages later is mainly a working out of the accompaniment and the lyrical piano melody, which was only hinted at previously by the opening interval. The meter has now been cast as 2/4, but a mixture of sharps and flats on different systems shows uncertainty about the key and mode. Neither text nor vocal line is yet present. Ex. 2 contains two sketched versions of the introduction and the melody of it in its final version. These sketches show that at the outset Strauss considered the piano as well as (or even more than) the voice capable of lyrical interpretation of the text. Here the poet's three verses recall his lover's song, upon which Strauss (in his final version) based his fifteen-measure prelude. He reiterated the melody later, also giving over parts of it to the voice, as on the appropriate words "Ich habe es gehört" (mm. 19–21). This theme brings to mind the long melodies found in certain songs of op. 66, particularly the one in nos. 8 and 12 that later became the basis for the "Mondscheinmusik" in the final scene of *Capriccio*.[17] This latter melody is also a long-breathed cantilena. It is not surprising that certain songs in both opp. 66 and 68 have similar elements of construction—such as the long piano solo sections—since they were composed in the same months.

How much time and how many sketches it took Strauss to arrive at the final version of *Als mir dein Lied erklang* cannot be fully determined on the basis of existing sources. (Were his diaries available, they would certainly be of some help in this matter.) Since he is known to have worked regularly and rarely to have been unable to put music on paper, the creation of this song need not have taken many days.

Ex. 1, *Als mir dein Lied erklang,* op. 68, no. 4 (motives from sketchbook 39, opening 2ʳ [top of each pair of lines], and final version [bottom of each pair]):

Ex. 2, *Als mir dein Lied erklang*, op. 68, no. 4 (two versions of accompaniment from sketchbook 39, openings 7ᵛ and 8ʳ, and complete melody from final version, mm. 1–16):

Ich wollt ein Sträusslein binden, op. 68, no. 2

Strauss presumably worked on *Ich wollt ein Sträusslein binden*, the only sketch dated in book 39, over a period of about two weeks. Its first appearance in the book is the briefest version, while its second accounts for nearly every measure found in the final copy, with about half of them filled out in the accompaniment. The second sketch is dated at the end 26 January 1918, and the final version dates from 2 February 1918. This song is second in appearance in both sketchbook pages and final copy. Its preliminary sketch includes the first eight measures of the vocal line and several more measures of chord sequences, most of which appear later in the song. A comparison of the opening vocal line in the two sketch versions and in its final form shows that most details were solidified between the writing down of the two sketches (Ex. 3). Throughout the song, the vocal part of the second sketch (the middle line of Ex. 3) is remarkably close to that of the final version, varying slightly in only some ten measures. Most of the accompanimental motives are present, although later they are more developed. One recurrent arpeggiated figuration of the left hand (given to harp

Ex. 3, *Ich wollt ein Sträusslein binden,* op. 68, no. 2 (two versions from sketchbook 39, openings 3^r and 35^v, and final version):

Ex. 4, *Ich wollt ein Sträusslein binden,* op. 68, no. 2 (two sections of accompaniment from sketchbook 39, openings 35^v and 36^v, and final version):

and violoncellos in the 1940 orchestration) is absent from the sketch. In most places only the root of the chord is indicated, while in a few others the lefthand measure remains entirely blank (Ex. 4). Since the figure is a simple one that reappears (on different chords) some thirty times, it may be that Strauss felt it unnecessary to write the figure down. Or possibly he had not yet decided what rhythmic configuration to give the accompaniment when he made his sketches. Whatever the explanation, the song is complete enough so that he could conceivably have prepared the final manuscript directly from the sketchbook.

Säusle, liebe Myrte, op. 68, no. 3

The third song in op. 68 to be completed, *Säusle, liebe Myrte* has a final manuscript dated 18 February 1918. Its first appearance in sketchbook 39, following the first versions of *Als mir dein Lied erklang* and *Ich wollt ein Sträusslein binden,* consists of only a title indication at the top left of an otherwise blank opening. Later in the book it appears basically complete. Nearly all measures of the text and vocal line are accounted for here. While some measures of the accompaniment, especially those of the bottom staff, are again left blank, the motives and harmonic outlines have been established. Strauss began with a rapid piano figuration (Ex. 5a) but abandoned it after two measures in favor of syncopated rolled chords. He retained these in the final version (Ex. 5b), later making them pizzicato string chords. The idea of the original figuration may have found its way into the accompaniment of *Als mir dein Lied erklang* (Ex. 6).

The isolation and analysis of the main motives in this sketch version of *Säusle, liebe Myrte* show that at the time of its writing Strauss had planned his principal motivic elements. Although there is no documentary evidence to suggest it, quite possibly some now lost earlier sketches

Ex: 5a and b, *Säusle, liebe Myrte,* op. 68, no. 3 (left hand of accompaniment from sketchbook 39, opening 10ᵛ, and final version of accompaniment):

mm. 1-3

mm. 1-4

Ex. 6, *Als mir dein Lied erklang,* op. 68, no. 4 (final version of accompaniment):

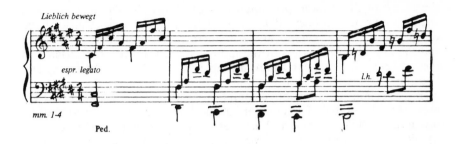

Ex. 7, *Säusle, liebe Myrte,* op. 68, no. 3 (sketchbook 39, opening 10^v [textless], and final version):

Ex. 8, *Säusle, liebe Myrte,* op. 68, no. 3 (sketchbook 39, openings 10^v, 12^r, 12^r,16^v, and 15^v; all except the last are retained in the final version):

Ex. 9, *Säusle, liebe Myrte,* op. 68, no. 3 (sketchbook 39, opening 12^r):

were made for this song; whether or not there were other sketches, Strauss must have worked out the motives mentally before setting down the music of the version presented in sketchbook 39. The first principal vocal motive was conceived to go with the initial words "Säusle, liebe Myrte" (Ex. 7) and reappears with them at the outset of the second stanza. The first four notes of the motive are not, however, restricted to these words; they appear again and again with other texts (Ex. 8) and become an important figure in the accompaniment as well. The ornamented versions of this motive found in the completed song are not yet present in the sketch. The idea for a turn-like figure does seem to have its origin in the sketch, where it illustrates the word "rauschen" (Ex. 9). This triadic version of the figure is also related to a winding accompanimental figure which represents the cooing turtledove (Ex. 10) and the murmuring fountain (Ex. 11). Ornamented variants of the original four-note figure that do not appear until the final manuscript version are given in Ex. 12. The first appearances of two other motives that are stressed in the sketch and even further developed in the finished song are included in Ex. 13.

Ex. 10, *Säusle, liebe Myrte,* op. 68, no. 3 (final version):

Ex. 11, *Säusle, liebe Myrte,* op. 68, no. 3 (final version):

Ex. 12, *Säusle, liebe Myrte,* op. 68, no. 3 (final version):

Ex. 13, *Säusle, liebe Myrte,* op. 68, no. 3 (final version):

An die Nacht, op. 68, no. 1

Strauss wrote out *An die Nacht* and *Amor* in final form in Zurich while on a concert tour. Both songs appear basically complete in sketchbook 39. Strauss actually sketched all of *An die Nacht* in 2/4 meter, while the final version is in 4/4, requiring a change to 3/2 for one measure (18).[18] The presumably earliest versions (openings 29ᵛ–30ʳ) are found in the center of the section devoted to *An die Nacht;* measures 1–26a, in a later version, precede this section and measures 26a–59b (the end of the song) follow. These middle four pages are filled with accompanimental material that does not survive in the song's final form. An important motive in this accompaniment derives from the six vocal measures found

on opening 30ʳ (Ex. 14a), which contains a partial inversion of the opening motive of the completed song (Ex. 14b). The version of this motive
found in Ex. 14a also appears seven times in the accompaniment of these
middle pages (Ex. 15), but is entirely absent from the published song; nor
is it taken up in the 1940 orchestration. The motive survives in the more
complete vocal sketch (Ex. 16), but it is not emphasized by being taken
over into the accompaniment of this version. Perhaps Strauss realized
that too frequent emphasis on this "Naturthema" in its two so obviously
related forms was too repetitious and ordinary. As in the other sketches
of op. 68, a few measures of the accompaniment are left blank here, but
the figurations appear elsewhere and could easily have been supplied by
the composer when copying out the next version. The vocal line—except
for the motive discussed above—is fairly well worked out in Strauss's
usual manner. It appears that in general he had a clear idea of his vocal
lines before writing them down, since there are rarely large-scale changes
of the sort encountered in measures 35–44 of *An die Nacht* (Ex. 17).
Other variants between the sketch and final version of this song appear in
Ex. 18. Ex. 19 includes examples of the types of small-scale alterations
Strauss effected between the sketch and final version of four other works.
Even where the notes of the vocal line are completely changed, the basic
rhythmic flow of the phrases is rarely altered more than a beat or two,
and there are no large-scale compressions or extensions.

Ex. 14a, *An die Nacht,* op. 68, no. 1 (motives from sketchbook 39, opening 30ʳ):

Ex. 14b, *An die Nacht,* op. 68, no. 1 (final version):

Ex. 15, *An die Nacht,* op. 68, no. 1 (sketchbook 39, openings 29^r–30^v):

Ex. 16, *An die Nacht,* op. 68, no. 1 (sketchbook 39, opening 32^v, and final version):

Ex. 17, *An die Nacht,* op. 68, no. 1 (sketchbook 39, opening 32, and final version):

Ex. 18, *An die Nacht,* op. 68, no. 1 (sketchbook 39, openings 27ᵛ, 27ʳ, 28ᵛ, and 31ʳ, and final version):

mm. 8-9 ge - schie - den ist ver - bun - den

mm. 13-14 A - bend - rot .

mm. 8-9 ge - schie - den ist ver - bund - den

mm. 13-14 A - - - bend - rot.

mm. 16-17 Bjel - bogs Speer [Bjel- bogs Speer]

mm. 30-31 nie - - der - taucht.

mm. 16-17 Bjel - bogs Speer, Bjel- bogs Speer

mm. 30-31 nie - - der - taucht.

Ex. 19a, *Salome,* scene iv, fourth measure after rehearsal number 275 (*Particell* in sketchbook 13, opening 11ʳ, and final version):

Was war's?

Was war's?

Ex. 19b, *Hab ich euch denn je geraten,* op. 67, no. 5 (sketchbook 18, openings 4ʳ, 5ᵛ, 5ʳ, and 5ʳ, and final version):

m. 8 schlies- sen woll- tet?

m. 8 schlies- sen woll-tet?

mm. 13-16 brauch-te dem ge-wand- ten Tisch- ler Win - kel- mass nicht ein- zu- schär- fen

mm. 13-16 brauch-ten dem ge- wand- ten Tisch - ler Win- kel - mass nicht ein- zu - schär - fen

mm. 25-26 schon zu mei-nem Ei - gen mach-te

mm. 37-38 so, so____ wollt er's ma-chen

mm. 25-26 schon zu mei- nem Ei- gen mach-te

mm. 37-38 so, so wollt er's ma- chen

Ex. 19c, *Intermezzo,* Act I, scene vi, beginning two measures before rehearsal number 230 (sketchbook 40, opening 33ᵛ, and final version):

sei - ne glän - zen - de Lauf- bahn die - se Mas- se

sei - ne glän - zen - de Lauf- bahn, die-se Mas- se

Ex. 19d, *Einerlei*, op. 69, no. 3 (sketchbook 17, opening 15ᵛ, and final version):

Amor, op. 68, no. 5

Except for the fragment *Abendständchen* and the incomplete version of *Als mir dein Lied erklang*, the sketch of *Amor* in book 39 has more missing measures than its companions. It is not whole sections that are left out (as for *Als mir dein Lied erklang* or the second and third songs of op. 67 in sketchbook 41), but a measure or two in various places.[19] In other sketchbooks, too, there are examples of Strauss's planning an entire song—even marking off measures and writing out the text over them to approximate the rhythmic movement.[20] As Ex. 17 shows, even when Strauss recast the rhythms and repeated different parts of the text he did not significantly alter the shape of the music or its duration. In this respect the early sketches of *Intermezzo*, Act II (in sketchbooks 40, 41, and 42), are interesting because they contain a number of text passages set to melodies that in the final version are actually spoken instead of sung. By setting out the words over the accompaniment in fixed rhythms (and pitches), Strauss planned the large-scale movement of the music. In parts of *Intermezzo* he later decided to remove the vocal melodies, but did not make extensive alterations in the length of the instrumental sections over which the text was to be spoken in free rhythms.

When sketching *Amor*, Strauss already had in mind the main musical ideas: present here are the repeated quarter-note motives for the word "Amor" (hinting at 2/4 meter); the "flickering" triplet motives for "Feuer," "Flügeln," etc., in both voice and piano; and the series of ornamental trills. A few variants worked into the final version are given here in Ex. 20. As in other sketches of op. 68, in some places the accompaniment is sparse or not filled in; further, in measures 25–46, 49.2–50, and 60–61 the voice part is lacking. The varying degrees of completeness

Ex. 20. *Amor,* op. 68, no. 5 (sketchbook 39, openings 20ʳ, 20ʳ, 21ᵛ, and 23ᵛ, and final version):

found in the sketches of this group of songs suggest that for some of them further sketches or manuscript versions must certainly have been created before the *Stichvorlagen.* Even if it appears to weaken Strauss's supposed claim that in the 1940's he was able to write out manuscripts of his tone poems from memory, the gradual working out of ideas found in sketchbooks such as no. 39 indicates that he did not carry all his music in his head and that the extant manuscript sources are not the only ones ever created.

Lied der Frauen, op. 68, no. 6

Lied der Frauen was the last song of op. 68 to be written out in final form (on 4 May 1918, some ten weeks after the last of the other five songs was completed), the only one known to occupy space in two sketchbooks, and the first of op. 68 to be orchestrated. The first set of sketches for *Lied der Frauen* in book 39 shows that Strauss had determined neither key, rhythm, nor melodic ideas for the first one and a half lines of text (see top line of Ex. 21). The second set of sketches (openings 40ʳ–42ᵛ) bears a somewhat closer relationship to the final version: here measures 1–27 are roughly drafted, with the text written out over the measures but set to notes in only a few of them. Next follows a third set of sketches (openings 42ʳ–53ᵛ), in even fuller form and extending through measure

169. This set includes the entire C minor portion of the song and five of its stanzas. Ex. 21 shows four versions of the opening vocal phrase, illustrating its transformation from the initial sketch to the final published version. The final C major stanza, an extended refrain on "Gelobt," and the postlude (mm. 170–296) do not follow in the same sketchbook. Although there would have been space here,[21] they were written out at the beginning of sketchbook 42 (openings 3ʳ–8ʳ).

Ex. 21, *Lied der Frauen,* op. 68, no. 6 (sketchbook 39, openings 6ʳ, 40ʳ, and 42ʳ, and final version):

The Orchestration of Op. 68

Several of the orchestrations Strauss made were of his most popular songs, for example, *Morgen!* or *Zueignung.* Others may have been intended as a means of popularizing neglected songs. One of his goals in orchestrating op. 68 was certainly the latter, as this letter to Clemens Krauss indicates:

> I've just chanced to play through my Brentano lieder, op. 68, again and find that they're quite good and rewarding. I wonder why they're so little done and want to orchestrate them now.[22]

Strauss immediately carried out his intentions, orchestrating the first five songs in the opus between 3 July and 2 August 1940. *Lied der Frauen,* along with these five, was created specifically for performance by Viorica Ursuleac, Krauss's wife. In September 1933 Strauss had declared to Krauss his intention of orchestrating *Lied der Frauen* to add to a group of three songs for her to sing in Berlin.[23] The other songs are *Mein Auge, Befreit,* and *Frühlingsfeier* (see Table 3 in Chapter IV). With *Lied der Frauen,* these three form an attractive orchestral song group. Krauss's statement about *Mein Auge* and *Frühlingsfeier* that "the orchestra will give a hymn-like expression that the piano could give only incompletely" could well be applied to all four.[24] Perhaps this is why the composer chose these songs instead of orchestrating all of op. 68, which contains a wide variety of vocal styles, at this time. Of all the songs in op. 68, *Lied der Frauen* could be said to be the most "symphonic" in its accompaniment; there is nothing, however, in the original 1918 sketches to indicate that Strauss conceived the accompaniment for orchestra—as there is, for example, in the sketches for *Die heiligen drei Könige aus Morgenland* (see Chapter IV, p. 112). A note on the orchestral manuscript of *Mein Auge* indicates the composer's desire to have it, *Frühlingsfeier,* and *Befreit* published together. (Before the appearance of GL IV in 1965, only *Frühlingsfeier* was published in its orchestral version, by Bote & Bock in 1934.) Although there is no evidence that he planned to orchestrate all of op. 68 until his 29 June 1940 letter to Krauss, perhaps Strauss was reserving *Lied der Frauen* for eventual completion of the other songs. It is well that he held back *Lied der Frauen,* because, after preparing the five new orchestral versions, he decided to revise its orchestration:

> I see in my manuscript that *Lied der Frauen* is orchestrated much too thickly; please be so kind as to send me your score and put in brackets all woodwind and brass you find dispensable. Remarkable, how one finds his own productions in need of revision after a few years![25]

By the end of September 1940 Strauss had the manuscripts of all six songs delivered to Fürstner, who released them early in 1941 in six separate scores.[26] The orchestral versions were first performed on 9 February 1941 in Düsseldorf by Erna Schlüter under the direction of Hugo Balzer. Strauss would have much preferred Ursuleac as the singer in the premiere, but he had no control over Balzer's programing. In a letter to Krauss on 12 October 1940 (in which he plays on the words "*Ur*suleac" and "*Ur*aufführung"), Strauss encouraged the Krausses to perform them before Balzer if at all possible.[27]

No sketches for the orchestrations of op. 68 appear to be extant. The manuscripts that do exist are final, clean copies, one for each song. Nos. 1–5, formerly belonging to the Strauss Archive and still listed as such in Asow and GL, were either given away or sold some time after the composer's death to Eugen Antosch of Vienna. At last report they were among the holdings of Musikantiquariat Hans Schneider, Tutzing (see Chapter I, pp. 15–16). Photocopies belonging to the Bayerische Staatsbibliothek (Mus. Mss. App. 44) show that—except for the errors pointed out here on p. 104 and a few other details—the manuscripts agree with the printed scores. The autograph full score of *Lied der Frauen* is still in the Strauss Archive, along with a few other orchestrations (including those prepared with it in 1933) and orchestral songs.

VI

THE STRAUSSES AS PERFORMERS OF HIS LIEDER

For Strauss the lied was clearly a secondary genre of composition, subordinate at first to the orchestral poems and later to the operas. His early biographers and critics were wont to repeat the phrase "Er ist kein Liednatur"; but it must be remembered that Strauss composed lieder throughout most of his life, producing over two hundred of them.[1] More validly than any other major operatic composer of the nineteenth century, he can also claim for himself a large and successful collection of songs. Furthermore, the lied is the only small-scale genre which continued to hold his attention throughout his lifetime. His professional activity—as a pianist and more importantly as a conductor—also bears witness to his interest in song. In Strauss's correspondence with his family, friends, and publishers, there are frequent references to the composition, performance, and publication of his songs. In the letters as well as in his other writings, he reveals that the lied is a vital part of his entire *oeuvre*. Significantly, his lifelong devotion to vocal music—particularly solo music for the female voice—is marked at its extremes by lieder: the songs from his childhood form the prelude and the *Four Last Songs* the postlude.[2]

The picture of Strauss as a family man is well known through works such as the *Symphonia domestica* (1904) and *Intermezzo* (1916–23). The songs also attest to the close relationship between his family life and his creative endeavors. Several songs and other compositions from his youth (as well as the later *Rosenkavalier*) were dedicated to the Pschorr family of Munich, relatives on his mother's side. He dedicated other songs to his mother, wife, and son, often choosing texts he felt were appropriate to the occasion that he wished to commemorate. For his marriage on 10 September 1894 to Pauline de Ahna (1862–1950), daughter of the Bavarian general Adolph de Ahna, he wrote the four songs of op. 27, which are among his best known and finest examples in the genre.

Strauss first met Pauline in August 1887 during a vacation with the Pschorr family in Feldafing, a Bavarian village near Munich. At that time she had studied at the Munich Conservatory but had had no experience as a professional singer, so that Strauss undertook to help train her for the stage. After his appointment to the court at Weimar in 1889, he introduced her there as a leading soprano. In 1891 Cosima Wagner engaged her for the part of Elizabeth in *Tannhäuser* at Bayreuth, a role which she sang again in 1894 when Strauss made his Bayreuth conducting debut. On

23 December 1893, he conducted and Pauline sang in the world premiere of Humperdinck's *Hänsel und Gretel.* Other operatic roles sung by Pauline during her short stage career include those of Mozart's Pamina and Elvira, Beethoven's Fidelio, Massenet's Lotte, Thomas' Mignon, and Wagner's Elsa, Eva, Isolde, Fricka, and Venus. She sang Freihild in Strauss's own Wagnerian opera *Guntram* (composed in 1887–93) for its first performance on 10 May 1894 in Weimar, under the composer's direction. A single unsuccessful performance of the opera in Munich (16 November 1895) signaled the end of her career as an opera singer and the temporary waning of his interest in operatic writing. In 1897–98, Strauss made plans for some operatic works, but these were left incomplete. One was an opera on the subject of *Till Eulenspiegel,* another on Otto Julius Bierbaum's *Lobetanz* (set by Strauss's boyhood friend Ludwig Thuille once Strauss abandoned his plans), and a third on Goethe's singspiel *Lila,* part of which he had set to music as a child. His next opera, *Feuersnot,* was not composed until 1900–01; its first performance was 21 November 1901 in Dresden. There is no evidence that either Strauss or his wife ever intended to have her participate in its production.

During the years following their marriage in 1894, both the composer and his wife turned instead to the lied. Together they gave evenings of lieder not only in Berlin, where Strauss was employed as conductor of the Court Opera from 1898 to 1919, but also on extensive tours throughout Germany and to other countries. Their journey to the United States from February to April 1904 included thirty-five concerts. About one quarter of them were recitals of lieder with piano accompaniment, but most were orchestral concerts at which Pauline performed a few songs, some with orchestra and others with Strauss at the piano. A short time after this moderately successful tour, she appears to have retired from the recital stage. Paralleling the couple's earlier cessation of operatic performance and composition, at about the time Pauline stopped giving *Liederabende* Richard stopped producing lieder. From the end of 1906 until 1918, he did not publish a single song.[3] (As can be seen from Appendix B of the present study, he may have begun some songs during this period, but none were completed.) From 1885 until this break, he had composed and published one hundred and twelve songs; together they comprise twenty-four collections containing two to eight songs each.[4] The rate of composition reached a peak in 1899–1901, the same period in which the Strausses' *Liederabende* were most numerous.

This chapter represents an effort to bring together for the first time the most important information about the Strausses' lieder performances. The data has been drawn primarily from his voluminous correspondence, from concert programs and announcements, from sections of German music periodicals (e.g., *Die Musik* and *Neue Zeitschrift für Musik*) that are devoted to concert life in German towns, and from a few foreign journals. The abundant secondary literature on Strauss has neglected this significant aspect of his professional (and family) life around the turn of the century. Only an occasional reference can be found in some of the biographies and other studies. Even Norman Del Mar, who in DM III devotes an entire chapter to the lieder ("A Lifetime of Lieder Writing," pp. 246–404), makes only a few brief references to Pauline's performances. Her career as a singer is mentioned no more than a handful of times in Alan Jefferson's *The Lieder of Richard Strauss* and in the chapter "Strauss and his Wife" (pp. 29–41) of his *Richard Strauss*. The best general surveys in English of German lied performances at the turn of the century barely touch upon the Strausses' concertizing.[5] Jefferson, along with such other recent writers as George Marek (*Richard Strauss: The Life of a Non-Hero*), has been much more interested in portraying Pauline as a domineering wife with an abrasive personality and a sharp tongue than as an artist.

The fairest assessment of Pauline's personality comes from those who knew her rather than from these latter-day writers with axes to grind. The Mahlers and Hofmannsthals are said to have avoided her company whenever tactfully possible, yet she got along well with Willi Schuh, Lotte Lehmann, and others in the musical world. Lehmann—whom Pauline once insulted at the intermission of a *Frau ohne Schatten* performance so that Lehmann could hardly return to sing the remainder of the opera—recognized that Pauline's tirades were intended to shock outsiders. Ernst Roth (for many years the director of publications for Boosey & Hawkes and a friend of the Strausses from 1922) portrayed her as a faithful wife and stern disciplinarian who surrounded the genius of her husband with "normality" and practicality. In spite of occasional frictions (most often in public and for the sake of exhibitionism, sometimes even on the recital stage), her untiring vigilance and self-denial achieved her main goal: "the establishment of a perfect equilibrium between a genius and the world."[6] Several critics who made less than complimentary comments about her vocal abilities nevertheless praised her personality and sincerity as they came across on the stage. For the most part they were also convinced that, among all singers of whatever stature, Pauline could provide the most authentic and intimate interpretation of her husband's songs. The comments Strauss himself made about her singing in letters and later in reminiscences concur with their opinions.

The performance history of Strauss's lieder actually began years before he met Pauline. Prior to writing op. 10 in 1885, he had composed some forty-five lieder, the majority of which remained unpublished and unknown to the public during his lifetime. They were intended primarily for private performance among relatives and friends. The young composer dedicated the earliest of his efforts at song to various members of the Pschorr family, particularly to Johanna, his favorite aunt, who was an ardent music lover with a good alto voice. According to the composer's younger sister, Johanna von Rauchenberger-Strauss, their aunt arranged family concerts of her nephew's works, at which he accompanied her. Some of the boy's twenty-five lieder dedicated to her were certainly performed at these gatherings, along with compositions by others. Lieder by Schumann, Franz, Loewe, and their contemporaries formed part of the family's repertoire. Their *Hausmusik* extended beyond lieder to include instrumental chamber music, "toy" symphonies, and dramatic presentations. Strauss was represented as a composer in some of these works as well.[7]

The first public performance of some of Strauss's early songs antedates his first appearance on the stage as a pianist or conductor. In the spring of 1879 he wrote three songs to poems by Emanuel Geibel, dedicating them to Fräulein Cornelie Meysenheym, a singer in the Bavarian Court Opera. She performed them in the Munich Museum Hall on 16 March 1881.[8] Up to that time, only his String Quartet, op. 2, had been given in public (by the quartet of Benno Walter, his father's cousin and for a time Richard's violin teacher). Later in the month the Symphony in D minor (once op. 4, now catalogued as AV 69) was played by the Munich Court Orchestra under Hermann Levi.

During the 1880's, Strauss played the piano parts of his Violin Concerto in D minor, op. 8 (in the 1882 Vienna premiere of the version for piano and violin), and the Violin Sonata in E-flat, op. 18 (in Munich). At Meiningen on 18 October 1885, he performed Mozart's Piano Concerto in C minor, K. 491, with his own cadenzas (AV 179). Strauss felt more at home with the chamber works than with the concerto, which, as he claimed, he had to practice for many months and even then did not thoroughly master. As well as playing the Mozart concerto in public, in 1885 he also tried out his own *Burleske* (AV 85) in rehearsals with the Meiningen Court Orchestra. After some reworking, this composition was given its premiere by the virtuoso Eugen d'Albert, to whom it was dedicated. For many years Strauss continued to perform the Violin Sonata along with two other early works, his Violoncello Sonata, op. 6, and the Piano Quartet, op. 13. His playing of these works during his 1921 American tour did not attract the crowds or create the enthusiasm of his orchestral appearances. Although certain critics negated the judgments of others, it was the general consensus that Strauss played these works as a composer, not as a pianist.[9]

Strauss was unable to meet the demands of the piano compositions of Chopin and Liszt, probably at least in part because he preferred reading through new music at the piano to developing his technical skills by concentrated practice. While he did not continue to perform solos in public after his early attempts, he did for many decades accompany lieder recitals. He never hesitated to play through his works for friends, and often held reading sessions of parts of new operas or entertained with lieder and arias at fashionable dinner parties.

Strauss himself considered his best efforts at the piano to be those as an accompanist of lieder, playing in a somewhat free manner and never taking the notes literally.[10] Once, after nearly ruining a performance of *Lied an meinen Sohn* (his op. 39, no. 5), Strauss exclaimed to the singer Ludwig Wüllner "the devil may play that," referring to the particularly difficult piano part he had written to describe a storm.[11] For the decades of the 1880's and 90's, which are the most important years as far as Strauss's composition of lieder is concerned, very little about his actual manner of performing can be ascertained. There is more evidence about his style of accompanying in *Liederabende* especially after World War I.

An American critic who recognized Strauss's skill as an accompanist described his playing as providing "a delicate perspective interwoven in the song instead of [a] strenuous and interfering solo."[12] If, as evidence seems to indicate, Pauline's voice was not a powerful one, his ability to keep his sometimes full and complex accompaniments well under control was certainly important. His skill in playing *pp* and *ppp*, and his refusal to treat the accompaniment as if it were the featured solo, were also praised.

During the last two decades of the nineteenth century, Strauss referred in letters to his playing of his own songs, and on a few occasions to those of other composers, both in public and at private gatherings. He took more care to report on the reactions of the audience or on which songs were done and which encored than to reveal details of his or the singer's performance. In March 1884, for instance, he accompanied the Berlin actress Johanna Schwartz (a pupil of Julius Stockhausen) in songs of Schubert and Brahms. He requested his mother to send some of his own lieder so that the actress might get to know them.[13] In December 1885 he read through some of his own songs at the home of Alexander Ritter, who was immensely pleased.[14] Two months later at the Hermitage in Weimar, Strauss accompanied the tenor Engelhardt in two of his songs, one of which had to be repeated.[15] The composer's letters never fail to note the encores; many songs, both those with piano and those with orchestra, were given "da capo" (Strauss's usual term). Rarely are there reports of additional songs (besides those on the program) being given as "encores" in the present-day sense.

Strauss began his duties as conductor with Eduard Lassen (1830–1904) at the Weimar Court Theater on 1 October 1889, remaining there until June 1894. His first concert program (29 October 1889) included two songs by Ritter and his own *Ständchen* (op. 17, no. 2), sung by Heinrich Zeller.[16] A few weeks later, Strauss wrote that he wanted to have a *Liederabend* of his own songs at the Liszt Verein in Weimar. What probably would have been the earliest of such evenings for the composer apparently came to nothing, and he had to wait another six or seven years before plans for an entire evening of his songs were realized. In the meantime, groups of songs were performed at orchestral concerts, quite in keeping with the general trend of programing in the last two decades of the nineteenth century.

Edward Kravitt has pointed out that orchestral concerts throughout the nineteenth century sometimes included melodramas, choral works, arias, lieder, and recitations of poetry interspersed with the major orchestral works.[17] After 1900 it became less common to fill a program with such a mixture of genres. Songs were by then usually relegated to *Lie-*

derabende, which had been gaining acceptance since about 1875.[18] In Vienna and Munich, the two centers in which *Liederabende* had first received approval, the interpreters were usually opera singers. In the 1880's Viennese *Liederabende* were given by the singers Eugen Gura, Ludwig Wüllner, Johannes Messchaert, Julia Culp, Lilli Lehmann, and others.[19] Some of the same singers later concertized with Strauss. Gura gave a concert of Strauss's lieder in Frankfurt during 1896. On the manuscript of a song dating from the following year, Strauss indicated the ideal performers, Gura and the pianist H. Schwartz, as an "anerkannter Verein." Above a high and florid passage, he wrote "Wer's kann, singe es Gura nach!"[20] Strauss dedicated his songs in op. 29 to Gura and recommended both him and his son Hermann as good interpreters for the orchestral songs in op. 33.

In Vienna, where Strauss was not well known until after 1900, his lieder gained him the acceptance that the less comprehensible larger works could not achieve. In addition to Pauline's successful recital there, in the five months from November 1901 to March 1902 twenty *Liederabende* that included Strauss's songs were given in the Bösendorfer Saal. Among the artists were Tilly Koenen, Lula Mysz-Gmeiner, Emilie Herzog, and Ferdinand Jäger.[21]

During his Weimar and Berlin years, Strauss considered Hans Giessen and Ludwig Wüllner his favorite male singers for *Liederabende.* Giessen was a court singer in Dresden and Weimar. "Hänschen mit dem höhen Cis," as Strauss called him, gave several *Liederabende* with the composer, singing only works by Strauss. Twenty songs were performed by the pair in Berlin on 18 February 1899. On 23 November 1900 they gave a recital in Leipzig; of the fifteen lieder presented one was so new that it was still in manuscript, and three were so well liked that they were encored.[22] Another operatic tenor, Raoul Walter of the Munich Opera, gave a lieder recital with Strauss in Berlin during 1900.[23] In November and December of the following year, Strauss made a number of tours through Germany with the singers Hermann Gura, Wüllner, Giessen, and Pauline, as well as with the actor Ernst von Possart. With Possart he gave his two melodramas, *Enoch Arden* and *Das Schloss am Meere,* which the two had premiered in 1897 and 1899, respectively. During preparations for and on the tour, which began just five days after the world premiere of *Feuersnot* in Dresden (21 November 1901), Strauss reported performances in Frankfurt (with Wüllner, on 27 November), Giessen (with Giessen [sic], on 4 December), Berlin (with Gura, 11 December), and Brünn (with Pauline, 8 December).[24] Other recitals were given in Wiesbaden, Freiburg, Constance, Stuttgart, Würzburg, and Prague. Strauss's letters repeatedly proclaimed success. To Franz Wüllner, Ludwig's father and a conductor in Cologne who gave first performances of some of Strauss's orchestral and choral works, he reported that the Frankfurt recital made a great impression and pleased him immensely. Of the many Strauss lieder in Wüllner's repertoire, twenty were given on that program.[25] Concert programs and reviews as well as the composer's correspondence show that Strauss's *Liederabende* usually included from ten to twenty songs selected from various opus groups. He tried to achieve a variety of musical and poetic style, mood, and subject matter in his programs. Even when several songs from one collection appeared on a program they were not necessarily sung in succession. Strauss himself remarked that critics and audiences did not properly recognize the variety in his songs; his programing was probably designed to show off the many sides of his lieder writing. His choosing of songs from different groups is not unusual for its time. Reger, for instance, who also accompanied singers in his own lieder, selected songs from different collections for recitals. His Berlin program with Ludwig Hess in the spring of 1903 included sixteen songs from his five groups between op. 51 and op. 68.[26]

As *Liederabende* grew in popularity and spread through Germany, many artists—Pauline Strauss among them—found that they could devote themselves exclusively to the lied. Pauline's career was even more selective, for she seems almost never to have sung lieder by any composer except her husband.[27] Along with recitals of lieder—always with Richard at the piano—she frequently presented lieder at his orchestral concerts. The first reports for both types of programs (in several German cities and also in London) date from 1896–97. These are the same years during which Strauss began to write orchestral songs and to orchestrate those written originally for voice and piano. Op. 33, a group of four songs for voice (specifically for tenor or soprano, for soprano, for baritone or mezzo-soprano, and for baritone or bass) with orchestra, was begun in June 1896 and completed at the end of the following January. It is Strauss's first group of songs originally conceived with an orchestral accompaniment.[28] Up to 1906, he wrote two other groups of orchestral lieder, op. 44 in 1899 (two songs for low voice), and op. 51 in 1902 and 1906 (two songs for a low bass). Eight songs originally written with piano accompaniments were orchestrated during this period (see Table 3). Of further interest are Strauss's orchestrations of Alexander Ritter's *Nun hält Frau Minne Liebeswacht* (AV 188); of Beethoven's *Wonne der Wehmut* (AV 189) and *Ich liebe dich* (not in Asow); and of Schubert's *Ganymed* (AV 187).[29] The Ritter orchestration (January 1898) was intended as a personal gift for the Ritter family a year and a half after Alexander's death; it may have been created for performance by Alexander's daughter Hertha (a well known singer) or by Pauline. The other three were certainly for Pauline to sing. *Ganymed* was presented in this version by the Strausses at a Schubert festival in Munich on 31 October 1897. Performances by Pauline of the Beethoven orchestrations (which were created just before the Ritter in January 1898) have not yet been documented.[30]

Toward the end of the nineteenth century many of Strauss's contemporaries also showed an interest in orchestral songs. The desire for more homogeneous concert programs was undoubtedly one factor that encouraged them to turn in this direction. There was, of course, the purely practical problem of moving the piano onto the stage during an orchestral concert. The aesthetic conflict between large orchestral works and the more intimate lied caused some critics to complain of such inconsistent programing. It was during this period, however, that the lied was losing much of its intimate aspect and was no longer looked upon exclusively as house or chamber music. The appearance of orchestrations of lieder and orchestral songs furthered this shift of focus from the salon to the larger concert hall.

Even after Strauss began to write orchestral songs, he and Pauline gave a mixture of lieder with orchestral and piano accompaniments on their concerts. Typical programs including three or four lieder with orchestra and a like number with piano were held on the following dates:

27 February 1898 in Madrid (with Wagner excerpts as well)
4 April 1898 in Weimar (a benefit concert)
7 February 1899 in Bremen[31]
23 January 1900 in Cologne (a Gürzenich concert)
23 January 1901 in Vienna

At some concerts, Pauline sang only orchestral songs, and at others only those with piano accompaniment. The sample program in Illustration 9 is typical of the Strausses' concerts, which were usually devoted to the works of the composer-conductor-accompanist of the evening, with perhaps an overture or symphony by Mozart, Beethoven, or Weber. Other typical concerts were those in Mannheim on 20 March 1901 (seven songs and *Ein Heldenleben*) and in Frankfurt on 23 March 1901 (six songs and *Also sprach Zarathustra*).

On a very few occasions Pauline was joined by other singers. For instance, at a concert in Prague on 14 March 1900, she gave three songs of each type (and was so well received that she had to repeat half of them), while a Frau Hunold sang two Mahler songs.[32] Evidence assembled so far shows that Pauline gave only a few concert programs with conductors other than Richard and no *Liederabende* with other accompanists. For the orchestral Gürzenich concert in Cologne on 23 January 1900, Franz Wüllner directed *Macbeth* and four orchestral lieder with Pauline as soloist. Even for this concert, however, the original plans had been for Strauss to conduct.[33]

After settling in Berlin in November 1898, the Strausses gave *Liederabende* and orchestral concerts that included songs both in Berlin and in other cities. The performances outside Berlin are more fully documented, since advance arrangements had to be made through letters. Strauss often went ahead to rehearse the orchestra, writing to Pauline not to forget the scores and parts or to send the texts so that they could be printed in the program. In one letter he requested that she bring along the music for all of his songs, including those not on the program, so that they could perform them if an appropriate social occasion should arise.[34] There are frequent references to such informal evenings with Pauline and

Illustration 9

Pauline and Richard Strauss: concert program from 25 January 1898.

Tonhalle Zürich.

—+— **Dienstag, den 25. Januar 1898** —+—
im grossen Saale:

�֍ **KONZERT** ✖

zum Besten der Hilfs- und Pensionscassa des Tonhalleorchesters

unter Mitwirkung von

Frau Pauline Strauss-de Ahna aus München,
des **Gemischten Chors** Zürich, des grossen **Konzertorchesters**

und unter Leitung des

Herrn Hofkapellmeister RICHARD STRAUSS aus München.

PROGRAMM:

I. Abteilung.

1. Wandrers Sturmlied von Göthe für sechsstimmigen
   Chor und grosses Orchester . . . . *Richard Strauss*
2. Vier Gesänge für Sopran mit Orchesterbegleitung *Richard Strauss*
   a. Rosenband, von Klopstock.
   b. Liebeshymnus, von Henckell.
   c. Morgen, von Mackay.
   d. Cäcilie, von Hart.
   Vorgetragen von Frau Strauss-de Ahna.

II. Abteilung.

3. „Also sprach Zarathustra", Tondichtung, frei nach
   Friedr. Nietzsche, für grosses Orchester . . . *Richard Strauss*
4. Drei Lieder mit Klavierbegleitung . . . . . . *Richard Strauss*
   a. Sehnsucht, von Liliencron.
   b. Traum durch die Dämmerung, von Bierbaum.
   c. Ständchen, von Graf Schack.
   Vorgetragen von Frau Strauss-de Ahna.
5. Ouverture zur Oper „Der Freischütz" . . . . . *Weber*

Oeffnung der Thüren um 7 Uhr. — Beginn des Konzertes punkt 7 1/2 Uhr. — Ende 9 1/4 Uhr.

Sonntag, den 30. Januar 1898:

V. Kammermusikaufführung.

Dienstag, den 8. Februar 1898:

VIII. Abonnementkonzert.

Solist: Frau Schumann-Heinck.

others throughout the composer's life. As late as the 1930's, he wrote to her about dinner parties at which he accompanied singers in his music.[35]

Concert tours just before the turn of the century took the Strausses to foreign countries as well as to numerous German towns. In 1897 alone, for example, they presented concerts in Amsterdam, Barcelona, Brussels, London, and Paris. Their concerts were predominantly orchestral, but Pauline's songs never failed to please the audiences, who demanded repetitions and curtain calls. According to the composer, she interpreted *Morgen!* (op. 27, no. 4), *Traum durch die Dämmerung* (op. 29, no. 1), and *Junghexenlied* (op. 39, no. 2) as no one else could.[36] A group of orchestrated songs that she presented on many of her concerts became known as the "Drei Mutterlieder."[37] They include *Meinem Kinde* (op. 37, no. 3, one of the songs written to celebrate the birth of the Strausses' son Franz in 1897), *Wiegenlied* (op. 41, no. 1), and *Muttertändelei* (op. 43, no. 2). The orchestration and performance of the "Mutterlieder" show once again Strauss's dual concern for his family and his profession. According to his diary, Pauline presented the first orchestral performances of them at the Bergische Musikfest in Elbersfeld on 8 July 1900; of *Muttertändelei*, Strauss said it was "brilliantly orchestrated." *Wiegenlied* was so well liked it had to be given "da capo."[38] In October 1900 he wrote to his parents that Pauline would soon be singing these new orchestral lieder; further performances followed on 14 and 23 March 1901 in Prague and Frankfurt.[39] Since only *Muttertändelei* survives in a dated manuscript (21 February 1900), their performance helps to establish dates for the other two orchestrations.[40]

The year 1901 began with a heavy schedule for Pauline: in January there were orchestral concerts at which she sang lieder in Leipzig (on 14 January), Munich (the 18th), and Vienna (the 23rd). She sang in Berlin on 21 and 26 February, then traveled to Düsseldorf (on 9 March), Prague (the 14th), Mannheim (the 20th), and Frankfurt (the 22nd and 23rd).[41] The Viennese concert gave Eduard Hanslick cause to write the second of what were to be only three favorable reviews of Strauss's music. He praised Richard's incomparable accompanying as well as Pauline's soft sweet voice and artistry, even making a request that Strauss send him copies of the songs.[42] Since Pauline was ill and unable to perform her program on 9 March, she was replaced by Alexander Ritter's daughter Hertha, who sang nine Strauss lieder.[43] There are other reports of Pauline's being tired and nervous at concerts, and of illnesses after performances; yet she continued to tour in 1902 and 1903, especially in the winter months. A second Viennese appearance—this time an evening of lieder with piano in the Bösendorfer Saal (31 January 1902)—won praise from critics such as Hanslick and Max Graf, who called her a moving, deeply musical singer and him an ideal accompanist. In the summer of 1903 she sang lieder at the Strauss Festival at St. James Hall, London, with the Amsterdam Concertgebouw; in October she appeared at the Heidelberg Music Festival. For performance at the latter event, Strauss wrote *Gefunden* (op. 56, no. 1) and dedicated it to Pauline in commemoration of his receiving an honorary doctorate from the University of Heidelberg on 8 August 1903.[44] This song was still in manuscript form when she performed it in America in 1904, and drew attention as Strauss's latest contribution to the lieder repertoire.

During 1903 each of the Strausses experienced periods of illness but went ahead with plans for another tour of England that was to include five orchestral concerts and one evening of lieder. They also planned their more strenuous trip to the United States, which took place in February–April 1904. In all, this tour included thirty-five orchestral concerts and lieder recitals; Pauline reported in letters to Richard's parents that she performed and/or rehearsed nearly every afternoon or evening. Her first recital was in Carnegie Hall on the afternoon of 1 March 1904, where she sang the following:

> *Ich trage meine Minne,* op. 32, no. 1
> *Ich schwebe,* op. 48, no. 2
> *Freundliche Vision,* op. 48, no. 1
> *Junghexenlied,* op. 39, no. 2

* * *

> *Du meines Herzens Krönelein,* op. 21, no. 2
> *Ach Lieb, ich muss nun scheiden!,* op. 21, no. 3
> *All mein Gedanken,* op. 21, no. 1
> *Winterweihe,* op. 48, no. 4

* * *

> *Ein Obdach gegen Sturm und Regen,* op. 46, no. 1
> *Gefunden,* op. 56, no. 1 (not yet assigned an opus number)
> *Traum durch die Dämmerung,* op. 29, no. 1
> *Heimliche Aufforderung,* op. 27, no. 3

Strauss accompanied her and also played his melodrama *Enoch Arden,* op. 38, with David Bispham as narrator. On this occasion Pauline was well liked by both the critics and the public: four songs had to be repeated, and she made many curtain calls and received several bouquets. Most of her other recitals were given in other large cities, including Boston, Chicago, Cleveland, Detroit, Minneapolis, Philadelphia, and Pittsburgh. The farewell recital on 26 April at the National Theater in Washington, D. C., is another good example of the mixed type of concerts that were in vogue at the time. Here vocal, instrumental, and spoken genres are combined:

> *Ich trage meine Minne,* op. 32, no. 1
> *Himmelsboten,* op. 32, no. 5
> *Einkehr,* op. 47, no. 4
> *Cäcilie,* op. 27, no. 2
> *Morgen!,* op. 27, no. 4

Traum durch die Dämmerung, op. 29, no. 1
Ein Obdach gegen Sturm und Regen, op. 46, no. 1
Heimliche Aufforderung, op. 27, no. 3

(Pauline and Richard Strauss)

* * *

Enoch Arden, op. 38

(Sydney Lloyd Wrightson and Richard Strauss)

* * *

Violin Sonata, op. 18

(Anton Kaspar and Richard Strauss)

* * *

The lieder were sung in German, but provided with English translations in the program. There is no text in the program for *Enoch Arden,* which was probably performed in English. (There is no mention in the program of A. Strodtmann as the German translator of Alfred Lord Tennyson's original text.)

After recovering from the American journey, Pauline presented lieder at several concerts in 1905, including some given during a spring tour through the Netherlands. With a single exception, these are the last references to her performances to be found in Strauss's correspondence and in the concert programs and periodical reports. The only verified performance after 1905 is an all-Strauss program given by the Munich Lehrergesangverein together with the Musikalische Akademie on 10 January 1908. The composer conducted some of his choral works and Pauline sang two groups of orchestral lieder (five songs altogether).[45] No primary sources appear to provide evidence for the claims made by Alan Jefferson in *The Lieder of Richard Strauss* that "They toured together giving lieder recitals from the time they were married and up to about 1915" (p. 4) and "Thus he kept up the [performing] partnership, which in fact continued until towards the end of the First World War" (p. 19). (Michael Kennedy, in his *Richard Strauss,* p. 208, repeats these claims.) It is an unfortunate coincidence that the letters in Strauss's *Briefe an die Eltern* end in 1906, a year after his father's death. His mother lived on until 1910, but the remaining family letters for the years 1907–10 are unpublished. Few of the Strausses' letters to other people—at least of the ones now published—mention their joint lieder recitals.

Pauline Strauss gave up her career without ever having made a recording, although by the time she retired other singers had recorded some of Strauss's songs.[46] She was considered a dramatic soprano in her years of opera performing, and then sang primarily young dramatic roles. Later, as a lieder singer she was said to have a small voice that was not well projected; some critics felt it not overly pleasant in tone. She was, nevertheless, constantly praised for her uncommonly poetical and emotional interpretations, "her accustomed fervor and intelligence," and her "clever dramatic delineations," good diction, and winning manner.[47] A performance in Cologne was judged to have been sung "with much more intelligence than charm of voice."[48] A critic of her American appearances wrote that

> whatever her vocal methods, her readings are infused with warmth and artistic conviction. . . . We must assume that Madame Strauss sings her husband's songs exactly as he wishes them to be sung.[49]

On another occasion, her sensitive performance and Richard's seeming lack of involvement caused a critic to write that it appeared that *she* was the composer.[50] Her performances, particularly of *Traum durch die Dämmerung* and *Morgen!*, two songs which were hardly ever given without being encored, drew much praise. Richard Specht claimed that no one else could interpret the "Drei Mutterlieder" as she, that no one sang them with the same power of experience or intimacy of tone.[51] Of *Junghexenlied* (op. 39, no. 2), Reinhold Muschler wrote that one would have to have heard Pauline sing it to grasp the depth of the song.[52] Del Mar expands upon this:

> It is one of the songs in which—according to Strauss himself—his Pauline used to excel, and this throws an interesting further light on her artistry and personality. For with all her sharpness of manner she clearly had an enchanting sense of fantasy and a liveliness of wit which never ceased to delight her admiring husband.[53]

Other singers offered their praises for Pauline's voice, among them Elena Gerhardt, who claimed that "she had a delightful lyrical soprano voice and sang his songs most warmheartedly."[54] Gerhardt was quite impressed with Pauline's lyrical voice, singling out her performance of *Wiegenlied* (op. 41, no. 1), a song she considered one of Strauss's most difficult because of the breath control it requires.[55] Lotte Lehmann is said to have been chosen to play the part of Christina Storch, the character modeled on Pauline in *Intermezzo,* because "her voice approximated more closely to Pauline's than any other known to Strauss and his circle."[56] A few years after Pauline stopped singing in public, Alexander Dillmann referred to her "bell-like silver voice, to which is added an expression, a rapture which forces everyone momentarily into its power and under its spell."[57] As late as 1948, when Ernst Roth was visiting with the Strausses while Richard was in a clinic in Lausanne, Pauline remembered one of the lieder of which she had been a superb interpreter. As Strauss tried to recall the title of his song beginning "Du wirst nicht weinen," she supplied it (*Befreit*) and proceeded to sing it from memory in half voice but still with a good sound.[58]

Probably as a result of the illnesses she suffered in the early years of the new century Pauline was not always in good form for her performances. On occasion she had trouble in the upper register, and it was suggested that her voice was not equal to her repertoire. During the American tour, she received less favorable criticism in New York than in other cities. To some extent this may reflect the less sophisticated public and critical audiences in some of the smaller towns, but there were also suggestions that Nellie Melba and Marcella Sembrich had bribed the New York critics.[59] Carnegie Hall was considered too large a hall both for her singing voice and for the speaking voice of David Bispham in his *Enoch Arden* narration. Pauline's strengths were clearly in her interpretation of the songs (many of which were already familiar to New York audiences) rather than in her vocal ability. One anonymous reviewer found her suffering from faulty breathing, constant tension in the tongue, and audible throat sounds.[60] After her second New York appearance, in the second Strauss Festival concert by the Wetzler Orchestra on 3 March 1904, another anonymous reviewer assessed her skills:

> Of Mme. Strauss it can only be said that a second hearing accentuates her lack of vocal equipment as well as the beauty of her interpretation and manner of singing her husband's songs.[61]

Faring somewhat better in Philadelphia, Pauline "won instant favor by her charming personality . . ." and invested "each song with such intense personal feeling, dramatic force and sympathy with the song's emotional content, that these qualities carry her on to triumph."[62] Although this critic thought that her never very powerful voice had lost its pristine freshness and lacked any great charm, he praised her for submerging her limitations as much as possible in order to let the positive aspects of her performance dominate. In Chicago, her orchestral songs were well received and her exquisite interpretations much applauded. The songs performed in Chicago, with the Chicago Symphony on 1 and 2 April, were the "Drei Mutterlieder" and another group of four songs orchestrated especially for her: *Liebeshymnus, Das Rosenband, Cäcilie,* and *Morgen!* Most of her performances with orchestra during the tour included one or both of these groups. The same recital she presented on 1 March in Carnegie Hall was given again in Boston on 28 March (and probably repeated in recitals in Chicago, Providence, and elsewhere). A long-winded Boston critic for *The Musical Leader* stated:

> She was several times encored for her especially excellent interpretation, although her German school of vocalization is devoid of actual beauty, and, instead, is full of very ordinary technic, which has marred her artistic prospects. She is "artistic" only in the fact that she covers up her defects in vocal equipment, but even so she is a sweetly gracious and simple mannered woman on the stage, almost too much so, be it kindly said, . . .[63]

Not everyone agreed with his last statement. Her need to be dominant on stage found its expression in the flourishing of a scarf or fan or in a deep bow, often designed to cover the piano postlude with applause.[64] She was also noted for her hats, which were quite extravagant, but very much in place on the recital stage in her day. In America her traditional German costumes provoked favorable comment, although *The New York Times* described her merely as "a very plain looking woman of about forty years."[65]

At about the same time Pauline abandoned her career as a lieder singer reports of Strauss's concerts and recitals with other vocal artists diminished as well. His increasing involvement in the composition, production, and conducting of operas at this period is certainly the primary explanation for this. After productions of *Elektra* and *Salome* established him as a major—if controversial—operatic composer, critics and reporters of news in the musical world centered their attention on his stage works. Still, reports of Strauss conducting concerts of the Berlin and Vienna Philharmonic Orchestras, the Berlin Court Orchestra, and festival orchestras in cities such as Dresden, Stuttgart, and Wiesbaden appear fairly regularly in German music journals. The tone poems continued to be the most frequently performed of his works, but lieder occasionally turned up—for instance at the Munich Strauss Week of 1910, when the composer accompanied nineteen of his songs at recitals given by Tilly Koenen and Baptist Hoffmann. The orchestral lieder from his opp. 33 and 44 were also given at this festival. Several other occasions also included the performance of these songs and op. 51, sometimes with excerpts from *Guntram* or *Feuersnot* also on the program. Anton van Rooy and Karl Scheidemantel, who performed op. 33 with Strauss conducting, were each honored with the dedication of a song in op. 44; Baptist Hoffmann of the Berlin Opera gave the premiere of op. 44. The two songs of op. 51 were dedicated to and premiered by the bass Paul Knüpfer, also of the Berlin Opera. Among the other singers who performed at concerts and music festivals with Strauss conducting (or occasionally at the piano) were Milka Ternina, David Ffrangcon-Davies, Fritz Feinhals, Friedrich Brodersen, Heinrich Rehkemper, Leo Slezak, Selma Niklas-Kempner, Frau Walter-Choinanus, Frau Dr. Hertmanni, and Rudolf von Milde. Scattered performances are reported up to the years of World War I. After the war, a slight resurgence in Strauss's touring and performing with lieder singers coincides with his return to the composition of lieder. Notable among the artists with whom he toured at this time are—besides Elisabeth Schumann—Richard Mayr, Elena Gerhardt, Claire Dux, and Franz Steiner. In addition to singing orchestral songs, Steiner was the first performer to give a "complete" concert of Strauss's lieder with piano; see Chapter I, p. 11.

A description of Strauss's manner of accompanying lieder at this period is provided by Alfred Orel, who turned pages for the composer at one of his many *Liederabende* with Elisabeth Schumann. The pair were giving an all-Strauss evening as one of the highlights of the wartime programs at the Wiener Hochschule für Musik. Beforehand, Strauss cautioned Orel, "You must not look at the notes, since I'll play it quite differently."[66] Confirming Strauss's remark, Orel reported that he used wider registers and different octave doublings than those in the score and played certain chords as arpeggios or with harmonic enrichment. He likened Strauss's use of the written accompaniment to an operatic coach's use of a vocal score in rehearsing a singer. To Orel's ears, while Strauss was able to evoke the sounds of an entire orchestra if he desired (as he did on this occasion for *Cäcilie*), he could also play quite literally (as in *Morgen!*). Orel also commented on Strauss's habit of occasionally tracing the outlines of themes from his other works during the applause between songs. At the Schumann recital, for instance, he created—as if for himself alone—an introduction to *Du meines Herzens Krönelein,* from the folksong-like final duet of *Der Rosenkavalier.*[67] On another occasion with Schumann, Strauss reportedly used the "presentation of the rose" theme from the same opera to "modulate" between *Der Stern* and *Schlechtes Wetter.*[68] Antoine Goléa also reports on Strauss's inclination to "allow himself sudden and very audacious improvisations in the piano part" while accompanying Schumann in opp. 68 and 69.[69]

While it is true that Strauss did not do his initial composing at the piano, it may well be that when he found himself in the role of pianist he could not resist the temptation to compose—or to improve upon his earlier compositions. Or he may have varied the written music in order to keep from showing the boredom for which his accompanying was sometimes attacked. For all his technical facility and the confidence of his accompanying, at this period Strauss's playing was criticized as lacking the musicality and expression that were characteristic of his compositions. *The New York Times* music critic Richard Aldrich found his accompaniments subdued, lacking in flavor, and without musical significance; they suggested to Aldrich that the composer had no interest in what he was doing.[70] Other critics too sensed that, in view of the style of his more recent compositions, Strauss probably retained little enthusiasm for his early works. There were, after all, nearly forty years, seven operas, and several other major works between the Strauss of *Zueignung* and the Strauss of *Schlagobers* or *Eine Alpensymphonie.*

Familiar as certain of his songs were to him by the 1920's, Strauss did not usually play them from memory. Upon arriving in some of the midwestern towns (Detroit, Madison, and perhaps others) and finding the luggage containing some of their music lost, Strauss and Elisabeth Schumann substituted some Schubert songs—for which scores could be located—for some of the Strauss lieder originally programed. For his own *All mein Gedanken,* Strauss improvised a completely new accompaniment, one which so pleased Schumann that she claimed she could scarcely continue to sing. When she later asked him to write it out, it had slipped from his memory.[71]

The various reports of Strauss's style of accompanying by singers, page turners, and critics can be supplemented by documentation from the composer himself: he can today be heard as accompanist in recordings of twenty-two of his songs. The recordings were made with Heinrich Schlusnus and Robert Hutt ca. 1921–22 and with Maria Reining, Lea Piltti, and Anton Dermota in a series of Austrian radio broadcasts ca. 1942. They present many of his best-known lieder, one (*Zueignung*) in three different performances and four others in two versions each.[72] The early acoustic recordings probably represent Strauss's typical accompanying during the period of his second U. S. tour. Like the recital described by Orel, they include strictly literal interpretations (a few of them lackadaisically hammered out) and those with considerable freedom, especially in tempo, rhythmic flexibility, and chord figurations. Since the 1942 recordings also contain some variants in these aspects of the songs, we may assume that his style of playing did not change drastically over the years.

Strauss's most striking departures from the printed piano part include arpeggiated or rolled chords where the chord is notated to sound as a simultaneity, rushed and even rhythmically incorrect piano postludes, one entirely new rhythmic pattern for the accompaniment, and a great flexibility of tempo where no *rit.* or *accel.* is marked. Examples of at least a few rolled chords are written into the accompaniments of many songs. In *Die Nacht*, for example, measures 40 and 41 are so designated; in accompanying this song, Strauss adds a few more rolls, both where they might be required because of the wide span of notes within one hand (as in m. 25, or in many places in *Ruhe, meine Seele!*) and where there is no technical reason (as in mm. 5, 14–15, and 26). On the other hand, *Freundliche Vision* has no rolls indicated in the steady quarter-note left-hand accompaniment; Strauss arpeggiates many of the four-note chords to add to the atmosphere of the poem.

The recordings suggest a few reasons for this style of accompanying, which threatens to become mannered and even trite in some songs. First, it appears that Strauss is attempting to support the singer by sustaining the sonorities of the piano longer. Since some of the chords are written to be held for several beats in slow tempos, they soon die away in the piano. In *Ruhe, meine Seele!*, Strauss restrikes an eight-beat chord on the fifth beat, but even then the sound has dwindled by the end of the measure. This song has perhaps the most static (and least "pianistic") of all his lieder accompaniments and thus seems a natural candidate for orchestration. In the orchestral version, which Strauss created only in 1948 (while at work on the *Four Last Songs*), the instruments not only sustain the chords better than the piano but also create a richer atmosphere. Capitalizing on the greater interest in the accompaniment made possible by the orchestra, he added two more measures to the original three of the introduction and four more to the original four of the postlude. The bell- or chime-like figure introduced originally in measure 7 now makes its first appearance—effectively scored for flute, piccolo, celesta, and harp (playing harmonics)—in measure 5 of the introduction and reappears more often than in the piano version.[73] (Some higher notes of this figure, in mm. 3–14, are entirely lost in the surface noise of Strauss's 1921 recording.)

In contrast to the expansion of the orchestral postlude, in this recording of *Ruhe, meine Seele!*, Strauss actually plays the last few measures in a slightly faster tempo, reducing the note values of three chords
by half and omitting a rest. Thus the original rhythm of measures 39–43

(C) becomes approximately

Similarly, in his accompaniments of *Cäcilie* and *Morgen!* he shortens the
endings by omitting beats. Since in these songs he accompanies three
different singers (two in 1921, one in 1942), we may suspect him of doing
this on other occasions as well.[74] Strauss also tends to rush some of the
interludes, chooses tempos faster than those commonly heard today, and
in *Ruhe, meine Seele!* omits beats under long notes of the vocal line (mm.
16, 19).

Another reason for Strauss's rolling chords appears to be an attempt
to introduce more rhythmic variety and nuance into certain phrases, particularly where the rolled chord coincides with a vocal tenuto or ritardando. Finally, in certain songs (for example, *Morgen!* or *Ich schwebe*)
there are already a number of written rolled chords; the rolls he adds to
other chords are in keeping with the style, although they were not indicated when the song was first written and engraved. (There are no published corrections or second editions incorporating any such changes.) On
the other hand, a few written arpeggio figures may have been too difficult
for Strauss as a pianist—or not suited to his mood when he played
them—because he simplifies a few of the arpeggios in *Kling!* and blocks
chords at the end of one of the versions of *Ich liebe dich.*

The most unusual example of Strauss's departure from the printed
accompaniment figuration also involves rolled or arpeggiated chords. For
his performance of *Breit über mein Haupt* with Dermota, Strauss replaces
the original accompaniment, which moves primarily in half-note chords,
with arpeggiated patterns on almost every quarter note. Even toward the
middle of the song where the original accompaniment moves more
quickly he incorporates into it fuller chords, while retaining the other
moving parts. Strauss did not always play *Breit über mein Haupt* in this
way and may have improvised this version on the spot. In his earlier
recording with Hutt, he plays the music as written, except for a few rolled
chords toward the end and the addition of an octave below the root after
the last chord has been struck. Surprisingly, he never orchestrated this
song, which has a static accompaniment similar to that of *Ruhe, meine
Seele!*

Strauss did not indicate metronomic markings in his printed scores
for the songs; further, his indications of breathing places, tenutos, *rit.,*
accel., and other small, subtle rhythmic nuances are rather sparse. None
of the accompaniments he plays is treated with unvarying metronomic
precision, nor where there are multiple versions does he always take the
same tempo. While choice of tempo may have been the singer's decision

rather than his, he obviously did not object to different basic tempos for a song or to different degrees of variety within the song. His three performances of *Zueignung* provide an interesting contrast in terms of tempo and a surprising coincidence in treatment of the vocal climax on "heilig, heilig an's Herz dir sank" (mm. 25–26). The early recording with Schlusnus takes the fastest basic tempo but includes more variety; there are changes every two to six measures as well as tenutos (m. 16) and a rushed interlude (mm. 19–20). Schlusnus's tempo averages out to ♩ = 82 and is the fastest version of *Zueignung* I have found among recordings from various years of this century. The tempo of most modern singers is ♩ = 60–69. Reining's and Dermota's recordings are also faster than usual (♩ = ca. 75), but maintain a more consistent tempo throughout. In both these versions measure 16 remains in tempo, but 19–20 are still slightly rushed. In all three recordings the vocal climax (mm. 25–26) is greatly broadened, with some of the notes stretched to more than one and a half times their original value. Strauss holds back the accompaniment in two of them so that no additional notes are required, but with Dermota he repeats an extra beat of triplet eighths under the first "heilig." Strauss's desire to make more of this climax than he had originally done when writing the song in 1885 is suggested not only by these three recordings but also by his 1940 orchestration, in which this passage is rewritten as fourteen beats instead of eight (see Chapter IV, Ex. 5–7).

A similar dissatisfaction with the vocal ending of *Ich liebe dich* is apparent in Strauss's (and his singers') distortion of measures 42–44 (different in the two recorded versions). He also changed this ending in the 1943 orchestral version; see Chapter IV, Ex. 3. In Strauss's recording of *Ständchen,* there is another example of rhythmic variation of the vocal climax (mm. 81–87). The slight slowing of the tempo is not so noticeable as are Piltti's changes of note values:

Ständchen, op. 17, no. 2 (mm. 81–87), as written and as performed by Lea Piltti with Strauss as accompanist:

In this connection it should be noted that Mottl's orchestration, which Strauss himself conducted numerous times (and recorded with Julius Patzak), doubled the length of the high a² on "heilig" by adding an extra measure at this point. Strauss is said to have approved of this addition for performance with piano too, although here he does not adopt this change.[75]

In other passages of *Ständchen* Piltti takes great liberties with the meter, drawing out words particularly on high notes or at the ends of phrases. In what sounds like one of his more "bored," almost mechanical interpretations, Strauss forges ahead in all the interludes, scarcely allowing the singer the liberties she attempts. The basic tempo they take in this song is similar to the tempos usually adopted today. In many of his other accompaniments, however, Strauss and his singers move more rapidly than most modern-day performers. There is an additional striking discrepancy between the composer's own performance and current orchestral recordings of a few of the songs. Table 5, which lists eleven of the songs Strauss recorded, includes those in which there are large discrepancies of tempos; in the remaining eleven songs, there is less difference or a smaller range of differences from one extreme to the other.[76]

The recordings that Strauss made with Piltti, Reining, and Dermota are the last evidence we have of him as a lieder accompanist, an aspect of his career which he had begun six decades earlier. He was active as a conductor of lieder with orchestra as late as 1944, when Julius Patzak sang four of his orchestrated lieder under his direction. The recording of these songs (now on the Rococo label, no. 5348) is one of several currently available examples of Strauss as a conductor. The composer himself would probably have agreed with the judgments of both his contemporaries and later generations that his talents on the podium exceeded those at the piano. Nevertheless, his activity as a composer and performer of lieder with piano—particularly during the years of partnership with Pauline—reveals yet another facet of a many-sided musician.

Table 5

Tempo in the Performance of Strauss's Lieder with the Composer and Other Accompanists

Title, op., no.	M. M. with Strauss (approximate)	M. M. with others* (approximate)	M. M. with orchestra (approximate)
Zueignung, op. 10, no. 1	♩ = 74, 75, 82	♩ = 61, 63, 65, 69	♩ = 63
Heimkehr, op. 15, no. 5	♪ = 54, 59	♪ = 46, 50	- - - -
Seitdem dein Aug', op. 17, no. 1	♩ = 49	♩ = 50, 54	- - - -
Breit über mein Haupt, op. 19, no. 2	♩ = 39, 55	♩ = 42	♩ = 29
Ruhe, meine Seele!, op. 27, no. 1	♩ = 60	♩ = 43, 47, 52	♩ = 46
Heimliche Aufforderung, op. 27, no. 3	♩. = 81	♩. = 70	- - - -
Traum durch die Dämmerung, op. 29, no. 1	♪ = 53	♪ = 41, 47	- - - -
Schlagende Herzen, op. 29, no. 2	♩ = 51	♩ = 41, 45	- - - -
Nachtgang, op. 29, no. 3	♩ = 59	♩ = 39, 53	- - - -
Meinem Kinde, op. 37, no. 3	♪ = 61	- - - -	♪ = 52
Freundliche Vision, op. 48, no. 1	♪ = 69	♪ = 71	♪ = 51

* Selected from currently available recordings.

VII

CRITICAL OPINIONS OF STRAUSS'S LIEDER 1900–1977

The Strauss *Lieder*—some very
nice, some very cheap stuff.
Alban Berg*

Strauss's lieder have never attracted as much attention among critics as have his operas and tone poems. Shortly after their completion, most of his larger works—at least those produced up to World War I—became known through public performances and subsequent reviews. Critics awaited Strauss's new works with great anticipation, and journalists even reported on his works in progress. The orchestral and stage works are the subjects of criticism in the forty-six entries devoted to Strauss in Nicolas Slonimsky's *Lexicon of Musical Invective* (New York, 1963), pp. 180–95; the songs are not even mentioned in any of these writings. Edward Kravitt's listing of Strauss's "Adversaries" (nine, among them some whose writings appear in Slonimsky's collection) and "Champions" (eight) includes critics whose emphasis was on the larger compositions, the subject matter of the operas, Strauss's use of large orchestras, his conducting, and other more visible aspects of his musical career.[1] Although they were well known to these critics, the lieder obviously aroused less comment; not only were they works of a smaller genre, but on the whole they were less modern in style than the operas and tone poems. Furthermore, they did not always appear in large concert series or in opera houses, where performances were likely to be reviewed.

An examination of selected issues of German, French, English, and American periodicals from the first two decades of the twentieth century has shown that Strauss's lieder are often mentioned when performed, less frequently when first published; they are seldom reviewed in a critical sense and are not often enumerated by title or opus number. In reports of contemporary concert life and music festivals, the tone poems (especially *Tod und Verklärung, Don Juan, Don Quixote, Till Eulenspiegel,* and *Also sprach Zarathustra*) and the operas (*Salome* and *Elektra*) are mentioned far more often than the lieder. Yet the lieder were not neglected in actual performance. An article by Ernst Challier, Sr., in *Die Musik* on the

*Alban Berg, *Letters to His Wife,* edited, translated, and annotated by Bernard Grun (New York, 1971), p. 249 (letter from Vienna, 19–20 September 1919, about a concert he was rehearsing).

control of performing rights in Germany reports for the year from July 1903 to July 1904 a total of 1,532 concerts with 10,885 compositions (i.e., performances of compositions, obviously including repetitions of works), among them 3,623 lieder and duets. Strauss is represented by 75 orchestral and 210 lied performances; only Brahms and Wolf had more of the latter to their credit.[2]

Among Kravitt's "Champions," five writers had the most to say about Strauss's lieder: Strauss's biographers Max Steinitzer and Richard Specht, the prolific English writer Ernest Newman, and the American author-compilers James Huneker and Henry T. Finck. Of these, Newman stands out as being the most enthusiastic about and full of praise for Strauss's larger orchestral and stage works, but yet uncomplimentary about his songs. The other four—and favorably disposed critics in general—repeatedly praised the more popular of Strauss's lieder, while rarely recommending the unknown ones as worthy of consideration or capable of being understood. While a few writers were bold enough to suggest that new and different songs ought to be performed—not just the same popular two dozen over and over—Richard Specht's claim that "if a singer were to go on tour with others, he'd soon be home!" is more representative of the majority's opinion, at least until recent years.[3]

Contrary to his high praise for Wolf's songs, Ernest Newman wrote predominantly negative criticism about those of Reger and Strauss. Of Reger's many lieder, Newman allowed that perhaps eight were worth hearing; otherwise, their composer was too theatrical, self-conscious, artificial, and lacking in simplicity or truth. Newman's criticisms of Strauss's lieder cover only some one hundred and ten songs, those from op. 10 to op. 56; he was not aware of the youthful songs antedating op. 10, and, at the time of his writings, considered op. 56 the last lied group Strauss would write. Newman suggested that a small volume containing the following songs would suffice to illustrate the composer's art:[4]

Zueignung	*Traum durch die Dämmerung*	*Befreit*
Allerseelen	*Schlagende Herzen*	*Die sieben Siegel*
Seitdem dein Aug'	*Nachtgang*	*Ich schwebe*
Ständchen	*Ich trage meine Minne*	*Winterweihe*
Morgen!	*Meinem Kinde*	*Blindenklage*

Newman felt that his careful study of all songs from op. 10 to op. 56 had shown that many of them were a "woeful waste of time and labour" on the part of the composer.[5] A number of the songs were to him "commonplace, or dull, or pretentiously empty, or stupid, or downright ugly."[6] Others he found tiresomely didactic; inane rather than funny, which the composer aimed to be; lacking in form, conciseness, and unity; overly elaborate in accompaniment but yet inexpressive in vocal line. Three of Newman's statements (and his cranky tone in general) call into question the objective validity of his criticisms. First, he found there to be no change or development (i.e., qualitative growth of a personal style) in

Strauss's lieder writing from 1885 to 1906. What he implied was that the quality deteriorated while the style remained static, neither of which is an accurate claim. Newman also was quick to point out that Strauss supposedly created lieder as merchandise with which to acquire the publishers' money. Along with Strauss's other detractors, Newman claimed that it was money, not inspiration, that drove Strauss to write his music. As shown in Chapter I of the present study, the money Strauss earned from the sale of his lieder was much less than what he earned from the sale of other works and from performing fees, which were not collectible for the lieder. Finally, Newman admitted that the orchestral lieder were more appealing to him than those with piano accompaniment.[7] This generalization reinforces his preference for the tone poems above all other works, but it is a generalization not echoed by many other critics.

Like Newman and others writing before 1918, Finck assumed that op. 56 would be the last of Strauss's lieder. Unlike Newman, however, Finck was favorably impressed with their quality and variety. He applauded the fact that they were difficult songs for both singer and accompanist. Admitting that a few of the songs were mediocre (for example, op. 26) and others clearly potboilers (various titles in the groups between opp. 41 and 56), Finck found the "most important and popular" songs in opp. 27, 29, 31, 32, and 39. Implicit in his criticism—in contrast to Newman's—is the assumption that Strauss's style did change and that the style of the middle groups of songs was perhaps the best. Somewhat overly (but not negatively) impressed by the abundance of accidentals in Strauss's songs, Finck preferred the simpler ones like *Die Nacht, Breit über mein Haupt, Ach lieb! ich muss nun scheiden, Ach, weh mir unglückhaftem Mann, Morgen!,* and *Nachtgang.* He claimed *Ständchen* to be the composer's *pièce de résistance.*[8] Finck attempted to place Strauss's lieder in their proper historical context, both citing the points of departure for his early lieder (Liszt, Franz, Brahms, Schumann, and even Schubert) and setting straight those critics who had tried to attribute to Strauss a new school of song writing merely because he chose to use texts by a new generation of poets.[9]

An even more positive early attempt to understand and appreciate Strauss's lieder was made by Arthur Elson in 1905:

> That Strauss can write music of exquisite charm, is fully shown by his songs. Containing many modulations that sound strange at first, and some that seem needless, they are imbued with an exquisite melodic charm that is all the more wonderful in contrast with the unpleasing character of many of his orchestral themes. Some of them are priceless musical gems of the first water.[10]

The good qualities Elson and others found in the songs were not obvious to Newman, who suggested that the composer's artistic sense had begun to degenerate by the early 1900's. Newman wrote

> If his gift were for sheer musical beauty, the melody that sings from pure joy in itself, it would certainly appear here if anywhere. Yet among all his songs I cannot recall

more than one or two that seem to be written out of the mere heart of lyricism itself . . ."[11]

It was Elson's generally favorable, not Newman's harshly negative judgments that were shared by the majority of English-speaking critics around 1900–08. In England, those who admired the songs and tone poems were nevertheless put off or puzzled by some of Strauss's new works, particularly the *Symphonia domestica, Enoch Arden,* and eventually *Salome.* One writer claimed that several people were disappointed in the choral work *Taillefer,* which was rather too straightforward for them and not treated "with sufficiently Straussian obscurity."[12] The songs and their performances by Pauline, Hans Giessen, Ludwig Wüllner, and others, however, generally drew high praise. The composer was said to be more "natural" in them than in other branches of his art and to display here the "sweet reasonableness" that had justly found him favor as a song writer.[13] Anticipating his visit to the United States in 1904, American journalists produced a number of biographical articles and appreciations of his works. Most of these were favorable, claiming him to be the most prominent figure in the present-day musical world. He was called "this greatest of living composers"[14] not only for his mastery of orchestration but also for the melodic invention, beauty of expression, and "dramatic and masterly exposition of the mood."[15] Interest in Strauss continued during his tour and after his return to Germany. Portraits, cartoons, reviews, and concert announcements appeared in American journals throughout the year, and the music of *Ständchen* was printed (with German and English texts) in the February 1904 issue of *The Musician.* An article on contemporary songs by Richard Saville judged Strauss's lieder to be the most worthwhile of any written recently, attributing to them "an ever-increasing richness and spontaneity of inspiration."[16] Saville did Strauss a service in evaluating a few of his lesser known songs as well as the more popular. Some critics in America expressed a genuine curiosity about Strauss's new compositions (the world premiere of the *Symphonia domestica* was given on 21 March 1904 in Carnegie Hall), while others were rather naively impressed by reports that his piano accompaniments were the most difficult ever written, sometimes continuing erratically and unexpectedly for over twenty pages. One reviewer was properly shocked by *Wenn* (op. 31, no. 2). It is in E-flat major until the last seven measures, where there is a sudden shift to E major, in which key the song ends. Anticipating reactions such as hers ("A *fin de siècle* touch indeed!"[17]), when Strauss first had the song printed in the Munich periodical *Jugend,* I/4 (1896), he provided the following footnote:

> The composer advises singers [and accompanists] who intend to sing this lied while still in the nineteenth century [tradition] to continue it from here on a half tone lower (thus in E-flat), thereby concluding the composition in the same key in which it began.[18]

As an example of the varied opinions expressed by writers on Strauss's lieder, one might look at early criticisms of the famous *Ständchen*. The most devastating view is that of Rudolf Louis (a decided devotee of Wolf), who lamented the fact that Strauss's fame rested on this trite, commonplace little idea.[19] Of the writers mentioned above, Finck, Huneker, Newman, and Saville all singled out *Ständchen* as one of Strauss's best lieder. Finck and later Otto Erhardt, who described the song as Strauss's box office success ("Reisser"), commented on the displeasure this song's excessive popularity brought to the composer. Although he continued to perform it and never went so far as to withdraw it from his *oeuvre*, Strauss regretted its poor text accentuation, all the more so as its popularity proved indestructible.[20] Strauss himself never orchestrated *Ständchen*, as he did other lieder of which he wanted to increase or reinforce the popularity. He did, however, apparently approve of Felix Mottl's orchestration of the song, which Mottl prepared for his own wife to sing and which he had published in 1912. Strauss himself conducted Mottl's version several times, and even recorded it, further indicating his full approval.

Various writers have pointed out that by the end of his life—or even by the end of his concertizing with Pauline—Strauss must have played and heard some of the songs hundreds of times; any negative or indifferent attitude on the part of the composer toward these songs would, they claim, be justified or at least understandable. Yet Strauss is not known to have made any disparaging remarks about others of his great favorites. On the contrary, he quoted *Traum durch die Dämmerung* in other compositions and referred to it in prose writings and in conversation; late in life he still remembered some of the other successful songs fondly.

Elisabeth Schumann and Otto Erhardt both viewed *Ständchen* as the bridge for the general public to understanding Strauss—an easy introduction to his vocal music. Typical descriptions of it in two of the life-and-works writings that attempt to convey to the reader in a few adjectives the effect of each of Strauss's songs are Theodor Schäfer's "a charming, silvery and glittering song"[21] and Del Mar's claim "that it is a masterpiece there can be little doubt."[22] The song has, in fact, come to be known as typical of Strauss's writing and is often one of a handful of songs singled out for presentation as examples of his lied style. Its popularity is regrettable on at least three counts. First, Strauss himself was apparently displeased with his treatment of the textual accentuation. Second, a variety of instrumental arrangements—going as far from the original medium as saxophone quartet and trombone solo—have overpopularized music like this, which out of context (i.e., without its text) becomes rather mediocre. Finally, it is a false assumption that any one song could be "typical" of a genre that occupied a composer for nearly eighty years and in which he produced such a wide range of examples.

Ständchen, Traum durch die Dämmerung, and two other songs that rank as Strauss's most popular (*Zueignung* and *Morgen!*) were chosen by

James Husst Hall for description in his book *The Art Song*. Although Hall does not consider Strauss a master of the genre, he admits to the success of certain lieder, among them the spontaneously inspired, glowing, ecstatic *Ständchen*. "It may be flashy, but its downright honesty is disarming," he declares of this example of salon romanticism.[23] Philip Radcliffe cites *Ständchen* as an example of Strauss's more "successful" songs, those in the lyrical—as opposed to declamatory—style; it has for him "an enduring freshness and charm."[24]

Ständchen is included in Finck's anthology *One Hundred Songs by Ten Masters* (Boston, 1917), in which each composer is represented by ten works. Neither *Ständchen* nor any other of Strauss's songs appears in collections where one would expect them, as in *Neue Meister-Lieder, Sammlung berühmter Lieder der Neuzeit* (Leipzig, [ca. 1894]), or in other lieder anthologies of this period. Later anthologies do include Strauss's songs, usually representing the most popular among them, including *Ständchen*. The same songs reappear in editions of selected Strauss lieder, for instance those compiled by James Huneker, Sergius Kagen, and Max Heinrich.

Critics writing during the very decades in which Strauss was creating many of his lieder did not fail to consider the poetry as an important aspect of the lied. The poetry he chose brought Strauss both the highest praise and the strongest condemnation. J. A. Fuller-Maitland in his not altogether complimentary article on Strauss in *Grove's Dictionary of Music and Musicians*, second edition [the first edition contained no entry for him], praised the beauty of Strauss's songs from all periods (i.e., from op. 10 to op. 56). He attributed the wide appeal of certain songs (*Ständchen, Heimliche Aufforderung, Morgen!, Traum durch die Dämmerung, Ich trage meine Minne*, and *Das Lied des Steinklopfers*) to "their musical worth and their fitness for the way in which the feeling of the words is followed."[25] Huneker, writing about the same time, expressed the opinion that Strauss's music shows

> absolute fidelity to the poetic theme—that is, fidelity as the composer conceives it. Of mere sensuous or decorative music-making there is none.[26]

Singers as well as critics praised the skill with which Strauss combined text and music in his songs. Elena Gerhardt claimed that

> The outstanding characteristic of his songs is the absolute simplicity with which he expresses almost every mood. The musical phrase seems to pour out of him as soon as the poem takes hold of him and you hardly ever come across a line which you feel has been contrived.[27]

According to Elisabeth Schumann, Strauss wanted every word intelligible to the audience and to that end preferred to have the complete text (and translation, if appropriate) in the program, rather than the usual summary of the text. In her "master lesson" on *Morgen!*, Schumann describes details of the text interpretation which Strauss insisted on, such as letting the "n" on the final word "schweigen" vibrate and emphasizing deliberately the descending quarter notes on "niedersteigen."[28]

Strauss's ability to create the atmosphere of the poem in the accompaniment and to write the vocal part "so the sense of the poem is never trammelled by melody" was applauded in England. In contrast to Strauss's rich and highly colored invention, Wolf's songs were at this time termed a pose—works revealing "a love of abnormal harmony and an anemic thinness of emotion."[29] Strauss fared somewhat better than Wolf among certain German-dwelling critics as well. In spite of an enthusiastic audience, an English reporter resident in Leipzig was ungrateful to Ludwig Wüllner for having introduced him to some of Wolf's lieder, which he considered "about the most unrefreshing products of modern times" he had yet heard. Shortly thereafter, he was pleased to hear a recital by Anton van Rooy devoted to Schubert and Schumann:

> It is a case for special gratitude when one is not compelled to hear *Lieder* by Hugo Wolf and similar declamatory and constantly modulating compositions.[30]

In a review of newly published Strauss lieder, Eugen Segnitz recommends opp. 39, 43, 44, 46, and 47 (all published between 1898 and 1900) as songs in which Strauss

> shows endless talent for mood painting and understands like none of his contemporaries how to interpret poetic contents in music and to make music serve words.[31]

For Segnitz, the highlights of these groups were *Junghexenlied* and *Der Arbeitsmann* (op. 39, nos. 2 and 3), which contrast the fantastic world with a most realistic one; and *Einkehr* and *Von den sieben Zechbrüdern,* both of which show Strauss as a humorist in the vein of *Till Eulenspiegel* and *Don Quixote.*[32] He applauded the variety of Strauss's lieder, a quality which Strauss himself felt that not enough critics appreciated in his works. Toward the end of his life, the composer told Roland Tenschert, the Viennese writer on music who devoted much study to his lieder, that this variety, especially in the humorous and characteristic songs, had not yet received its due recognition.[33]

Other critics reacted negatively to the humor in Strauss's lieder: Newman, for example, cited a long list of "intolerably facetious" works which to him resulted only in inanity.[34] J. M. P. Steinhauer, reviewing a performance of op. 44, was unable to comprehend or take seriously the second of the two songs, *Nächtlicher Gang,* because of its literal representation of the storm and a general feeling that Till Eulenspiegel himself had escaped into the orchestra and made havoc of Strauss's attempt at writing a humoreske.[35] Strauss was criticized not only for the inappropriateness of his humor but also for the heavy-handed and overdone pomposity. Both the songs and the tone poems beginning with *Ein Heldenleben* (op. 40, completed toward the end of 1898) were called pretentious,

inflated expressions which lacked the sincerity and directness of his earlier works.

Alfred Kalisch's article on Strauss, which appeared in both the third
and fourth editions of *Grove's Dictionary,* cited many of the same songs
that Fuller-Maitland had singled out as noteworthy for their "lyrical charm
of melody and extraordinary insight into the meaning of the text and
picturesque accompaniment."[36] Kalisch did not agree with Fuller-Maitland, however, that *Das Lied des Steinklopfers* was a successful setting.
Rather, he found it a song in which the text is not about the beautiful or
romantic (as he implies a lied text should be), but about the "ugly side of
the world, and violent, subversive feelings."[37] He questioned the value of
setting such a text to music and suggested—as Newman had also—that
Strauss's literary judgment sometimes failed him. Years earlier, Erich Urban had not known what to make of this song, which he considered totally
new and revolutionary.[38]

Other critics considered that songs such as *Das Lied des Steinklopfers* and *Der Arbeitsmann,* both of which are settings of the new
"social lyric" ("Soziallyrik"), were important milestones in the history of
the lied. They attempted to understand the new and different text, tone,
and musical style of these works. Finck, for example, found the unpleas-
ant and harsh harmonies ugly but still appropriate in expression for the
lied idiom. Upon first hearing David Bispham sing *Das Lied des Steinklopfers* in 1904, a New York critic judged it

> extremely striking, extremely novel, expressing in the music the grimness, the hard
> hopelessness, the anarchistic tendency of the words. There is potent effect in the
> repetition of the few most significant phrases after the poem has been sung through.[39]

Some expected that Strauss might continue to write lieder in the style of
these songs and thus enter into an entirely new type of song writing. He
did not, however, pursue this course, and few of his lieder texts belong to
the category of social lyric. Within a few years, he abandoned the lied;
perhaps he felt the anguish and oppression expressed in these songs was
better suited to a more dramatic medium and therefore turned his efforts
to composing works for the stage.

It was not only these settings of the "Soziallyrik" (meaning "socially-
conscious" lyric) that audiences found hard to understand. At the premiere of *Der Einsame* (op. 51, no. 2) on 5 March 1906, for instance, there
was much astonished shaking of heads at Strauss's noteworthy and powerful orchestral setting. This often "deeply shocking" declamatory setting
for low bass voice was still in manuscript, having been completed as
recently as 18 February 1906. Most of the audience considered it less
comprehensible than *Im Spätboot* (op. 56, no. 3), performed with Strauss
at the piano on the same program.[40]

Of Strauss's songs written around 1900, those of op. 48 were the
favorites for most listeners and reviewers. Upon hearing Hermann Gura
sing this opus, a Berlin critic to whom it was new described the songs as

peaceful, lucid, and basically simple creations of unusually effective power and beauty.[41] *Waldseligkeit,* op. 49, no. 1, which became part of Pauline's repertoire soon after its composition, was considered an immediately understandable song. Most of its seven companions in op. 49, however, remained among Strauss's less frequently performed lieder. In general it was the lyrical songs, evoking a single mood or thought in the manner of *Morgen!* or *Traum durch die Dämmerung,* that were the most accessible. Romain Rolland, whom Strauss met for the first time in 1899, wrote to the composer of his enthusiasm for two collections of newly published songs which Strauss had sent him:

> . . . May flowers and September fruits, and they really are fresh and fragrant like the seasons. . . . They exude a breath of youth—the most beautiful of all beautiful things. . . .[42]

Concerning the influence of earlier lieder composers on Strauss, there is little agreement among critics. Almost every major composer of the nineteenth century is claimed by some writer as influential, and nearly as many are denied as having had any effect on Strauss at all.[43] It is my belief that the songs of his predecessors did have a marked influence on Strauss's lieder writing; in his wide variety of songs certain ones can be singled out as particularly reminiscent of Brahms, Schubert, Schumann, Liszt, and other composers. Especially in Strauss's early songs (the youthful songs and at least those through op. 29) there are echoes of earlier lieder, the ones he grew up playing and hearing.

The majority of writers on Strauss agree in tracing a line of musical succession from Liszt through Wagner to Strauss. Strauss's first exposure to Wagner—forestalled as long as possible by his anti-Wagnerite father—and his subsequent declaration to Ludwig Thuille "I have become a Wagnerian," along with his somewhat later association with Alexander Ritter, determined the direction that Strauss's future orchestral and operatic writing would take.[44]

In contrast to the strong influences from the past, there is little in Strauss's music (and even less documentary evidence) to suggest that the music of his contemporaries affected his own writing. Strauss took great interest in conducting the works of his contemporaries (Mahler, Thuille, Schillings, Korngold, and others); he also promoted the publication of Reger's compositions, prepared keyboard reductions of works by Ritter and others, and founded *Die Musik,* a series of monographs (not to be confused with the periodical of the same name) that included articles on composers, musical genres, and the cultural life of past and present. Yet he formed no close ties with any other living composer—except for Thuille and Ritter in his early years—and did not allow their works to touch his own musical style. Critics such as Rudolf Louis considered this a fault: he suggested that if Strauss had known Wolf's songs, his own might have benefited.[45] Suggestions by Finck (*Richard Strauss,* p. 286) and a few other writers that Wolf's song writing was familiar to (and therefore influential on) Strauss cannot be supported. Though writing in the same genre at the same time, the two composers moved in very different geographical, social, and musical spheres. They never met, although they once came close to it when both visited a singer with new lieder on the same day.

Strauss's freedom from outside influences—or his refusal to be constrained by them—may be the key to the entire course of composition he pursued after writing *Salome* and *Elektra*. Just after 1900 he stood at the forefront of modern composition, with the tone poems and these two dramatic works to his credit. At the time of his 1904 tour to America, U. S. critics echoed statements such as this one from *The Musical Leader:* "As everyone knows, Strauss is the most advanced of the 'ultra-modern' school."[46] Preparing *New York Times* readers for Strauss's visit, Richard Aldrich referred to him as the "most commanding figure in the musical world of today . . . the man who has most deeply impressed himself upon current music."[47] Shortly after this tour, at a crucial point in the musical history of the early twentieth century, Strauss stopped moving forward at his usual pace and began looking instead to the past. This looking back does not really entitle him to the claim of being the first neo-classicist of the century because he was never far enough removed from his Classical-Romantic inheritance to make a distinct turn back to it. Yet many of his twentieth-century works—from *Der Rosenkavalier* to the *Four Last Songs*—depend much more on this inheritance than on the prevailing musical languages of their day or on the idiom of *Salome* and *Elektra*.

There is no less disagreement among critics of Strauss's new lieder of 1918 than there is in earlier writings on the songs up to op. 56. Richard Specht suggested that in opp. 67, 68, and 69 Strauss's harmonic, melodic, and declamatory trademarks had deteriorated to mere mannerisms. Specht found op. 67 joyless, the coloratura style of *Amor* unbearable. On the other hand, an anonymous writer reporting in the *Neue Zeitschrift für Musik,* LXXXVII (1920), p. 38, on the recent publication of op. 69 praised these songs as creations having an altogether surprising simplicity of character and freshness of expression.

Not as much attention as might be expected was focused on these new works of 1918. Except for the controversial op. 66, which immediately attracted some notice in the journals (in spite of its being published by a non-musical firm in a limited edition of only 120 copies), Strauss's return to the lied was not considered as important at this time as was the creation of new works in other larger and more visible genres. Less than three months after he had completed op. 66, a gossip column in the *Signale für die musikalische Welt* reported that Strauss had shown the singer Franz Steiner a group of ten [sic] new songs with which the composer indirectly declared war on the publishing industry.[48] In the 2 October 1918 issue of the same journal (pp. 641–43) August Spanuth made public the story behind the creation of this opus and the satirical verses used for it. He quoted a few of the more innocuous texts (those without publishers' names in them), described them as mocking and derisive, as vulgar hackwork, but made no mention of the musical quotations and passed no judgment on the quality of the songs. A few years later an American summarizing the story of the work's creation reported that

> The cycle is written in the best Strauss vein and [is] declared to be the best musical inspiration he has had for years.[49]

Of all the songs written in 1918, opp. 68 and 69 were reviewed most favorably in contemporary critics' reports, while op. 67 remained almost unmentioned. As stated in Chapter II, Strauss was praised for the Brentano, Arnim, and Heine texts he chose to set in opp. 68 and 69. His awareness of tradition in the choice of poems by earlier Romantics is reflected particularly in the comparatively simple settings of op. 69, a group which he called *Fünf kleine Lieder.* Although certain writers (e.g., Erhardt, *Richard Strauss,* p. 178) have argued that Strauss's approach to lieder composition was altered after World War I by the events and pressures of the war, these songs hark back to the idiom of his earlier lieder just as the *Four Last Songs* later reaffirm his Romantic heritage. To be sure, the vocal writing—especially in op. 68—had been much influenced by the operatic writing in *Ariadne auf Naxos,* but the harmonic and formal structures owed nothing to the existence of the twentieth-century avant-garde. Elisabeth Schumann's 1922 Salzburg performance of op. 68 caused one reviewer to proclaim it the highlight of the festival:

> [the songs] showed how agonizing and problematic all this experimental music appears next to the genius of a man who has the opportunity and the courage to reveal it. These songs are splendid, priceless; the maturity of late summer lies over them, a fullness of new inspirations and musical charms is poured out over them.[50]

The final two groups of songs that Strauss intended to be included among his works published with opus numbers were the orchestral *Drei Hymnen,* op. 71 (1921), and the five songs with piano, *Gesänge des Orients,* op. 77 (1928). Although they remain relatively unknown today and never attracted the attention of many singers even in Strauss's lifetime, upon their publication both collections received favorable notices in the press. A writer for the *Musical Courier,* for instance, claimed op. 71 to be true to its composer's genius, of exquisite color and warm sentiment, and wonderfully orchestrated.[51] Reviewing op. 77, Ernst Rychnovsky cited the extreme difficulty (especially in range and breath control) of these "masterpieces of small form" that results from the influence of Strauss's operatic writing. Although Rychnovsky felt that Strauss may have gone too far in his demands upon the singer in order to create his artistic image, he thought that the musical rendering of the poems more than did them justice.[52]

Op. 71 was given its first performance in Berlin on 9 November 1921 by Barbara Kemp with the Berlin Philharmonic conducted by

Gustav Brecher. As of 1930, when Strauss recommended op. 71 (along with others of his orchestral songs) to Rose Pauly, only one other singer had done them in public with orchestra. Op. 77 was premiered in Vienna, also within a year of its completion. On 5 June 1929 Koloman von Pataky and the composer presented the five songs for the first time. Whether they were ever performed by Elisabeth Schumann and her husband, Karl Alwin, to both of whom they are dedicated, is not known. Only one recording of each opus is thought to have been made, that of op. 71 by Phyllis Curtin (1964) and of op. 77 by Dietrich Fischer-Dieskau (1970).[53]

The degeneration Specht saw in Strauss's vocal compositions of 1918 had already been suggested by Newman as present in those written before 1906; other writers echoed their criticisms, especially in reference to the later works. Specht generalized that a youthful composer was more subjective, an older one more objective; he considered the lied a subjective medium and found the highest quality only in those of Strauss's songs written before 1906. On the occasion of the composer's sixtieth birthday, *The New York Times'* critic Aldrich declared that Strauss had written himself out early, not producing much of quality in recent years, or since about op. 60.[54] Strauss himself is said to have considered the medium of the lied most suited to a composer's youthful expression, but did not let that attitude dampen his desires to express himself in vocal composition. Like Strauss, both Brahms and Pfitzner created the majority of their lieder in their younger years. (One wonders if this would have proved true of Schubert, had he lived longer.) And, like Schumann, Strauss concentrated most heavily on the creation of lieder at one period in his life. For him, the years 1894 to 1901 may be compared to Schumann's "lieder year" of 1840. Franz Grasberger, citing the parallel of Schumann's lieder year having coincided with his marriage to Clara Wieck, considers Strauss's op. 27—dedicated to Pauline on the occasion of their marriage in 1894—as the beginning of Strauss's "Liederfrühling."[55]

From 1918 onward, Strauss's lieder were widely discussed by reviewers on the following occasions: in 1921 (Strauss's second concert tour to America), 1949–50 (at his death and upon the publication and world premiere of the *Four Last Songs*), 1958–59 (the publication and performance of some newly discovered early songs, collected together as *Drei Liebeslieder;* the publication of op. 66 by Boosey & Hawkes), and 1964 (the centenary of the composer's birth).

Although Strauss's first American tour had not been totally successful financially or critically for the sponsoring organizations (Strauss himself was well paid and received favorable criticism), by 1921 American enthusiasm for a second appearance was high. Interest—if not controversy—was increased by a supposed interview with the composer by one Henrietta Straus. In the article which appeared in *The Nation* the composer purportedly spoke negatively about Americans and their musical culture.[56] This interview, the prevalent anti-German sentiment in certain quarters, and the reputation that Strauss had gained on his first visit for being commercially rather than artistically minded all attracted attention to his arrival. There was a curiosity, too, about the composer whose musical standing had so greatly altered in the first decades of the twentieth century. Aldrich deplored what he considered the scandalous way in which Strauss let his artistic standards and personal dignity be sacrificed to his desire to earn money. He was probably referring to the two concerts Strauss and Pauline presented in 1904 at the auditorium of the Wanamaker store in New York. The concerts were open to the public free of charge and attracted thousands of people; Strauss was paid one thousand dollars for each concert. Aldrich further stated that, except for *Der Rosenkavalier,* few of Strauss's compositions in the intervening years enhanced his reputation or proved that his creative ability was enduring.[57]

Arriving in the country in late October, Strauss toured until 1 January 1922, conducting major orchestras and accompanying lieder and chamber recitals. Elisabeth Schumann was his principal soloist for eighteen programs; in addition, he performed lieder with either orchestral or piano accompaniment with Claire Dux, Elena Gerhardt, and George Meader. (Frieda Hempel was scheduled to sing in his farewell concert, but did not appear; Birgit Engell was also to have sung with him, but did not.) As during the earlier tour with Pauline, the tone poems, a few chamber works, and the more popular of his lieder dominated the programs. At least forty different songs were given by the various singers. More works of other composers (especially Mozart, Weber, Beethoven, and Wagner—all Strauss's favorites) were presented than during the earlier tour. This time arias appeared on the orchestral programs, usually with a few orchestral lieder. At lieder recitals in Detroit, Madison, and possibly other cities, Schumann and Strauss presented some Schubert lieder when their luggage containing the Strauss scores had gone astray.[58]

While about half of the lieder that appeared on the recitals of this tour were the very ones Pauline had presented in 1904 and were also those often sung in New York by other artists,[59] Strauss's new songs of 1918 were not totally neglected. An article on the composer in *Musical America* during his visit stated that he had written "a group of songs or arias—*grosser Lieder*—for high voice and orchestra" which would be heard in the concerts of his tour.[60] Another article, entitled "Elisabeth Schumann to Sing New Songs of Richard Strauss" mentioned *Ich wollt ein Sträusslein binden, Säusle, liebe Myrte, Der Stern,* and *Einerlei* as works she would sing and which had never before been heard in America.[61] Before Schumann's Town Hall recital, it was announced that she would sing several new Strauss songs. The program was to be the same as those she had given in other cities, including the songs mentioned above and another from op. 69, *Schlechtes Wetter.* The program and reviews of the recital, however, indicate that none of op. 68 was sung. *Schlechtes Wetter* was so well liked that it was repeated, as were two other songs.

Schumann's recital was the first of Strauss's "Intimate Matinee Recitals" at Town Hall, Elena Gerhardt's the second. Gerhardt programed eight of Strauss's songs which she had never before given in public. These songs were not newly written ones, but were merely new to her. The most recently composed was *Gefunden,* which Pauline had sung in the U. S. while it was still in manuscript. A third recital in Town Hall, given by the composer with the Metropolitan Opera tenor George Meader, was judged by some reviewers to be the best in terms of vocal quality and technique. It is also of interest because some less frequently sung Strauss songs were included. Table 6 gives the programs sung by the three artists in this series. The songs on Meader's program which may have been unfamiliar to the audience are those from opp. 17, 22, and 49.

Other relatively new works sung during the 1921 tour were the orchestrations of *Die heiligen drei Könige aus Morgenland* (dating from and published during 1906 but claimed by reviewers as new to them in 1921), and the 1918 orchestration of *Freundliche Vision.* The latter, one of the five songs orchestrated for Schumann, was sung several times by her and also by Claire Dux.

In general, by 1921 the critics appear to have accepted Strauss's songs as an established part of the repertoire, works no longer requiring critical assessment before their position would be taken for granted. A few writers found new interest in them for their foreshadowing of the composer's more recent works, but they did not elaborate upon this observation. Strauss's songs were by this time an established part of singers' repertoires at least along the Eastern seaboard; by contrast, very few of Wolf's songs appear in American programs of this period, while the names of Reger, Pfitzner, and others of Strauss's contemporaries can hardly be found at all.

None of the New York critics was overly impressed by the performances of Strauss and his singers, saying that they were used to hearing his songs given by better singers and better pianists. Nevertheless, after more than forty concerts and recitals, Strauss closed his American tour with earnings reported at fifty thousand dollars, or—at the prevailing rate of exchange—ten million German marks.[62]

From the end of this tour until his death, Strauss attracted little attention as a lieder composer or accompanist. Aside from op. 77, the few lieder that he wrote between 1922 and the *Four Last Songs* remained relatively unknown; some were not published or performed in public until after his death. Although he found a new "ideal" interpreter in the soprano Viorica Ursuleac, the performances of his lieder—both orchestral and with piano—diminished somewhat in these years, as did his interest in writing lieder.

The publication and premiere of the *Four Last Songs,* which neither Richard nor Pauline lived to see, created a resurgence of interest in Strauss as a lieder composer. The extant sketches of *Im Abendrot* (dating from 1946) and of the three Hesse songs (1947–48) show that he worked on these orchestral lieder over a longer period of time than was usual in his earlier years. (In general, the orchestral songs appear to have been longer

Table 6

Strauss's Series of "Three Intimate Matinee Recitals" in Town Hall, New York (1921)

I. ELISABETH SCHUMANN, soprano, 3 p.m. Thursday, 15 December 1921.*

1. *Zueignung*, op. 10, no. 1
Junghexenlied, op. 39, no. 2
Du meines Herzens Krönelein, op. 21, no. 2
All mein Gedanken, op. 21, no. 1
Traum durch die Dämmerung, op. 29, no. 1
Wiegenlied, op. 41, no. 1

2. *Glückes genug*, op. 37, no. 1
Muttertändelei, op. 43, no. 2

Einerlei, op. 69, no. 3
Der Stern, op. 69, no. 1
Schlechtes Wetter, op. 69, no. 5

3. *Ich trage meine Minne*, op. 32, no. 1
Ich schwebe, op. 48, no. 2
Schlagende Herzen, op. 29, no. 2
Freundliche Vision, op. 48, no. 1
Ständchen, op. 17, no. 2

II. ELENA GERHARDT, mezzo-soprano, 3 p.m. Saturday, 24 December 1921.

1. *Allerseelen*, op. 10, no. 8
Frühlingsgedränge, op. 26, no. 1
Die Nacht, op. 10, no. 3
Hat gesagt—bleibt's nicht dabei, op. 36, no. 3
Zueignung, op. 10, no. 1

2. *Gefunden*, op. 56, no. 1
Wie sollten wir geheim sie halten, op. 19, no. 4
Mein Auge, op. 37, no. 4

Meinem Kinde, op. 37, no. 3
Cäcilie, op. 27, no. 2

3. *Ruhe, meine Seele!*, op. 27, no. 1
Anbetung, op. 36, no. 4
Schlagende Herzen, op. 29, no. 2
Morgen!, op. 27, no. 4
Heimliche Aufforderung, op. 27, no. 3

III. GEORGE MEADER, tenor, 3 p.m. Saturday, 31 December 1921.

1. *Breit über mein Haupt*, op.19, no. 2
Mit deinen blauen Augen, op. 56, no. 4
Sie wissen's nicht, op. 49, no. 5
Zueignung, op. 10, no. 1

2. *Kornblumen*, op. 22, no. 1
Mohnblumen, op. 22, no. 2
Epheu, op. 22, no. 3
Wasserrose, op. 22, no. 4

3. *Freundliche Vision*, op. 48, no. 1
Wozu noch, Mädchen, op. 19, no. 1
Das Geheimnis, op. 17, no. 3
Nichts, op. 10, no. 2

4. *Morgen!*, op. 27, no. 4
Die Nacht, op. 10, no. 3
Ich trage meine Minne, op. 32, no. 1
Heimliche Aufforderung, op. 27, no. 3

---

* The program for this recital is reconstructed from newspaper announcements before the recital and reviews afterward. Actual programs of the other two recitals are preserved in the Town Hall archives.

in gestation than those with piano.) The final manuscript scores were not completed until May–September 1948. *September,* the last of the group to be scored (ending on 20 September), was his last completed work. Coming at the end of his life as they do, these songs emphasize the importance of the lied in his life's work and represent his crowning achievement in the realm of the orchestral lied. Nor are they four isolated examples of Strauss's interest in song during his last years. During and after working on a series of abstract instrumental compositions and arrangements of excerpts from stage works, Strauss turned to the composition of these lieder, to the orchestration of *Ruhe, meine Seele!,* and to the creation of other vocal works which were never completed. He orchestrated *Ruhe, meine Seele!* between the final scorings of *Im Abendrot* and *Frühling.* Like the *Four Last Songs,* its text expresses thoughts that were very much Strauss's own, when he knew he had not long to live. The scores of these five works followed one another at about a month's interval: *Im Abendrot* was completed on 6 May 1948 (the short score on 27 April), *Ruhe, meine Seele!* on 9 June, *Frühling* on 18 July (the short score on 20 June), *Beim Schlafengehn* on 4 August, and *September* on 20 September (sketches dated at the end 10 August 1948).[63] In the same sketchbooks that contain drafts for the *Four Last Songs* are sketches for a work for six-part chorus and orchestra, *Besinnung* (AV 306), also using a text by Hesse; for another orchestral song based on Hesse's poem *Nacht* (AV 303); for a lied, apparently with piano accompaniment, to a poem by Betty Knobel (*Malven,* AV 304); and possibly for another lied, *Höhe des Sommers* (see Appendix B).[64] The last of these is not catalogued in Asow, nor is the poet (Hesse) indicated by Strauss. The text, which appears opposite that of *September* in sketchbook 141, is one of several other Hesse texts Strauss may have intended to set. Willi Schuh, who examined the volume of Hesse's poetry used by the composer—*Die Gedichte,* second edition (Zurich, 1942)—reported that Strauss had marked off a total of twelve poems, including those for three of the *Four Last Songs.*[65]

Less than a year after Strauss's death (on 8 September 1949) and within days of Pauline's death (13 May 1950), the world premiere of the *Four Last Songs* was given in London by Kirsten Flagstad with Wilhelm Furtwängler and the Philharmonia Orchestra. This performance followed close upon the publication of the orchestral—in full and pocket size—and piano versions. Together these events resulted in many reviews, articles, and analytical studies. Almost all writers agreed that in both text and music the *Four Last Songs* were a most appropriate ending to a long and for the most part brilliant career as a composer of vocal music. Their valedictory nature is emphasized, and parallels drawn between them and Brahms's *Four Serious Songs, Abschied* in Mahler's *Das Lied von der Erde,* Wolf's *Three Michelangelo Songs,* and other last works. More recently, there are Vaughan Williams' *Four Last Songs* (1954–58), which, like Strauss's, were given a title and published together after their composer's death.

Unlike these other songs and collections, however, Strauss's *Four Last Songs* were of a definitely retrospective musical character, quite removed in time and style from the musical world of the 1940's. Critics of a conservative persuasion judged them "a true oasis in the desert of modern concert life."[66] These songs were thought of as a summary of the increasingly distant romantic age from which Strauss never entirely separated himself. Their musical language was "a serener continuation of a viewpoint maintained by the composer for over half a century."[67] Michael Kennedy has even gone as far as to call them "escapist," the works of "an old man turning his back finally on the madness of the world" (*Richard Strauss*, p. 217). Reminders of Strauss's much earlier writing were obvious, both literally and in a more general sense, only now the overdone, self-important affectations were tempered by a depth of purpose and a refined sensibility. Rich, evocative, lush, opulent, magical, autumnal, and glowing are some of the adjectives repeatedly applied to Strauss's "swan-song." This "musical sunset" of an octogenarian master not only called up memories of the Strauss of the past, but also reaffirmed the importance of his inheritance from the nineteenth century, especially from the opposing forces, Brahms and Wagner.

Though dedicated to friends of his last years rather than to his wife, the *Four Last Songs* were nevertheless a last, intimate musical message to her. The poems were obviously chosen with as much care as were those of earlier songs which he dedicated to her for their marriage, Franz's first birthday, and other important events in their family life. The significance which the lied continued to hold for Pauline long after she stopped singing had its final expression in her request that three of Strauss's most famous lieder—*Allerseelen, Morgen!* and *Freundliche Vision*—be sung at his funeral. (In fulfillment of Strauss's own wish, the final trio of *Der Rosenkavalier* was also sung.[68]) While the *Four Last Songs* may never rival in popularity these three songs or a dozen others from the same period, they easily surpass the other songs that Strauss conceived originally with orchestral accompaniment. A report by the Berlin Strauss Society estimated that by 1958 the *Four Last Songs* had been given at least two hundred public performances with orchestra.[69]

Despite his advanced age and poor health, Strauss was able to maintain the high quality of his luxuriant and masterly writing for both voice and orchestra in the *Four Last Songs*. In his concern for words as well as music he is remarkably disciplined in allowing the voice to float atop the rich but discreetly light orchestral textures. One writer, Alan Frank, considers the similarity of tempo and mood in the four songs (three are marked Andante, and *Frühling* is an only slightly faster Allegretto) too static for modern ears. He expresses the same reservations about Strauss's *Metamorphosen* of 1945, but goes on to point out that not all four of the songs need be performed together.[70] The coloratura writing, reminiscent of passages in both operas and lieder, is evocative and atmospheric rather than pictorially detailed. As in the vocal lines of many of his earlier works, Strauss could not resist the opportunity to illustrate a few words through melismas and other types of word painting. Mosco Carner suggests that *Frühling* is the least inspired of the four songs: its somewhat forced expression, he claims, lacks the spontaneity and freshness of melodic invention found in Strauss's earlier songs, and the vocal line is uncomfortable and angular. He laments that Strauss was here unable to conjure up the "spring" atmosphere of earlier songs such as *Frühlingsgedränge* (op. 26, no. 1) or *O süsser Mai!* (op. 32, no. 4).[71] Yet the success of the *Four Last Songs* lies at least in part in their delicate, subdued expression and in their simple, understated, and almost static moods. As Carner himself points out, the tenderness and emotion of the texts are expressed in very sublimated musical terms. The smooth lines and gently undulating phrases require a singer with accomplished breath control and the ability to sustain uniformity and intensity throughout a wide range. The "usual *frisch und fröhlich* style" of performance that lieder singers indulge in when singing Strauss "is the last thing this kind of music will suffer."[72]

In 1958–59 the rediscovery of three early Strauss songs and the publication of op. 66 in a form more widely available than the 1921 limited printing (which was done by a publisher who did not specialize in music) again caught the attention of reviewers. The three songs, issued under the Henmar Press imprint of C. F. Peters with the title of *Drei Liebeslieder,* are *Die erwachte Rose* (AV 66), *Begegnung* (AV 72), and *Rote Rosen* (AV 76). The first of Strauss's youthful songs to be published in a performing edition, they were sung with great success by Elizabeth Schwarzkopf in New York, London, and Wiesbaden (30 November 1958, 18 January 1959, and 1 March 1959, respectively). As of 1958, it was thought that all three songs dated from 1883, or about the time of op. 10. *Die erwachte Rose* and *Begegnung,* however, were actually written earlier, in 1880, while op. 10 is now known to date from the late summer and fall of 1885. On 19 October 1883 Strauss sent his autographs of these two songs from 1880—along with that of the newly composed *Rote Rosen*—to Lotti Speyer, whom he had met the previous summer and with whom he carried on a correspondence for the next few years. Through her family, they eventually reached Peters and were published in handsome editions that included facsimiles of the first pages of the autographs. In later printings, two of Strauss's letters to Speyer (the nature of which obviously suggested the title *Drei Liebeslieder* to the publishers), articles about the discovery of the songs, and reviews of their first performances were reproduced in the editions as well. The reviewers thought the songs well written and effective, much in the style of op. 10. The main attraction that they held was, of course, that they were new discoveries and welcome additions to the lieder repertoire.

Although Strauss's *Krämerspiegel,* op. 66, had not gone unnoticed or unperformed since its creation in 1918, about the time of Strauss's death at least one writer considered the cycle "now as good as extinct."[73]

The 1959 publication of the cycle by Boosey & Hawkes created new interest. As the prefatory note in the edition points out, Strauss had long since made peace with his publishers. The occasional texts of the songs could be viewed as humorous and historical commentary, thus seen in a different light than they had been four decades earlier.[74] Herbert Brauer, one of two singers who was to record the group of songs in Strauss's centenary year, sang them in 1958 at a successful Berlin *Liederabend*.

The largest and most important of the many publications issued in 1964, the centenary of Strauss's birth, was the *Gesamtausgabe der Lieder*. In addition to collecting together all the previously published songs that were formerly available from a dozen different publishers, the edition includes both early and late songs and orchestrations printed here for the first time. A facsimile edition of *Im Abendrot* also appeared in 1964, along with special issues of periodicals devoted to the composer, and essays and books by Anton Berger, Franz Grasberger, Ludwig Kusche, Willi Schuh, Walter Thomas, and others. Commemorative issues of *Music and Musicians, Oesterreichische Musikzeitschrift*, and *Tempo* honored the composer as had earlier issues of *Die Musik, Schweizerische Musikzeitung, Tempo*, and other journals on various birthdays and upon his death. Special performances and recordings were plentiful throughout the year. Asow's thematic index, originally intended to be an eightieth (and then eighty-fifth) birthday offering, could not be completed because of the editor's untimely death: he was buried on 11 June 1964, the exact date of Strauss's one hundredth birthday. The first fascicle had been completed in 1954, but the entire project was not to be finished until 1974. In 1964, Munich, Koblenz, Vienna, and Salzburg held special Strauss exhibitions. Lieder performances were given in connection with the Viennese exhibit, which included a generous sampling of lieder manuscripts, programs and posters, books of poetry used by Strauss, and related photographs, letters, and cards. At the Munich Festival, the world premiere of the recently published three Rückert songs (*Vom künftigen Alter, Und dann nicht mehr*, and *Im Sonnenschein*) was given on 2 August 1964. The *Four Last Songs* were sung at Strauss celebrations in places as distant as Buenos Aires, where Strauss had conducted the Vienna Philharmonic in 1920 and 1923, and Aspen, Colorado. The Bavarian Radio announced that it would broadcast a complete series of Strauss's lieder during 1964.[75]

It must be admitted that Strauss's lieder, over two hundred completed songs in all, are uneven in quality. In the other genres in which he composed extensively there is likewise a mixture of more and less successful compositions. Perhaps this is to be expected in a career as long as Strauss's: his creative life as a composer spans eight decades during the course of which musical styles changed drastically and new compositional techniques came into being. Many of his compositions have stood the test of time and continue to be performed today; at least five of the operas, for instance, are now internationally considered repertoire pieces. Performances of these five (*Salome, Elektra, Der Rosenkavalier, Ariadne auf Naxos,* and *Die Frau ohne Schatten*) and a sixth, *Arabella,* formed a two-week Strauss cycle at the Vienna State Opera in January 1977. At the opposite extreme, *Intermezzo* has only recently received its first staged performance in the U. S. (Philadelphia, 25 February 1977), *Die aegyptische Helena* is occasionally revived in concert form, and *Guntram* has yet to be given in this country.

Like the operas, certain songs are performed and recorded again and again while others remain virtually unknown. This situation is hardly unique to Strauss: on the contrary, it is characteristic of Schubert, Brahms, and almost all other lied composers who wrote prolifically. While this will probably not change in the future, one can hope that some songs, especially the Rückert settings and more of those dating from 1918, will become more widely appreciated. Their importance lies not only in the effectiveness of their musical interpretation of the text but also in their position as connecting links between Strauss's well known nineteenth-century songs and his crowning achievement in the lied genre, the *Four Last Songs.*

Contrary to the opinions of writers like Ernest Newman, who saw no line of development in Strauss's lieder of different periods, more recent critics have recognized changes of style, technique, function, and means of expression over the years. His earliest songs show Strauss beginning as a composer brought up on the music of the earlier nineteenth century. They follow the somewhat narrow tradition of the lied as *Hausmusik* and draw on the same type of Romantic poetry set by his predecessors. The songs from op. 10 through op. 56 represent a wide selection of poets and types of poetry, including a number of then living writers. New modes of musical expression appear in some of these songs: prominent are the increasingly "orchestral" or "symphonic" piano parts and the actual orchestrations as well as the use of extremes and contrasts in vocal range and a wider variety of melodic/declamatory vocal lines. The broadening of the definition of the lied in Strauss's works begins in the songs of the late nineteenth century and continues up to the 1940's. Not only the orchestral songs but also the shorter occasional and dedicatory pieces expand the concept of the lied even further, as do the twentieth-century works of Strauss's contemporaries and the younger generations writing at the same time.

The influence of Strauss's operatic writing also contributes to the changing nature of his songs and to his lessened interest in them in the early 1900's. I cannot agree with the following recent statement by Michael Kennedy:

> It is curious how he kept his composition of songs in a separate compartment, as it were: there are few links with the operas, few quotations and little relevance to his other works of the same periods.[76]

As evidence provided in the present study (particularly in Chapter III) should indicate, both the accompaniment and the solo vocal line in Strauss's lieder were greatly influenced by his other writings. The fact that actual quotations are few is hardly convincing proof that the composer compartmentalized the different genres in which he composed. On the contrary, the various aspects of his career as composer, pianist, and conductor, and even his family life, seem to be well integrated and mutually beneficial.

Appendix A

CHRONOLOGICAL LIST OF STRAUSS'S LIEDER WITH DATES OF COMPOSITION AND PUBLICATION

(Including an Index to Significant References in the Text of this Study)

NOTE:

Collection titles are given according to the first editions (including peculiarities of spelling, but with numerals spelled out). The original title is followed by the opus or AV number; for sketches not included in Asow, the reader is referred to Appendix B of this study. The city, publisher, and date of the first edition appear in parentheses, with abbreviations for GL and NL where appropriate. All orchestrations of lieder originally published with piano accompaniment are listed under the original versions, not in chronological order; for the latter, see Table 3. Page references in the righthand column are to significant discussions (generally longer than one sentence) in the present study. Boldface page numbers indicate music examples. If the entire opus is discussed, the page reference is listed on the appropriate line; if an individual song is singled out, then the reference is on the line for that song only.

Index to Significant References

Title of collection or individual song if not part of collection when first published Individual song within collection	Date of composition or completion	Page references
Weihnachtslied (Schubart), AV 2 once op. 5, no. 1; op. 1, no. 1 (*Berliner Lokalanzeiger,* Christmas 1898 Beilage)	December 1870	65, 224 nn. 32 and 35
Einkehr (Uhland), AV 3 once op. 1, no. 2 (*Die Musik,* IV/8 Beilage, 1904)	21 August 1871	105–6, 224 n. 32
Winterreise (Uhland), AV 4 once op. 2, no. 5; op. 1, no. 2 or 3 (GL III)	1871?	
Waldkonzert (Vogel), AV 5 once op. 9 (NL)	1871?	91–92
Der weisse Hirsch (Uhland), AV 6 (NL)	1871?	91–92, 216 n. 1
Der böhmische Musikant (Pletzsch), AV 7 (NL)	1871?	91–92
Gute Nacht (Geibel), AV 193 (unpublished sketch)	1871?	
Herz, mein Herz (Geibel), AV 8 (unpublished sketch)	1871?	
Des Alpenhirten Abschied (Schiller), AV 151 (lost)	1871–72?	
Der müde Wanderer (Fallersleben), AV 13 once op. 7, no. 1; op. 1, no. 3 or 4 (GL III)	1873?	41–43
Husarenlied (Fallersleben), AV 14 once op. 7, no. 2; op. 1, no. 4 or 5 (GL III)	1873?	65
Der Fischer (Goethe), AV 33 once op. 14, no. 1 (?); op. 4, no. 1 (GL III)	1877?	41, 43, 51
Die Drossel (Uhland), AV 34 once op. 14, no. 2; op. 4, no. 2 (GL III)	1877?	58, **59**
Lass ruhn die Toten (Chamisso), AV 35 once op. 14, no. 3; op. 4, no. 3 (GL III)	1877?	63
Lust und Qual (Goethe), AV 36 once op. 14, no. 4; op. 4, no. 4 (GL III)	1877?	
Alphorn (Kerner), AV 29 once op. 15, no. 3 (GL III)	1878? (or 1876?)	
Spielmann und Zither (Körner), AV 40 once op. 12, no. 1; op. 6, no. 1 (GL III)	beg. January 1878?	41, 43

Title of collection or individual song if not part of collection when first published Individual song within collection	Date of composition or completion	Page references
Wiegenlied (Fallersleben), AV 41 once op. 12, no. 2; op. 6, no. 2 (GL III)	beg. 1878?	
Abend- und Morgenrot (Fallersleben), AV 42 once op. 8, no. 1 (GL III)	1878?	
Im Walde (Geibel), AV 43 once op. 20, no. 1; op. 15, no. 1; op. 8, no. 2 (GL III)	early February 1878	**49**
Der Spielmann und sein Kind (Fallersleben), AV 46 once op. 20, no. 2; op. 15, no. 2; op. 8, no. 3 (NL)	15–28 February 1878	16, 41, 43, 45
Nebel (Lenau), AV 47 once op. 18, no. 1; op. 10, no. 1 (GL III)	1878?	
Soldatenlied (Fallersleben), AV 48 once op. 18, no. 2; op. 10, no. 2 (GL III)	1878?	5
Ein Röslein zog ich mir im Garten (Fallersleben), AV 49 once op. 18, no. 3; op. 10, no. 3 (GL III)	1878?	41
Weihnachtsgefühl (see 8 December 1899)	1879?	107
Für Musik (Geibel), AV 158 (lost)	7 April 1879	
Waldesgesang (Geibel), AV 55 once op. 14, no. 4; op. 19, no. 4; op. 23, no. 4 (GL III)	9 April 1879	16, 106
O schneller, mein Ross (Geibel), AV 159 once op. 23, no. 5 (lost)	9–10 April 1879	
Die Lilien glühn in Düften (Geibel), AV 160 (lost)	12 April 1879	
Das rote Laub (Geibel), AV 161 once op. 26, no. 1 (lost)	May 1879	
Frühlingsanfang (Geibel), AV 162 once op. 26, no. 2 (lost)	21–24 May 1879	
Die drei Lieder (Uhland), AV 164 once op. 30, no. 1 (lost)	11–18 December 1879	
In Vaters Garten heimlich steht (Heine), AV 64 once op. 30, no. 2 (NL)	19–24 December 1879	41

Title of collection or individual song if not part of collection when first published Individual song within collection	Date of composition or completion	Page references
Der Morgen (Sallet), AV 165 once op. 30, no. 4 (lost)	9–10 January 1880	
Die erwachte Rose (Sallet), AV 66 once op. 30, no. 3 (New York: C.F. Peters, 1958)	12 January 1880	180
Immer leise wird mein Schlummer (Lingg), AV 166 (lost)	17 December 1880	
Begegnung (Gruppe), AV 72 (New York: C.F. Peters, 1958)	18 December 1880	180
Mutter, o sing mich zur Ruh (Hemans), AV 167 (lost)	29 December 1880	
John Anderson, mein Lieb (Burns/ Freiligrath), AV 73 (NL)	31 December 1880	
Geheiligte Stätte (Fischer), AV 170 (lost)	24 December 1881	
Waldesgang (Stieler), AV 172 (lost)	10 December 1882	
Ballade "Jung Friedel . . ." (Becker), AV 173 (lost)	December 1882	
Rote Rosen (Stieler), AV 76 (New York: C.F. Peters, 1958)	11 September 1883	180
Mein Geist ist trüb (Byron/Böttger), AV 175 (lost)	12 May 1884	
Der Dorn ist Zeichen der Verneinung (Bodenstedt), AV 176 (lost)	12 May 1884	
Acht Gedichte aus "letzte Blätter" von Herrmann von Gilm für eine Singstimme mit Klavierbegleitung, op. 10 (Munich: Aibl, 1887)		1–2, 9, 98–99, 101
1. *Zueignung*	13 August 1885	12, 13–14, 20, **50,** 101, 109, **111,** 159, 161, 177
Zueignung orchestration (GL IV)	19 June 1940	11, 108, 109, **111,** 224 nn. 36 and 37
2. *Nichts*	15 August 1885	79, 177
3. *Die Nacht*	11 August 1885	78, 177
4. *Die Georgine*	18 August 1885	79
5. *Geduld*	29 August 1885	70, 218–19 n. 35
6. *Die Verschwiegenen*	11 November 1885	**46, 50**
7. *Die Zeitlose*	12 November 1885	

Title of collection or individual song if not part of collection when first published Individual song within collection	Date of composition or completion	Page references
8. *Allerseelen*	31 October 1885	11, 12, 13–14, 22, 177
(nos.6, 7, 8 once numbered 7, 8, 9)		
Wer hat's gethan? (Gilm), AV 84 A once op. 10, no. 6 (Tutzing: Schneider, 1974)	13 November 1885	9, 15, 16, 99, 222–23 n. 13
Fünf Lieder für eine Singstimme mit Begleitung des Pianoforte, op. 15 (Hamburg: Rahter, 1887)		9
1. *Madrigal* (Michelangelo Buonarroti)	1886?	37, 215 n. 73
2. *Winternacht* (Schack)	27 November 1886	44
3. *Lob des Leidens* (Schack)	30 November 1886	
4. *Aus den Liedern der Trauer* "Dem Herzen ähnlich" (Schack)	3 December 1886	
5. *Heimkehr* (Schack)	1886?	11, 161
Sechs Lieder von Adolf Friedrich von Schack, für eine hohe Singstimme mit Klavierbegleitung, op. 17 (Hamburg: Rahter, 1888)		9
1. *Seitdem dein Aug'*	1886–87?	161
2. *Ständchen*	22 December 1886	11, 12, 13, 14, 72, **73–75**, 149, **159–60**, 166, 167–68, 177, 207 n. 4, 220 n. 50
3. *Das Geheimnis*	1886–87?	177
4. *Aus den Liedern der Trauer* "Von dunklem Schleier"	1886–87?	**50**
5. *Nur Mut!*	1886–87?	
6. *Barkarole*	1886–87?	73, **74**
Sechs Lieder aus "Lotosblätter" von Adolph Friedrich Graf von Schack für eine Singstimme mit Klavierbegleitung, op. 19 (Munich: Aibl, 1888)		9, 208 n. 13
1. *Wozu noch, Mädchen*	5 February 1888	70, 177
2. *Breit über mein Haupt*	1 February 1888	22, 158, 161
3. *Schön sind, doch kalt*	2 January 1888	
4. *Wie sollten wir geheim sie halten*	2 January 1888	177
5. *Hoffen und wieder verzagen*	early 1888?	
6. *Mein Herz ist stumm*	12 January 1888	

Title of collection or individual song if not part of collection when first published Individual song within collection	Date of composition or completion	Page references
"Schlichte Weisen." Fünf Gedichte von Felix Dahn für eine Singstimme mit Begleitung des Pianoforte, op. 21 (Munich: Aibl, 1890)		2, 10
1. *All mein Gedanken*	12 February 1889	20, 22, 39–**40**, 70–71, 81–83, 156, 177
2. *Du meines Herzens Krönelein*	7 April 1889	22, 81, 83, 177
3. *Ach Lieb, ich muss nun scheiden!*	19 April 1889	
4. *Ach, weh mir unglückhaftem Mann*	17 April 1889	
5. *Die Frauen sind oft fromm und still*	20 January 1890	233 n. 18
Mädchenblumen. Gedichte von Felix Dahn, für eine Singstimme mit Pianofortebegleitung, op. 22 (Berlin: Fürstner, [1891])		2, 3, 28, 177, 207 nn. 5 and 6
1. *Kornblumen*	28 March 1888	
2. *Mohnblumen*	29 March 1888	100
3. *Epheu*	March 1888?	**51**
4. *Wasserrose*	March 1888?	
Zwei Lieder (Gedichte von N.v. Lenau) für eine Singstimme mit Begleitung des Pianoforte, op. 26 (Munich: Aibl, 1894)		
1. *Frühlingsgedränge*	2 December 1891	177
2. *O, wärst du mein!*	2 December 1891	**46**
Vier Lieder für eine Singstimme mit Begleitung des Pianoforte, op. 27 (Munich: Aibl, 1894)		15, 177
1. *Ruhe, meine Seele!* (Henckell)	17 May 1894	30–31, 60, 62–63, 157–58, 161, 214 n. 41, 218 n. 31
Ruhe, meine Seele! orchestration (GL IV)	9 June 1948	108, 157, 178
2. *Cäcilie* (Hart)	9 September 1894	22, 79
Cäcilie orchestration (Vienna: Universal-Edition, 1911)	20 September 1897	108, 149
3. *Heimliche Aufforderung* (Mackay)	22 May 1894	22, **46**, 161
4. *Morgen!* (Mackay)	21 May 1894	12, 13, 16, 22, 43, 84, **86**, 168–69, 221 nn. 58, 59, and 61, 233 n. 28

Title of collection or individual song if not part of collection when first published Individual song within collection	Date of composition or completion	Page references
Morgen! orchestration (Vienna: Universal-Edition, 1911)	20 September 1897	108, 149
Drei Lieder (nach Gedichten von Otto Julius Bierbaum) für eine Singstimme mit Klavierbegleitung, op. 29 (Munich: Aibl, 1895)		2
1. *Traum durch die Dämmerung*	4 May 1895	12, 13, 22, 27, 32, 44, 87–**88,** 149, 161, 177, 208 n. 10
2. *Schlagende Herzen*	5 June 1895	79, 161, 177
3. *Nachtgang*	7 June 1895	20, 22, 64, 161
Drei Lieder von Carl Busse für eine (hohe) Singstimme mit Pianofortebegleitung, op. 31 (Berlin: Fürstner, 1896)		
1. *Blauer Sommer*	1 January 1896	43–44
2. *Wenn* (also in *Jugend*, I/4, 1896)	15 June 1895	166, 233 n. 18
3. *Weisser Jasmin*	24 June 1895	
Stiller Gang. (Dehmel). Lied für eine Singstimme mit Klavierbegleitung, op. 31, no. 4 (Berlin: Fürstner, 1896)	30 December 1895	31, 44
Fünf Lieder für eine Singstimme mit Klavierbegleitung, op. 32 (Munich: Aibl, 1896)		
1. *Ich trage meine Minne* (Henckell)	26 January 1896	22, 72, 76–**77,** 101, 177
2. *Sehnsucht* (Liliencron)	24 January 1896	149
3. *Liebeshymnus* (Henckell)	25 February 1896	
Liebeshymnus orchestration (Vienna: Universal-Edition, 1911)	27 September 1897	108, 149
4. *O süsser Mai!* (Henckell)	28 March 1896	
5. *Himmelsboten (Des Knaben Wunderhorn)*	3 January 1896	39–**40**
Vorüber ist der Graus der Nacht (Henckell?), AV 221 A (unfinished sketch)	1896?	
Wir beide wollen springen (Bierbaum), AV 90 (Munich: *Jugend*, I/42, 1896 [in facsimile])	7 June 1896	16, **61**
Vier Gesänge für eine Singstimme mit Begleitung des Orchesters, op. 33 (Berlin: Bote & Bock, 1897)		147, 155
1. *Verführung* (Mackay)	6 June–5 July 1896	

Title of collection or individual song if not part of collection when first published Individual song within collection	Date of composition or completion	Page references
2. *Gesang der Apollopriesterin* (Bodmann)	7 July–10 September 1896	33
3. *Hymnus* (attributed to Schiller)	25 December 1896– 5 January 1897	
4. *Pilgers Morgenlied* (Goethe)	21 December 1896– 25 January 1897	31, 112
Vier Lieder für eine Singstimme mit Klavierbegleitung, op. 36 (Munich: Aibl, 1898)		
1. *Das Rosenband* (Klopstock)	10–20 September 1897	112, **114,** 115
Das Rosenband orchestration (Vienna: Universal-Edition, 1911)	22 September 1897	108, 112, 115, 149
2. *Für funfzehn Pfennige (Des Knaben Wunderhorn)*	20 August– 2 September 1897	72, 115, 229 n. 20
3. *Hat gesagt–bleibt's nicht dabei (Des Knaben Wunderhorn)*	31 March 1898	79, 88–**89,** 177, 217 n. 15
4. *Anbetung* (Rückert)	24 March 1898	65, 177
Sechs Lieder für eine Singstimme mit Klavierbegleitung, op. 37 (Munich: Aibl, 1898)		29
1. *Glückes genug* (Liliencron)	8 February 1898	22, 83–84, **85,** 177
2. *Ich liebe dich* (Liliencron)	7 February 1898	**109–11**
Ich liebe dich orchestration (Vienna: Universal-Edition, n.d.; or GL IV)	30 August 1943	108, **109–11**
3. *Meinem Kinde* (Falke)	7–8 February 1897	22, 161, 177
Meinem Kinde orchestration (Vienna: Universal-Edition, 1911)	1897–1900?	29, 108, 150
4. *Mein Auge* (Dehmel)	16 April 1898	32, 177, 214 n. 45
Mein Auge orchestration (Vienna: Universal-Edition, n.d.; or GL IV)	5 September 1933	108, 138–39
5. *Herr Lenz* (Bodmann)	9 June 1896	33
6. *Hochzeitlich Lied* (Lindner)	1 February–30 March 1898	33
Fünf Lieder für eine Singstimme mit Klavierbegleitung, op. 39 (Leipzig: Forberg, 1898)		
1. *Leises Lied* (Dehmel)	2 July 1898	

Title of collection or individual song if not part of collection when first published Individual song within collection	Date of composition or completion	Page references
2. *Junghexenlied* (Bierbaum)	31 May 1898	153, 177
3. *Der Arbeitsmann* (Dehmel)	12 June 1898	58, 169, 170
Der Arbeitsmann orchestration (unpublished)	12 December 1918	58, 108, 119, 218 n. 29
4. *Befreit* (Dehmel)	2 June 1898	32, 67, 153
Befreit orchestration (GL IV)	10 September 1933	108, 138–39
5. *Lied an meinen Sohn* (Dehmel)	8 July 1898	144–45
Fünf Lieder für eine Singstimme mit Pianoforte, op. 41 (Leipzig: Leuckart, 1899)		
1. *Wiegenlied* (Dehmel)	22 August 1899	20, 44, 177
Wiegenlied orchestration (Leipzig: Leuckart, 1901)	1899–1900?	108, 150
2. *In der Campagna* (Mackay)	24 August 1899	
3. *Am Ufer* (Dehmel)	15 August 1899	**76**, 218 n. 30
4. *Bruder Liederlich* (Liliencron)	16 August 1899	79
5. *Leise Lieder* (Morgenstern)	4 June 1899	33
Drei Gesänge älterer deutscher Dichter für eine Singstimme und Clavier, op. 43 (Berlin: Challier, 1899)		
1. *An Sie* (Klopstock)	14 August 1899	
2. *Muttertändelei* (Bürger)	15 August 1899	177
Muttertändelei orchestration (Berlin: Challier, 1911)	21 February 1900	108, 150
3. *Die Ulme zu Hirsau* (Uhland)	4 September 1899	60
Zwei grössere Gesänge für eine tiefere Stimme mit Orchesterbegleitung, op. 44 (Leipzig: Forberg, 1899)		155, 169, 234 n. 35
1. *Notturno* (Dehmel)	11 July–16 September 1899	15, 65, 67, 101–2, 210 n. 39, 223 n. 24
2. *Nächtlicher Gang* (Rückert)	10 September–10 November 1899	169
Weihnachtsgefühl (Greif), AV 94 (Berlin: *Die Woche,* I/41, 1899 [in facsimile])	8 December 1899 (revised version of 1879 song?)	107
Fünf Gedichte von Friedrich Rückert für eine Singstimme mit Klavierbegleitung, op. 46 (Berlin: Fürstner, 1900)		6
1. *Ein Obdach gegen Sturm und Regen*	16 January 1900	**69**, 79
2. *Gestern war ich Atlas*	21 November 1899	69

Title of collection or individual song if not part of collection when first published Individual song within collection	Date of composition or completion	Page references
3. *Die sieben Siegel*	18 November 1899	
4. *Morgenrot*	4 February 1900	7, 44, 65
5. *Ich sehe wie in einem Spiegel*	7 February 1900	**51**
Fünf Lieder (Ludwig Uhland) componirt für eine Singstimme mit Klavierbegleitung, op. 47 (Berlin: Fürstner, 1900)		5, 208 n. 12
1. *Auf ein Kind*	5 May 1900	
2. *Des Dichters Abendgang*	8 May 1900	
Des Dichters Abendgang orchestration (Berlin: Fürstner, 1918)	15 June 1918	108, 119
3. *Rückleben*	23 May 1900	41
4. *Einkehr*	30 May 1900	**61,** 105–6
5. *Von den sieben Zechbrüderñ*	11 June 1900	38
Fünf Lieder nach Gedichten von Otto Julius Bierbaum und Karl Henckell für eine Singstimme mit Klavierbegleitung, op. 48 (Berlin: Fürstner, 1901)		
1. *Freundliche Vision* (Bierbaum)	5 October 1900	32, 44, 161, 177, 221 n. 60
Freundliche Vision orchestration (Berlin: Fürstner, 1918)	1 July 1918	108, 119
2. *Ich schwebe* (Henckell)	25 September 1900	**87,** 177
3. *Kling!* (Henckell)	30 September 1900	31, 214 n. 41
4. *Winterweihe* (Henckell)	23 September 1900	20
Winterweihe orchestration (Berlin: Fürstner, 1918)	28 June 1918	108, 119
5. *Winterliebe* (Henckell)	2 October 1900	
Winterliebe orchestration (Berlin: Fürstner, 1918)	29 June 1918	108, 119
Acht Lieder für eine Singstimme mit Klavierbegleitung, op. 49 (Berlin, Fürstner, 1902)		
1. *Waldseligkeit* (Dehmel)	21 September 1901	
Waldseligkeit orchestration (Berlin: Fürstner, 1918)	24 June 1918	108, 119
2. *In goldener Fülle* (Remer)	13 September 1901	79
3. *Wiegenliedchen* (Dehmel)	20 September 1901	20
4. *Das Lied des Steinklopfers* (Henckell)	24 September 1901	62–63, 78, 170
5. *Sie wissen's nicht* (Panizza)	14 September 1901	177
6. *Junggesellenschwur (Des Knaben Wunderhorn)*	11 May 1900	72
7. *Wer lieben will muss leiden* (Alsatian folksong)	23 September 1901	41

Title of collection or individual song if not part of collection when first published Individual song within collection	Date of composition or completion	Page references
8. *Ach, was Kummer, Qual und Schmerzen* (Alsatian folksong)	23 September 1901	
Zwei Gesänge für eine tiefe Basstimme mit Orchesterbegleitung, op. 51 (Berlin: Fürstner, 1903, 1906)		155
1. *Das Thal* (Uhland)	11 December 1902	**51**
2. *Der Einsame* (Heine)	18 February 1906	55–**56, 57,** 170
Lied des Gefangene (?). See Appendix B. (unpublished)	ca. 1903–04	
Blumenglöckchen (Goethe). See Appendix B. (unpublished)	1 August [1903]	95
Freundliches Begegnen (Goethe). See Appendix B. (unpublished)	2 August [1903]	95
Lesebuch (Goethe). See Appendix B. (unpublished)	1903–04?	95
Sonnensegen (Henckell). See Appendix B. (unpublished)	ca. 1903–04?	
Der fromme Hirtenknabe (Greif). See Appendix B. (unpublished; choral sketch?)	1903–04?	
Frühling (Heine). See Appendix B. (unpublished)	1904–05?	
Nachts in der Kajüte (Heine). See Appendix B. (unpublished)	ca. 1904–06 with 4 other Heine songs?	56
Sechs Lieder für eine Singstimme mit Klavierbegleitung, op. 56 (Berlin: Bote & Bock, 1906)		
1. *Gefunden* (Goethe)	31 July 1903	21, 41–**42,** 95, 101, 177
2. *Blindenklage* (Henckell)	1904–06?	
3. *Im Spätboot* (Meyer)		
4. *Mit deinen blauen Augen* (Heine)	1904–06? (sketch 5 September 1905)	177
5. *Frühlingsfeier* (Heine)	1904–06?	79
Frühlingsfeier orchestration (Berlin: Bote & Bock, n.d. [1934])	3 September 1933	108, 138–39
6. *Die heiligen drei Könige aus Morgenland* (Heine)	1904–06?	**60**
Die heiligen drei Könige aus Morgenland orchestration (Berlin: Bote & Bock, 1906)	7 October 1906	60, 108, 112

Title of collection or individual song if not part of collection when first published Individual song within collection	Date of composition or completion	Page references
Zwei Lieder aus Calderón's *Der Richter von Zalamea*, AV 96 (Bonn: Boosey & Hawkes, 1953 [*Richard Strauss Jahrbuch 1954*])		37, 97–98
1. *Liebesliedchen*	16 August 1904	
2. *Lied der Chispa*	16 August 1904	
[Chispa III] (Calderón). See Appendix B. (unpublished)	1903–04?	37, 97–98
Kein Frühling (Rückert). See Appendix B. (unpublished)	ca. 1904–05?	
Stiller Festzug (Henckell). See Appendix B. (unpublished)	ca. 1905–06?	
Wald, jetzt noch du! (?) (Meyer). See Appendix B. (unpublished)	ca. 1905–06?	
Nähe des Geliebten (Goethe). See Appendix B. (unpublished)	ca. 1905–06?	
Der Graf von Rom (textless), AV 102 (Berlin: Programmheft der Städtischen Oper, 1961 [in facsimile])	17 January 1906	
Bleiben, Gehen, Gehen, Bleiben (Goethe). See Appendix B. (unpublished)	ca. 1906 with other Goethe settings?	97
Mailied (Goethe). See Appendix B. (unpublished; choral sketch?)	ca. 1904–06 or later?	
Wanderlied (Goethe). See Appendix B. (unpublished)	ca. 1906 or later?	97
Wiegenlied (Raabe). See Appendix B. (unpublished)	1906–18?	
Sonnett (Hebbel). See Appendix B. (unpublished)	1906–18?	
Herbstabend (?), AV 244 (unpublished sketch, perhaps lost)	before 1910?	
Krämerspiegel. Zwölf Gesänge von Alfred Kerr für eine Singstimme mit Klavierbegleitung, op. 66 (Berlin: Cassirer, 1921)		26, 33–34, 43, 52, 61–**62**, 118–20, 172–73, 180–81, 209 n. 20, 225 nn. 4–7, 226 nn. 8 and 9

Title of collection or individual song if not part of collection when first published Individual song within collection	Date of composition or completion	Page references
1.	15 March 1918	
2.	19 May 1918	
3.	16 March 1918	
4.	24 May 1918	
5.	16 March 1918	78, 80
6.	25 May 1918	
7.	17 March 1918	
8.	20 May 1918	**51**, 125
9.	21 May 1918	**62**, 218 n. 32
10.	21 May 1918	
11.	23 May 1918	**49**
12.	23 May 1918	125
Sechs Lieder für eine hohe Singstimme mit Klavierbegleitung, op. 67 (Berlin: Bote & Bock, 1919)		52, 119–20, 209 n. 20, 225 nn. 6 and 7
1. *Wie erkenn' ich mein Treulieb?* (Shakespeare/Simrock)	1918	36, 45
2. *Guten Morgen, 's ist Sankt Valentinstag* (Shakespeare/Simrock)	1918	36
3. *Sie trugen ihn auf der Bahre bloss* (Shakespeare/Simrock)	1918	36, 45
4. *Wer wird von der Welt verlangen* (Goethe)	1918	
5. *Hab' ich euch denn je geraten* (Goethe)	1918	58, **135**
6. *Wanderers Gemütsruhe* (Goethe)	1918	
Abendständchen (Brentano?). See Appendix B. (unpublished)	early 1918?	97
Sechs Lieder nach Gedichten von Clemens Brentano für eine Singstimme und Klavier, op. 68 (Berlin: Fürstner, 1919)		15–16, 91, 117–39, 172–73, 175, 209 n. 20, 225 nn. 2 and 3
1. *An die Nacht*	18 February 1918	64–65, 78, 80, 131–**34**
An die Nacht orchestration (Berlin: Fürstner, 1941)	27 July 1940	108
2. *Ich wollt ein Sträusslein binden*	6 February 1918	41–**42**, 126–28
Ich wollt ein Sträusslein binden orchestration (Berlin: Fürstner, 1941)	6 July 1940	108

Title of collection or individual song if not part of collection when first published Individual song within collection	Date of composition or completion	Page references
3. *Säusle, liebe Myrte*	9 February 1918	58, 80, **128–31**
Säusle, liebe Myrte orchestration (Berlin: Fürstner, 1941)	2 August 1940	108
4. *Als mir dein Lied erklang*	4 February 1918	8, 124–**26, 129**
Als mir dein Lied erklang orchestration (Berlin: Fürstner, 1941)	22 July 1940	108
5. *Amor*	21 February 1918	47, 64–65, 80, 136–37
Amor orchestration (Berlin: Fürstner, 1941)	3 July 1940	108
6. *Lied der Frauen*	4 May 1918	58, 71, 137–**38**
Lied der Frauen orchestration (Berlin: Fürstner, 1941)	22 September 1933	108, 138–39
Fünf kleine Lieder nach Gedichten von Achim von Arnim und Heinrich Heine, op. 69 (Berlin: Fürstner, 1919)		118–20, 172–73, 209 n. 20
1. *Der Stern* (Arnim)	June–July 1918	123, 177
2. *Der Pokal* (Arnim)	summer 1918?	
3. *Einerlei* (Arnim)	25 June 1918	77–78, 80, **136,** 175, 177, 227 n. 20
4. *Waldesfahrt* (Heine)	26 June 1918	**54**–55
5. *Schlechtes Wetter* (Heine)	21 June 1918	54–55, 175, 177
Es ist gut (Goethe). See Appendix B. (unpublished)	ca. 1918–22?	
Sinnspruch (Goethe), AV 105 (Berlin: Mosse, 1920 *Almanach . . . 1920)*	24 June 1919	
Drei Hymnen von Friedrich Hölderlin für eine hohe Singstimme und grosses Orchester, op. 71 (Berlin: Fürstner, 1921)		44–45, 173–74, 216 n. 7, 234 nn. 51 and 53
1. *Hymne an die Liebe*	6 April 1921	
2. *Rückkehr in die Heimat*	2 January 1921	
3. *Die Liebe*	20 January 1921	
Erschaffen und Beleben (Goethe), AV 106 (Berlin: Oertel, 1951)	25 December 1922	50, **52,** 217 n. 19
Durch allen Schall und Klang (Goethe), AV 111 (Zurich: Rotapfel, 1926 [in facsimile])	11 June 1925	

Title of collection or individual song if not part of collection when first published Individual song within collection	Date of composition or completion	Page references
Gesänge des Orients. Nachdichtungen aus dem Persischen und Chinesischen von Hans Bethge, op. 77 (Leipzig: Leuckart, 1929)		36, 173–74
1. *Ihre Augen* (Hafiz/Bethge)	14 August 1928	
2. *Schwung* (Hafiz/Bethge)	15 August 1928	220 n. 51
3. *Liebesgeschenke (Die chinesische Flöte*/Bethge)	14 August 1928	**49, 71**–72, 80
4. *Die Allmächtige* (Hafiz/Bethge)	15 August 1928	**71,** 80
5. *Huldigung* (Hafiz/Bethge)	24 September 1928	
Vom künftigen Alter (Rückert), AV 114 (op. 87, no. 1) (Vienna: Universal-Edition, 1964, & GL III)	early 1929	20, 66, 68, 219 n. 40
Und dann nicht mehr (Rückert), AV 115 (op. 87, no. 2) (Vienna: Universal-Edition, 1964, & GL III)	11 February 1929	68, 80
Spruch (Goethe), AV 116 (Vienna: Verlag Journalisten- und Schriftsteller-Verein Concordia, 1930)	9 January 1930	
Akkord (Wildgans), AV 266 (probably not composed)	24 April 1931	34–35
Das Bächlein (attributed to Goethe), AV 118 (op. 88, no. 1) (Vienna: Universal-Edition, 1951)	3 December 1933	
Das Bächlein orchestration (GL IV)	6 April 1935	108
Trunken müssen wir alle sein (Goethe). See Appendix B. (unpublished)	ca. 1934–35?	52–**53**
So lang man nüchtern ist (Goethe). See Appendix B. (unpublished)	ca. 1934–35?	52–**53**
Die Göttin im Putzzimmer (Rückert). See Appendix B. (unpublished solo version)	before 6 February 1935	**57,** 69–70, 106–7
Im Sonnenschein (Rückert), AV 121 (op. 87, no. 4) (Vienna: Universal-Edition, 1964, & GL III)	24 February 1935	68, 80
Zugemessne Rhythmen (Goethe), AV 122 (Bonn: Boosey & Hawkes, 1953 [*Richard Strauss Jahrbuch 1954*])	25 February 1935	
In tausend Formen (Goethe). See Appendix B. (unpublished)	ca. 1938?	227 n. 20

Title of collection or individual song if not part of collection when first published Individual song within collection	Date of composition or completion	Page references
Schlusslied (Rückert). See Appendix B. (unpublished; choral sketch?)	ca. 1938?	
Sankt Michael (Weinheber), AV 129 (op. 88, no. 3) (Vienna: Universal-Edition, n.d.; or GL III)	3 February 1942	35
Blick vom oberen Belvedere (Weinheber), AV 130 (op. 88, no. 2) (Vienna: Universal-Edition, n.d.; or GL III)	11 February 1942	35
Xenion (Goethe), AV 131 (Bonn: Boosey & Hawkes, 1960 [*Richard Strauss Jahrbuch 1959/60*])	20 September 1942	
Wiegenlied (Brentano). See Appendix B. (unpublished)	1944–45?	235 n. 64
[Vier letzte Lieder], AV 150 (London: Boosey & Hawkes, 1950)		14, 35, 64, 174, 176, 178–80, 235 nn. 63 and 70
1. *Frühling*, AV 150/I (Hesse)	18 July 1948	53–**59**, 112, **113**
2. *September*, AV 150/II (Hesse)	20 September 1948	
3. *Beim Schlafengehn*, AV 150/III (Hesse)	4 August 1948	96
4. *Im Abendrot*, AV 150/IV (Eichendorff)	6 May 1948	16, 58–**59**, 65, 210 n. 40
Nacht (Hesse), AV 303 (unpublished sketch)	1947–48?	94–**96**, 178, 222 n. 7
Malven (Knobel), AV 304 (unpublished)	1948–49?	95, 178, 222 n. 7
Höhe des Sommers (Hesse). See Appendix B. (unpublished)	1948–49?	178, 235 n. 65

Appendix B

INCOMPLETE SONGS AND CHORAL WORKS IN STRAUSS'S SKETCHBOOKS

Title/"First line" (POET)	Sketchbook no. (opening)*	Approximate date of book	Description of sketch
Abendständchen/ ["Hör, es klagt"] (BRENTANO/GEORGES)**	39 (17^v–20^v)	1918	piano part only, ca. 20 measures on two staves with two main musical motives
"Bleiben, Gehen, Gehen, Bleiben" (GOETHE)	? (?)	?	Cited in Schuh, *Goethe-Vertonungen*, p. 16; see *Wanderlied*, of which this text is the second stanza (not in sketchbook 17 with *Wanderlied*).
Blumenglöckchen "Ein Blumenglöck- chen vom Boden hervor" (GOETHE)	11 (41^f–42^v)	1903–04	first half of song (4 of 8 lines of text set); Goethe's title is *Gleich und Gleich*; dated in sketchbook Marquartstein, 1. August
[*Chispa III*]/"Ich bisher liebelos" (?) (CALDERON)	11 (46^f–48^v)	1903–04	duet for soprano and baritone; 34 measures with text and alternating voice parts; accompaniment (for guitar?) partially filled in; additional 40 vocal measures with only a few echoes in accompaniment but without more text
"Der fromme Hirtenknabe" (MARTIN GREIF)	13 (42^f–43^v, 44^f)	1903–04	text copied out complete on back cover; perhaps for a cappella chorus *a 4*, with all except last line and a half sketched out

Title/"First line" (POET)	Sketchbook no. (opening)*	Approximate date of book	Description of sketch
Die Göttin im Putzzimmer/"Welche chaotische Haushälterei" (RÜCKERT)	87 (7ᵛ–10ᶠ, 15ᵛ–17ᶠ)	1934–35	full text copied on 17ᶠ; sketch of solo (bass voice) version and accompaniment of same text used in AV 120, a 8 a cappella chorus written 6 February 1935 (in same key and time signature, with same initial motive)
Es ist gut/"Bei Mondenschein im Paradies" (GOETHE, West-östlicher Divan)***	18 (21ʳ)	1918–22	complete text only, copied in Strauss's hand inside back cover on same page as text for Hans Adam war ein Erdenkloss (25 December 1922) and in same sketchbook as sketches for op. 67, nos. 4–6 (1918), which are also settings of texts from the West-östlicher Divan
Freundliches Begegnen/"Im weiten Mantel bis ans Kinn verhüllet" (GOETHE)	11 (42ʳ)	1903–04	4 measures of introduction and 11 with voice; first 3½ of 14 lines in poem set; marked by Strauss "(Sonnett von Goethe)"; dated in sketchbook Marquartstein, 2. August
Frühling/"Die Wellen blinken und fliessen dahin" (HEINE)	14; 40 (48ʳ–49ᵛ; 2ʳ–4ᵛ)	1904–05	taken together, the two versions show that the entire song was planned, but with about half of the voice and accompaniment filled in; text includes 9 of 16 lines of poem: 1–2, 5–9, 15–16 (Sketches in book 5 headed with the title Frühling are for an unrelated instrumental work of the same name; neither is listed in Asow.)

Höhe des Sommers/"Das Blau der Ferne klärt sich schon" (HESSE)	141 (12ʳ)	1948–49	complete text written in opposite text of *September*, on same page as music for mm. 8–15 of *September*
"In tausend Formen" (GOETHE, *West-östlicher Divan*)	101 (2ᵛ–4ᵛ)	ca. 1938	complete text copied in; vocal line for first 4 out of 6 stanzas of text, with measures marked out for fifth; accompaniment not full under voice part; blank page left on 4ʳ intended for 6th stanza (?)
Kein Frühling/"Ist der Frühling da?" (RÜCKERT)	5; 40 (9ᵛˑ; 4ʳ–5ᵛ)	1904–05	31 measures of piano part with 14 including voice, but only 4 of them with text; several additional pages in sketchbook 5 may pertain to this work or to the instrumental *Frühling*
Lesebuch/"Wunderlichste Buch der Bücher" (GOETHE, *West-östlicher Divan*)	11 (44ᵛ)	1903–04	10 measures: 4 of piano introduction, 6 with voice and text for first 3 lines of 22-line poem; 5 of 6 measures accompanied
Lied des Gefangene für Bass No. 11/ (?)	11 (13ᵛ)	1903–04	title only at top of page; 5 measures at bottom of page marked "Schluss" include text and music
Mailied/"Wie herrlich leuchtet mir die Natur" (GOETHE)***	17; 40 (26ʳ–27ʳ; 7ʳ–8ʳ)	1904–06 (or later?)	text and vocal music (choral *a 4?*) for lines 12–14 and 35–36 of 36-line poem; ca. 50 measures of keyboard part (including bird calls which may be totally unrelated since they are not suggested by the text)
Nachts in der Kajüte/"Das Meer hat seine Perlen" (HEINE)	? (?)	?	Cited by Kravitt, "The Late Romantic Lied," p. 257. Perhaps dating from early 1900's along with other Heine settings; 6 measures sketched; marked "Heines doppeltnatur"

Title/"First line" (POET)	Sketchbook no. (opening)*	Approximate date of book	Description of sketch
Nähe des Geliebten/"Ich denke dein" (GOETHE)***	40 (8ʳ)	1905–06	1 measure of piano introduction, first 2 measures of voice and piano with first 3 words of poem
Schlusslied/"Du Duft, der meine Seele . . ." (RÜCKERT)	101 (5ʳ–8ʳ, 24ʳ)	ca. 1938	complete text copied on back cover; 7 pages of chorus *a 8*
"So lang man nüchtern ist" (GOETHE, *West-östlicher Divan*)	87 (2ᵛ, 3ʳ, 4ᵛ?)	1934–35	poem copied into book marked "Neue Liederskizze"; sketches of music for first half of text
Sonnensegen/? (HENCKELL)	11 (44ᵛ)	1903–04	only 2 measures of accompaniment
Sonnett/"Was ist ein Hauch? Ein Nichts" (HEBBEL)	17 (11ʳ)	1906 or later	printed text pasted in; ca. 4 measures of melody line without text
Stiller Festzug/"Geliebter Tritt und den Zalte" (?) (HENCKELL)	40 (5ʳ–6ᵛ)	1905–06	8 measures of piano introduction, 23 of piano coda; 8 measures of voice with text and a few piano chords
"Trunken müssen wir alle sein" (GOETHE, *West-östlicher Divan*)	87 (2ᵛ–3ᵛ,6ᵛ⁻ʳ)	1934–35	complete poem copied into book marked "neue Liederskizze"; sketches of music with voice in bass clef for first half of text and a second draft for lines 1–3

Wald, jetzt noch du! (?)/? (C.F. MEYER)	15; 40 (12r; 7v)	1905–06	both versions are for piano only, and are almost identical in their 23 measures followed by double bar (I have not located a poem of this or a similar title in Meyer's works.)
Wanderlied/"Von dem Bergen zu den Hügeln" (GOETHE)***	17 (47f)	1906 or later	8 measures of vocal part with 4 lines of text; 4 measures of piano introduction; later 8 more of piano; see *Bleiben, Gehen*
Wiegenlied/"Schaukeln und Gaukeln" (WILHELM RAABE)	17 (11f)	1906 or later	printed text pasted in (on same page as Hebbel's *Sonnett*) with ca. 6 measures of accompaniment
Wiegenlied/"Singt leise, leise, leise" (BRENTANO)	132; 133	1944–45	poem only, copied in by Strauss onto back cover of both sketchbooks (no musical examples in either book clearly connected with the text)

* See Chapters IV (nn. 3 and 4) and V (nn. 11 and 12) on the numbering of sketchbooks and openings.

** Strauss gives the poet as "Georges"; the poem may well be Brentano's popular *Abendständchen* ("Hör, es klagt die Flöte wieder"), since the remaining pages of the book are devoted to Brentano songs. It is rare to find a sketchbook containing only lieder, particularly a single set of them.

*** Not indexed in Schuh, *Goethe-Vertonungen.*

NOTES

CHAPTER I

1. See "Richard Strauss als Vorkämpfer für die Rechte der Komponisten. Das andere Lebenswerk des Meisters," *Internationale Richard-Strauss-Gesellschaft. Mitteilungen* (hereafter cited as IRSGM), no. 2 (July 1953), p. 2.

2. The commissioned compositions were the 1934 *Olympisches Hymne* (AV 119) for chorus and large orchestra, which Strauss conducted at the opening ceremonies of the now infamous 1936 Berlin Olympics, and the orchestral *Festmusik zur Feier des 2600 jährigen Bestehens des Kaiserreiches Japan*, op. 84 (1940).

3. Excerpts from Strauss's letters to Spitzweg, along with dates and other information about the circumstances of publication of many of his works, are found in Alfons Ott, "Richard Strauss und sein Verlegerfreund Eugen Spitzweg," in *Musik und Verlag. Karl Vötterle zum 65. Geburtstag am 12. April 1968*, edited by Richard Baum and Wolfgang Rehm (Kassel, 1968), pp. 466–75 (hereafter Strauss/Spitzweg). A bound volume of 124 of Strauss's original letters and postcards dating from 1889 to 1904 is to be found in the Stadtbibliothek in Munich; according to Ott, Spitzweg's letters are no longer in existence. Transcriptions of ten of Strauss's letters, along with two of Spitzweg's, appear in "*Der Strom der Töne trug mich fort.*" *Die Welt um Richard Strauss in Briefen*, edited by Franz Grasberger in collaboration with Franz and Alice Strauss (Tutzing, 1967). (Future references to this last collection will be identified as Grasberger, *Briefe*.)

4. Strauss contacted other publishers as well about the publication of lieder, but in the end offered them works in other genres. I have not been able to obtain information about the amounts Rahter paid for the two groups of songs. Elisabeth Schumann's recollection that Strauss received only twenty-five marks for *Ständchen* (op. 17, no. 2) is probably an underestimation. See H. G. Owen, "Elisabeth Schumann," *The Record Collector*, VII (1952), 227 (where she is also reported as saying that Strauss was only fourteen [instead of twenty-two] when he wrote *Ständchen*).

5. According to a letter I received from U[rsula] F. R. Fürstner (21 August 1972), the contract was dated 7 November 1890, with publication following at the end of 1890 or early in 1891. It was for a time believed that op. 22 was first published not by Fürstner but by O. B. Boise in London; see, for example, E. H. Mueller von Asow, *Richard Strauss. Thematisches Verzeichnis* (Vienna, 1955–74), p. 103, or *Richard Strauss. Gesamtausgabe der Lieder*, edited by Franz Trenner (London, 1964–65), I, 346. (Hereafter references to Asow's thematic catalogue will be identified as Asow; for works not having opus numbers, the abbreviation AV [ohne Opus Asow Verzeichnis] will be used, as in n. 2 above.) The letter from Fürstner and evidence from Strauss's own correspondence prove that there was no publication by Boise. Norman Del Mar, *Richard Strauss. A Critical Commentary on His Life and Works* (London, 1962–72), III, 281–82 (n. 20), explains that Boise's name became connected with Strauss's op. 22 because Boise lived in Berlin from 1888 to 1901, teaching and editing composers' manuscripts for publication. I have further determined that the confusion probably arose from the fact that in the first edition of op. 22 a notice reads "Copyright 1891 by O. B. Boise." The copyright presumably covers his editing, which is acknowledged on the first page of each of the songs. In subsequent reprints (including that of the *Gesamtausgabe der Lieder*) all references to Boise were omitted.

6. A facsimile of Strauss's card to Fürstner offering op. 22 for 800 marks appears in IRSGM, no. 50 (September 1966), p. 7, accompanying Ursula Fürstner's article cited below in n. 9. See Illustration 1 for the decorative cover of the first edition of op. 22.

7. Strauss/Spitzweg, p. 470 (Strauss's letters of 13 October and 13 November 1890).
8. Gustav Bock, "Richard Strauss und der Verlag Ed. Bote & G. Bock, Berlin," *Musikhandel,* I (1949), 35.
9. Ursula Fürstner, "Richard Strauss und der Fürstner-Verlag," IRSGM, no. 50 (September 1966), p. 9.
10. Ernest Newman, *Richard Strauss* (London, 1908; reprint, New York, 1969), p. 90: "A number of his songs may be frankly written off as not music but merchandise." That this merchandise benefited the publisher more than Strauss is suggested by Alfred Kalisch in his personal note in Newman's book ("Richard Strauss: The Man," p. xix). *Traum durch die Dämmerung,* Kalisch claims, was sold to the publisher Aibl for the equivalent of thirty shillings. Within the first two years it brought in four hundred pounds, none of which went to the composer. Although I have not been able to verify Kalisch's figures, they at least suggest the inequities of such outright sales.
11. Horst Riedel, "Dem Musikverlag Fürstner zum 100jährigen Bestehen," IRSGM, no. 56 (October 1968), p. 10. The songs transferred to Boosey & Hawkes in 1943 include opp. 31, 46, 49, 51, 68, 69, and 71.
12. Norman Del Mar, *Richard Strauss: A Critical Commentary on His Life and Works* (London 1962–72), III (hereafter DM III), 336, attempts to claim for op. 47 a unity by key relationships, with the third song as a pivot between flat keys and sharp keys. Strauss's own suggestions for transpositions upset this scheme, which was probably not an intentionally planned one anyway. The original sequence moves from C - E - b♭/ending in D - A - e, the transposed one from A - D - g/ending in B - F - c (upper case letters indicate major keys, lower case minor).
13. In a letter of 15 January 1890, Strauss makes this suggestion to Spitzweg, just after the 1889 appearance of the six songs in op. 19 as two volumes of three songs each. He also requests that a low-voice version of the songs be issued. Excerpts from this letter are found in Strauss/Spitzweg, p. 469. Rahter published Strauss's opp. 15 and 17 in two formats, singly and as a complete opus.
14. See p. 99 (as well as pp. 222–23, n. 13), concerning the omission of the ninth song from this publication.
15. In *Richard Strauss: Gesamtausgabe der Lieder,* edited by Franz Trenner, 4 volumes (London: Boosey & Hawkes/Fürstner Ltd., 1964–65; hereafter GL I–IV), modern title pages have been added before each group of songs. At the bottom of these pages there are dates and names of the original publisher. (Aibl is, however, replaced by Universal-Edition.) These dates must not be mistaken for publication dates; nor are they accurate dates of composition. For the most part, they repeat dates given in early fascicles of Asow's thematic index as dates of composition. Many are incorrect: in the case of op. 10, for example, both sources (and a large number of other writings) err in giving 1882–83 as the composition date.
16. This list is believed to represent a complete account of all versions published up to World War I. Information for it is taken from secondary sources and from copies of op. 10 examined in the following libraries: Bayerische Staatsbibliothek (Munich), Deutsche Staatsbibliothek (Berlin), Library of Congress, New York Public Library, Österreichische Nationalbibliothek (Vienna), Staatsbibliothek der Stiftung Preussischer Kulturbesitz (Berlin), and Städtische Musikbibliothek (Munich).
17. The date of Fürstner's *Lieder-Album* is probably ca. 1909. It certainly could not have predated 1906, the year in which Strauss composed and had Fürstner issue his piano version of the orchestral song *Der Einsame* (op. 51, no. 2), one of the songs included in the anthology.
18. Alan Jefferson, *The Lieder of Richard Strauss* (London, 1971), p. 18. Although Jefferson does not name a singer for this program, his context misleadingly implies that Pauline Strauss was the singer. Some of the programs she actually did give are discussed here in Chapter VI.
19. I have been unable to locate programs or other details for these performances, which are mentioned in *"Göttlich ist und ewig der Geist." Richard-Strauss-Ausstellung zum*

100. Geburtstag. . . . , edited by Franz Grasberger and Franz Hadamowsky (Vienna, 1964), p. 131, in explanation of an item in the commemorative exhibit.

20.   As of early 1920, op. 66 was still unpublished; its first private performance was in 1921, the first public hearing in 1926. Although published in 1919, the three Ophelia songs in op. 67 (nos. 1–3) would not have been appropriate for Steiner's voice; the remaining Goethe songs in the opus could have been done by him. (To date there does not appear to be any documentation of the first performance of op. 67.) Nor would much of op. 68 (newly published in 1919) have been suitable for the baritone. Furthermore, no. 6 in this group is known to have been premiered in September 1920. Op. 69 (published in 1919) could possibly have been included in Steiner's recitals. Although I believe his recitals probably did not include opp. 66–69, there is a suggestion that at least some of these songs were known to him by the report in "Kleine Mitteilungen von hier und dort," *Signale für die musikalische Welt*, LXXVI (1918), 546. Here an anonymous reporter writes of Strauss's showing Steiner ten [sic] satirical songs directed at music publishers (i.e., op. 66) while visiting the singer in Aschau.

21.   Hüsch recorded the song with an orchestra directed by Otto Dobrint; the record appeared as Gramophone Co. EG 3056 and has since been re-released as Lebendige Vergangenheit no. 76.

22.   GL IV, 1–7. The volume bears a copyright date of 1965, this orchestration of 1964.

23.   The Vindibona-Collection includes these songs: *Allerseelen, Du meines Herzens Krönelein*, all four lieder in op. 27, *Traum durch die Dämmerung, Ich trage meine Minne*, and *Liebeshymnus*. The Walhalla and Pantheon series contain *Gefunden, Blindenklage, Mit deinen blauen Augen*, and *Die heiligen drei Könige aus Morgenland*. Leuckart's versions of *Wiegenlied* were for mandolin orchestra arranged by Ferdinand Kollmaneck and for chamber orchestra by Curt Goldmann. Alfred Pagel arranged *Muttertändelei* for chamber orchestra for Challier, while Eduard Rudolf arranged *Freundliche Vision* and *Winterweihe* as well as *Schlechtes Wetter* for large orchestra, chamber orchestra, and "Parisian" orchestra. Only the Vindibona series is dated; it was issued between 1926 and 1930.

24.   According to Ernst Krause, *Richard Strauss. Gestalt und Werk,* fifth edition (Leipzig, 1975), p. 196, it was Strauss who negotiated with Aibl about the publication of Reger's works, of which Strauss was an "unenvious promoter." Similar statements are to be found in Adalbert Lindner, *Max Reger. Ein Bild seines Jugendlebens und künstlerischen Werdens,* third edition (Stuttgart, 1938), p. 177, and elsewhere. Strauss's own recollections concerning Aibl's publication of Reger's works are slightly inaccurate. In "Aus meinen Jugend- und Lehrjahren" (AV 326), Strauss claims to have gotten Reger's first twenty-five works published by Aibl (*Betrachtungen und Erinnerungen,* edited by Willi Schuh, second edition [Zurich, 1957], p. 217); before giving works to Aibl, however, Reger had in fact had some songs published by Schott (1890–94).

25.   Both Reger and Taubmann probably made these transcriptions at the request of the publisher. Taubmann also prepared two- and four-hand piano arrangements of Strauss's *Salome* and orchestrated some excerpts from *Der Rosenkavalier* (under the name of N. Nambuat) for Fürstner.

26.   Edward Kravitt, "The Late Romantic Lied. Performance, the Literary Approach, and the Naturalistic Movement" (Ph.D. dissertation, New York University, 1960), p. 101, for instance suggests that the voice is treated as an instrumental medium for the beauty of its sounds in the *Four Last Songs* and others of Strauss's songs dating from 1918 ff. Others have found the agility required in songs such as *Amor* (op. 68, no. 5) or arias such as Zerbinetta's rondo in *Ariadne auf Naxos* and the textless singing of Daphne after her transformation (in *Daphne*) to be more instrumental than vocal in character.

27.   Gieseking's autobiographical *So würde ich Pianist* (Wiesbaden, 1963), p. 135, lists these arrangements as having been published by Johannes Oertel of Munich. A letter of 25 May 1971 from that firm to me reports no records at all concerning these

arrangements. Asow and GL both list Fürstner as the publisher, a fact that is confirmed by printed copies in the Library of Congress.

28.   This recording is listed in Peter Morse and Christopher Norton-Welsh, "Die Lieder von Richard Strauss—Eine Diskographie/The Songs of Richard Strauss—A Discography," *Richard Strauss-Blätter*, no. 5 (August 1974), p. 87. The accompanist is not listed here or in the original entry in the Bettini-Katalog (April 1900). The official publication of the Viennese Internationale Richard Strauss-Gesellschaft, the *Richard Strauss-Blätter*, will hereafter be referred to as RSB.

29.   Ibid., pp. 88, 91, and 101. These Ampico piano rolls date from ca. 1921. The recordings with Patzak, now available as Rococo 5348, are excerpted from a concert of 15 September 1944. See also Chapter VI, nn. 9 and 72, p. 228 and p. 232.

30.   Ibid., p. 90, erroneously lists two acoustic recordings of *Allerseelen* as with orchestral accompaniment, both dated ca. 1910. The only known orchestration of this song is Robert Heger's, which dates from 1933.

31.   The unrecorded orchestral versions are of *Mein Auge, Der Arbeitsmann, Befreit, Des Dichters Abendgang*, and *Winterliebe*. See Chapter III, n. 29 (p. 218), concerning the authorship of the orchestration of *Der Arbeitsmann*.

32.   Robert Craft, " 'Elektra' and Richard Strauss," *The New York Review of Books*, XXIII/10 (10 June 1976), 32. Craft overemphasizes the neglect in claiming that fewer than a dozen of the orchestral lieder have been recorded. In fact, at latest count thirteen of the fifteen orchestral songs and twenty-one of the twenty-six orchestrations have been recorded at one time or another. Many of the recordings are not, admittedly, available easily, nor are these songs often heard in live performance.

33.   Concerning the Beethoven and Ritter lieder (and an unauthenticated orchestration of a Schubert song), see Chapter VI, p. 147 and n. 29 (p. 230).

34.   A description of the first three issues appears in my review of RSB, nos. 1–3, *Notes*, XXIX (1973), 463–64.

35.   This essay, appearing in RSB, no. 5, pp. 79–81, has been expanded into Chapter VI of the present study.

36.   Again, Dietrich Fischer-Dieskau deserves the credit. The song is included on his "Lieder der Jahrhundertwende" (Elektrola C 065-02 675), part of his series *Stilwandlungen des Klavierliedes 1850–1950*.

37.   See Chapter IV, n. 12 (p. 222).

38.   This information, which does not appear in Asow or GL, was kindly given to me by Alice Strauss. Although I have not located a citation, Schneider has presumably listed them in at least one of his catalogues. They are not mentioned among the manuscripts in his *Katalog Nr. 194. Richard Strauss. 1. Teil: Manuskripte und Briefe* (Tutzing, 1975), but may appear in its forthcoming *2. Teil: Autographen- Erstausgaben-Musikdrucke-Literatur*.

39.   In contrast to this current high price, the autograph version of *Notturno* was acquired by Broadcast Music Inc.—some time between 1947 and 1963—for only a few hundred dollars. (On this manuscript, see p. 101.)

40.   The four-page facsimiles appeared with Herrmann's "Das letzte Lied von Richard Strauss. Eichendorffs 'Im Abendrot,' " *Aurora. Eichendorff-Almanach*, XIX (1959), 79–80 (facsimile inserted after p. 80); and his "Mit Eichendorff beschloss Richard Strauss sein Schaffen . . . ," *Schlesien*, IX (1964), 107–08 (facsimile folds out following p. 108). Herrmann is not entirely accurate, of course, in calling *Im Abendrot* Strauss's last composition. Neither of these articles nor their facsimiles is listed in Asow, which mentions only the 1967 facsimile issued by Peter-Presse, Christoph Kreickenbaum, Darmstadt (Asow, p. 1658).

41.   Except for the newly printed works and the three Goethe settings on pp. 95–98, NL was produced from the same original pages as GL III, with new typesetting for headings and a few corrections in the music.

42.   *Der Spielmann und sein Kind* was actually preceded in January 1878 by *Arie der Almaide* (AV 44) for soprano and orchestra and by *Auf aus der Ruh* (AV 45) for tenor, chorus, and orchestra. Probably intended to be part of a larger work (both

texts are from Goethe's singspiel *Lila*), these excerpts were abandoned before the orchestration was completed and have never been published.

43. For Schuh's writings which list or discuss some of the song sketches, see the entries in the bibliography of this study (including NL, pp. 101–08). The lists of works found in the first volume of Schuh's biography (hereafter *Lebenschronik*), pp. 543–52, extend only through 1898. They include only a few sketched or incomplete compositions, only one of them a song. An examination of the sketchbooks (or even of Asow's catalogue) makes it clear that Strauss left fewer unfinished works in the years from 1885 to 1900 than in later periods.

CHAPTER II

1. Each song from op. 10 through op. 56 is listed in one of the biennial supplements of Challier's *Lieder-Katalog* (1888–1914). Strauss's name receives only a passing reference in, for example, Jack M. Stein, *Poem and Music in the German Lied from Gluck to Hugo Wolf* (Cambridge, Mass., 1971), and in Elaine Brody and Robert A. Fowkes, *The German Lied and Its Poetry* (New York, 1971). Stein's chronological boundaries should not preclude the consideration of Strauss, most of whose songs were written before Wolf's death and who began to publish his songs some three years before Wolf. There is no mention at all of Strauss in Günther Müller, *Geschichte des deutschen Liedes vom Zeitalter des Barock bis zur Gegenwart* (Munich, 1925; reprint Darmstadt, 1959); in Fritz Egon Pamer, "Das deutsche Lied in neunzehnten Jahrhundert," *Handbuch der Musikgeschichte*, edited by Guido Adler, second edition (Berlin, 1930), II, 939–55; in Walter Wiora, *Das deutsche Lied . . . Zur Geschichte und Ästhetik einer musikalischen Gattung* (Wölfenbuttel, 1971); or in similar surveys of the lied. Strauss fares somewhat better in a few other German publications, particularly in Hans Joachim Moser's *Das deutsche Lied seit Mozart,* second, revised edition (Tutzing, 1968), and in Kurt Gudewill's "Das Kunstlied in deutschen Sprachgebiet," section A of the article "Lied" in *Die Musik in Geschichte und Gegenwart* (Kassel, 1949–), VIII, cols. 746–75. Even among German publications, Moser's is exceptional in that it carries the lied tradition through the last works of Strauss and his contemporaries to Distler, Henze, Krenek, and Pepping in the present century.

2. Berg's corruption of the title is repeated by Hans Redlich and others in listing his early works. Alan Jefferson silently amends the reading to *Nachtgang* in his *Lieder,* Appendix D, "Poems set by Strauss and other composers," p. 125. Nicholas Chadwick in "Berg's Unpublished Songs in the Österreichische Nationalbibliothek," *Music and Letters,* LII (1971), 124 (footnote), verifies that *Nachtgang* is the poem set by Berg.

3. Strauss did not totally neglect Eichendorff even in his early works: choral compositions on his texts were written in 1876 (AV 25) and 1880 (AV 67, no. 1). A later work for chorus, *Die Tageszeiten,* op. 76 (1928) also employs Eichendorff's verses. Not until the late 1940's did Strauss turn to the poet for a solo song, *Im Abendrot* (1948). The composer discovered Rückert's suitability for his composition around 1897, using his poems for ten lieder, five choruses, and a few incomplete works between 1897 and 1935.

4. Jefferson does not explain the absence of Goethe, or his omission from the biographical sketches of poets which follow in Appendix E (pp. 126–30). Nor does he refer to the index that lists these settings, Willi Schuh, *Goethe-Vertonungen. Ein Verzeichnis* (Zurich, 1952).

5. At various times in his career, Reger published both orchestrations and solo piano arrangements of lieder by other composers. These include orchestrations of songs by Schubert, Brahms, and Wolf, along with solo versions (always with the text indicated above the original vocal melody) of songs by Schumann, Wolf, Brahms, and Strauss. The arrangements of Strauss's lieder, the first of all these works to be published,

appear to have been made at the suggestion of Eugen Spitzweg, head of the Munich firm of Joseph Aibl; see Chapter I, n. 24, (p. 209). Aibl issued nine groups of Reger's songs from 1898 to 1901 as well as these transcriptions and other works.

6. Elisabeth Schumann, in her *German Song,* translated by D. Miller Craig (London and New York, 1948), for example, generalizes that Strauss's songs "are practically all settings of poems which no other composer had chosen. It looks as though he had deliberately avoided any which previously had been adopted."

7. Jack M. Stein, "Was Goethe Wrong about the Nineteenth Century Lied? An Examination of the Relation of Poem and Music," *Publications of the Modern Language Association,* LXXVII (1962), 238.

8. Reger also set texts by Stefan Zweig, Strauss's librettist for *Die schweigsame Frau* and the man who drew his attention to the subject that later became *Capriccio.* Strauss did not set any of Zweig's texts in lieder. Librettists are excluded from the present study because Strauss worked with their writings in very different ways than with poets' verses in the lied. (Although Hofmannsthal wrote much poetry before devoting himself to dramatic works, Strauss did not draw on any of his poems for lieder texts.)

9. Kravitt, "The Late Romantic Lied," p. 38. Reger's settings listed here in Table 1 are, of course, an exception to his stated preference.

10. Ibid.

11. Wilhelm Mauke, "Liliencron als Befruchter der musikalischen Lyrik," *Die Musik,* III (1904), 438 (with statistics compiled by George Brandes).

12. Strauss's extant letters are published in *Richard Strauss und Ludwig Thuille. Briefe der Freundschaft, 1877–1907,* edited by Alfons Ott (Munich, 1969), hereafter cited as Strauss/Thuille. Franz Trenner is now preparing for publication Thuille's side of the correspondence, which until recently was believed lost. Some of Strauss's letters are the only record remaining of certain of his early songs that are now lost.

13. Strauss/Thuille, p. 185. All translations into English are mine, unless otherwise noted. In December 1875 Strauss composed a setting of Heine's *In Vaters Garten heimlich steht.* No other Heine settings from this period are known; Strauss appears not to have returned to the poet's works until ca. 1904–06.

14. Ibid. The earliest known Lenau setting by Strauss is *Nebel* ("Du trüber Nebel hüllst mir") from 1878. Lenau's work later reappears in the songs of op. 26 (1891–93) and as the inspiration for *Don Juan* (1887–89), a work which Strauss dedicated to Thuille.

15. Three quite late works for unaccompanied voice, which can hardly be considered lieder, do have texts by Strauss. They are occasional works of one page each, one written for a publisher, the other two for prominent figures of the Third Reich; see Asow, pp. 1282–83 and 1305–06 (AV 126, 127, and 136).

16. Henry T. Finck, *Richard Strauss. The Man and His Work* (Boston, 1917), p. 287. The same statement is quoted or paraphrased in several other sources. It originated as a letter written in 1893 to Friedrich Hausegger (not his son, Siegmund, as Finck states on p. 287). Newman, in his *Richard Strauss,* p. 94, incorrectly claims it to be from a 1903 letter, but names the correct Hausegger. Finck's and Newman's errors are set right in DM III, 248.

17. Finck, p. 287.

18. Ibid.

19. Johanna von Rauchenberger-Strauss, "Jugenderinnerungen," *Richard Strauss Jahrbuch 1959/60* (Bonn, 1960), p. 13.

20. Ibid.

21. Richard Strauss, *Briefe an die Eltern 1882–1906,* edited by Willi Schuh (Zurich, 1954), p. 82, from a letter of 22 January 1886 (hereafter cited as Strauss/Eltern).

22. *Richard Strauss und Joseph Gregor. Briefwechsel 1934–1949,* edited by Roland Tenschert (Salzburg, 1955), p. 182, from Strauss's letter of 12 May 1939 (hereafter cited as Strauss/Gregor). An extensive passage of this letter is quoted (in a slightly different translation from mine) in DM III, 247.

23. Walter Thomas, *Richard Strauss und seine Zeitgenossen* (Vienna and Munich, 1964),

p. 291. Hans-Esdras Mutzenbecher suggests that the influence of Hofmannsthal on Strauss's choice of poets, combined with his own feeling for literary quality, caused him to be more demanding in the years after World War I; see Mutzenbecher's "Marginalien um Richard Strauss/Marginal Jottings on Richard Strauss," RSB, no. 8 (December 1976), p. 18.

24. Susanne Langer, *The Problems of Art* (New York, 1957), p. 84.

25. According to Karl Böhm, Strauss happened upon the Bierbaum poem, read it through, conceived the idea for the music, and immediately began to write it down. At this moment, Pauline informed him that he was to accompany her on a walk. After being told that he was at work, she allowed him twenty minutes to continue, at the end of which time he had completed the setting. The story is repeated by William Mann in his *Richard Strauss. A Critical Study of the Operas* (London, 1964), p. 317 (note), and elsewhere. A slightly different version is given in Schuh, *Lebenschronik*, p. 470; it is based on Strauss's reply to a questionnaire from Julius Bahle (see AV 352, dating from 1931).

26. Albert Gutmann, *Aus dem Wiener Musikleben: Künstler-Erinnerungen 1873–1908* (Vienna, 1914), p. 125.

27. DM III, 280.

28. Frida Leider, *Playing My Part*, translated by Charles Osborne (New York, 1966), p. 28.

29. Adalbert Mercier, "Richard Strauss et ses nouveaux lieder," *Revue d'histoire et de critique musicale,* IV (1904), 419.

30. See *Hugo von Hofmannsthal. Richard Strauss. Der Rosenkavalier. Fassungen, Film-szenarium, Briefe,* edited by Willi Schuh (Frankfurt, 1971), pp. 27–156 and 196–220.

31. Ernst Krause, *Richard Strauss. The Man and His Work,* translated from *Richard Strauss. Gestalt und Werk,* third edition (Leipzig, 1955), by John Coombs (London, 1964), p. 264.

32. All three librettists have entire volumes devoted to their correspondence with Strauss: Strauss/Gregor; *Richard Strauss/Stefan Zweig. Briefwechsel,* edited by Willi Schuh (Frankfurt, 1957); and, in the most complete version, *Richard Strauss/Hugo von Hofmannsthal. Briefwechsel. Gesamtausgabe,* edited by Willi Schuh in collaboration with Franz and Alice Strauss, fourth, enlarged edition (Zurich, 1970).

33. My attempt in connection with the present study to locate volumes of correspondence has met with little success. Many poets were not significant enough to warrant such a volume. Where collections of their letters do exist today, Strauss's may be considered of only peripheral importance, or may not even have been preserved, since he was not directly involved in their creative work.

34. As witnessed by the English-language title of the Strauss/Hofmannsthal correspondence, *A Working Friendship* (London, 1961), even their prolonged collaboration did not result in much socializing. Aside from the formalities of greetings and leave-takings, Strauss's other letters too are generally devoid of any personal matters. The exceptions are frequent references to physical illness, especially in the later years, as in *Richard Strauss. Briefwechsel mit Willi Schuh,* edited by Willi Schuh (Zurich, 1969), and to matters of family interest in Strauss/Eltern. (Since many of the published collections omit portions of some letters, such topics may possibly have been covered in these sections of his correspondence.)

35. These include August Becker (1828–91), Friedrich von Bodenstedt (1819–92), Oskar Pletzsch (1830–88), and Karl Stieler (1842–85).

36. This letter, included in Grasberger, *Briefe,* pp. 82–83, concerns the plan for an opera, *Das erhabene Leid der Könige,* AV 217; see Asow, p. 1426. Strauss's acquaintance with Dahn's dramatic writings predates his songs on Dahn's poems. In 1885 the composer made a piano reduction of the score of Alexander Ritter's one-act opera *Der faule Hans,* based on a libretto by Dahn. (Strauss's reduction is catalogued in Asow as AV 184 A.)

37. Walter Thomas, in his *Richard Strauss,* briefly discusses the poets set by Strauss in his chapter "Von den Lied-Autoren zu Hofmannsthal" (pp. 289 ff.); Strauss's personal

acquaintance with the Berlin poets is mentioned on p. 290 and also by Edmund Wachten, *Richard Strauss * 1864. Sein Leben in Bildern* (Leipzig, 1940), p. 20.

38. Grasberger, *Briefe*, pp. 94–95; this is one of two letters from Henckell to Strauss included in the collection.

39. Ibid., pp. 136–37 (here and elsewhere Grasberger does not include or footnote the enclosures, which probably do not survive in the collections of letters). Henckell outlined a format of lieder (sung)/recitation/lieder/recitation/lieder.

40. Strauss/Eltern, p. 255.

41. Descriptions of these books, neither of which have I been able to locate, are taken from bibliographies and from the card catalogue of the Deutsche Staatsbibliothek (where the copies were typically reported as "lost"). *Kling!*, composed on 30 September 1900, may even have been written especially for inclusion in *Mein Lied*. The entire song is engraved in this volume; an incipit in Strauss's hand follows the printed poem. There is also an incipit (and perhaps the complete engraved music?) for *Ruhe, meine Seele!*.

42. According to Schuh (*Lebenschronik*, p. 462), Strauss made similar annotations in his editions of poems by Busse, Meyer, Mackay, Dehmel, Hesse, and others.

43. *Lebenschronik*, p. 448; on p. 450, Schuh contradicts his earlier statement by saying that Bierbaum was the one who sent Strauss the poem. I have been unable to locate a letter from either man for that date. That Dehmel sent the poem would be consistent with Schuh's mention (also on p. 450) of Dehmel's sending to Strauss proof sheets of his poem *Ballade von der schönen wilden Welt*. No sketches for this text have been found, and there is no other evidence that Strauss worked at a setting of the poem. It is not included in the Asow catalogue.

44. Ibid., p. 450.

45. Dehmel's letter in Grasberger, *Briefe*, pp. 116–17, is his only letter to Strauss now in print. Portions of a second letter (26 April 1898) are given in Schuh, *Lebenschronik*, pp. 448–49. According to this letter, Dehmel deleted *Mein Auge* from subsequent editions of *Erlösungen*. The poem was apparently completely withdrawn from Dehmel's works; it does not appear in the fourth edition of *Erlösungen*, which was issued as part of his *Gesammelte Werke in drei Bänden* (Berlin, 1916). Two letters from Dehmel to other people but concerning Strauss's lieder are quoted in part by Schuh (*Lebenschronik*, p. 451).

46. Schuh, *Lebenschronik*, p. 450; on p. 449 is a facsimile of the inscription from Strauss's copy in the Strauss Archive.

47. Richard Dehmel, "Offenherzige Erklärung," *Die Musik*, III/15–16 (May 1902), 1461–62; this statement is quoted in its entirety in Asow, pp. 239–40.

48. Grasberger, *Briefe*, p. 131 (14 May 1900). Schuh, *Lebenschronik*, p. 445, includes a brief statement from another Bierbaum letter (5 October 1900) about the ballet.

49. An excerpt from this unpublished letter of 6 October 1900 appears in Schuh, *Lebenschronik*, p. 445.

50. Ibid., pp. 454–55.

51. Strauss/Eltern, pp. 283–84 (26 November 1903).

52. To date, I have been unable to locate a copy of his two-volume *Ausgewählte Briefe* (Berlin, 1910).

53. The work is *Der Sonnenaufgang* (AV 231), a symphonic poem sketched in 1900 but not extant in complete form; see Asow, pp. 1433–34.

54. Grasberger, *Briefe*, pp. 92–93.

55. An excerpt from this letter is given in Schuh, *Lebenschronik*, p. 463. Strauss composed his *Gesang der Apollopriesterin*, op. 33, no. 2, between 7 July and 10 September 1896. *Unterwegs* appears not to have interested him; it is not listed in Asow.

56. See Strauss/Eltern, p. 257, for mention of Lindner's project (but not the opera's name) in Strauss's letter of 20 April 1902.

57. The original letter is in the Kerr Archive of the Berlin Akademie der Künste, along with others of Kerr's and seven letters, one postcard, and one telegram from Strauss. A transcription of this particular letter appears in IRSGM, no. 47 (December 1965), p. 8.

58. The first suggestion of this project was made by Strauss on 21 January 1920. This letter is transcribed in IRSGM, no. 48 (March 1966), p. 17; a facsimile of its first page appears on p. 16 of the same issue.
59. See Asow, p. 1446.
60. Strauss/Schuh, pp. 23–24 (14 March 1938).
61. Walter Huder, "Alfred Kerr und Richard Strauss," IRSGM, no. 48 (March 1966), pp. 19–20. (On p. 18, Huder wrongly states that the Kerr/Strauss correspondence began in 1913 instead of 1918; 1913 is merely the date of publication of *Die Harfe.*)
62. Three letters appear in Grasberger, *Briefe:* on p. 324 is one from Wildgans to Strauss concerning the poem for *Austria (Österreichisches Lied),* on pp. 330–31 Strauss's report that the work has been delivered to the publisher, and on pp. 335–36 Strauss's request for poems.
63. Ibid., p. 335 (24 April 1931). The reference to *Du bist die Ruh* is puzzling; Grasberger does not footnote this probable slip of Strauss's memory. The famous Schubert setting of this Rückert text was certainly known to Strauss, and he may have confused it with the title of his own *Ruhe, meine Seele!* (by Henckell). (Or, he may have been referring to the poems only, and not his own settings of them.) Both the text and music of the Henckell lied would make it a likely companion to the other two songs; all three remained favorites of Strauss, his wife, and lieder singers in general.
64. This suggestion is made not without some caution, since Strauss refers to having found the poem for *Durch Einsamkeiten* after a return from Italy in 1938. He states this in a letter to Viktor Keldorfer, director of the Wiener Schubertbund (to which the work was dedicated), dated 17 May 1938 (nine days after completion of the chorus). This letter was sent to Keldorfer along with the manuscript; see Asow, p. 1279. On the other hand, I have not found any other Wildgans poem with the word "Einsamkeiten" in its title or first line.
65. See Strauss/Gregor, pp. 135 and 137 (Strauss's letter of 23 October and Gregor's reply of 27 October).
66. Grasberger, *Briefe,* pp. 415–16 (27 April 1943).
67. The poem was subsequently printed in Weinheber's *Hier ist das Wort* (Salzburg, 1947), p. 169, and in *Richard Strauss. Dokumente seines Lebens und Schaffens,* compiled by Franz Trenner (Munich, 1954), pp. 209–10.
68. See Asow, pp. 1192–93, and items in the bibliographic listing there.
69. While throughout the nineteenth century a number of German composers were attracted to German translations and imitations of Oriental poetry, in the early twentieth century it was primarily American song composers who were drawn to Oriental themes.
70. These songs do not appear as part of Brahms's lieder publications in the nineteenth century. They were printed only in 1935 in a publication edited by Karl Geiringer (New York: G. Schirmer).
71. I have not yet found the date for Simrock's *Hamlet;* it is not necessarily later than the Schlegel/Tieck translations of 1839–41, for Simrock published his Shakespearean criticism in the 1830's. (Certain of his comedy translations did not appear until the 1860's.)
72. Schumann used the translations found in *Lord Byrons sämtliche Werke,* edited by his father, August Schumann, volume I translated by J. Körner, volume II by K. Kannegiesser (Zwickau, 1821–27). Wolf's two songs from 1896 use translations by Otto Gildemeister, Strauss's 1884 *Aus den Hebräischen Melodien* ("Mein Geist ist trüb," AV 175, a song now lost) that of Adolf Böttger.
73. Strauss's source appears to have been *Michelangelo. Sämtliche Gedichte in Guasti's Text,* translated by Sophie Hasenclever (Leipzig, 1875). The original untitled poem begins "Porgo umilmente all'aspro giogo il collo." Wolf used translations by Walter Robert-Tornow.
74. The settings of *Des Knaben Wunderhorn* poetry are found in opp. 32, no. 5; 36, nos. 2 and 3; and 49, no. 6. Op. 49, nos. 7 and 8, are translations from the Alsatian by

Curt Mündel. While the last two songs are rarely performed, the others fare somewhat better.

75. Strauss was not alone in finding the melodrama a suitable musical medium for the
ballad. Several works by Liszt come to mind, along with Schumann's opp. 106 and
122 (the latter of which consists of two miniature melodramas) and Wolf's *Der
Feuerreiter.* Choral settings were popular among Strauss's contemporaries, who
created several examples of mixed and male choruses on ballad texts.

76. E.g., by Mutzenbecher, "Marginalien um Richard Strauss," p. 18.

77. This is not to say that their texts have prevented other songs from becoming well
known. The explanations lie elsewhere, in factors such as the extent of the songs'
availability in publications and recordings, public interest in the lied genre, and other
differences attributable to the time in the history of the solo song during which they
were written.

CHAPTER III

1. The vocal line of one nearly complete early sketch, *Der weisse Hirsch* (AV 6), from
ca. 1871, is divided among three parts: alto (narrator), stanzas 1, 2, 6, 7, and (second
hunter), stanza 4; bass (first hunter), stanza 3; and tenor (third hunter), stanza 5.
This sketch is obviously a part-song, unlike the Brahms example and the others of
Strauss discussed here, which are intended for performance by only one singer.

2. Norman Del Mar (DM III, 299) recommends that the stage direction be taken
literally.

3. Grete Wehmeyer, *Max Reger als Liederkomponist. Ein Beitrag zum Problem der
Wort-Ton-Beziehung* (Regensburg, 1955), p. 223, cites examples in Reger's op. 76 of
songs (in particular no. 6) that do not have a coincidence of musical and textual
forms.

4. Roland Tenschert, *3 × 7 Variationen über das Thema, Richard Strauss* (Vienna,
1944), p. 135.

5. Wehmeyer, *Max Reger,* p. 88, describes certain songs of Reger's (op. 62, no. 8;
op. 35, no. 4; and others) as compositions for piano with obbligato voice.

6. Other less familiar examples with piano parts constructed on the same principle
include *An Sie* (op. 43, no. 1), *Des Dichters Abendgang* (op. 47, no. 2), and *Waldseligkeit* (op. 49, no. 1).

7. Timings given in the present study are approximate; some are based on a recording
or a consensus of recordings, where they exist (there are none of op. 44). Strauss
almost never indicated metronomic rates for his lieder. Op. 71 (of which no recording
is available) is the only group which has metronomic markings in the score; since
each of the three hymns in this opus has several sections in different tempos, Strauss
marked each change carefully.

8. At the opposite extreme are Strauss's five Goethe songs from the *West-östlicher
Divan* and *Zahme Xenien,* with durations of a minute or less. The dedicatory settings
Spruch (AV 116, 1930) and *Xenion* (AV 131, 1942) are the shortest at five and six
measures (less than twenty seconds) each.

9. Wehmeyer, *Max Reger,* p. 98, claims that Reger used the title "Gesänge" for some
collections of songs because he treated the texts in these groups more as prose than
as poetry.

10. Wolf used the term "Gedichte" instead of "Lieder" similarly in his song collections
based on poems by Goethe, Eichendorff, Mörike, Keller, et al. Universal-Edition,
after taking over Aibl's publications, changed the title of Strauss's op. 10 to *Acht
Lieder. . . .*

11. Good examples of monotone recitation can be found in *Heimliche Aufforderung,
Befreit,* and *Notturno;* of a confined range in *Stiller Gang* and *Ich wollt ein Sträusslein
binden;* and of leaps in *Das Lied des Steinklopfers* and *Sie trugen ihn auf der Bahre
bloss.*

12. Kravitt, "The Late Romantic Lied," pp. 289, 290. He further states that the idea of insanity is reinforced by the thin, linear texture, chromatic and tritone intervals, vague tonality, and monotonous rhythmic ostinato (the last as a musical equivalent of Ophelia's fixation).

13. *Richard Strauss/Hugo von Hofmannsthal. Briefwechsel. Gesamtausgabe,* edited by Willi Schuh in collaboration with Franz and Alice Strauss, third edition (Zurich, 1964), p. 498 (letter of 14 October 1923). (Hereafter references to this edition will read Strauss/Hofmannsthal [1964].)

14. Philip Radcliffe, "Germany and Austria" in *A History of Song,* edited by Denis Stevens (New York, 1961), p. 260.

15. The songs are *Wozu noch, Mädchen, Wie sollten wir geheim sie halten,* and *Bruder Liederlich.* Of the second, in which there are six examples of portamento, Del Mar suggests that Strauss let his enthusiasm for the apparently new discovery of this device get the upper hand (DM III, 275). In *Hat gesagt—bleibt's nicht dabei,* a portamento (or glissando) is certainly appropriate on "[da-]bei" in mm. 30–31, where an ascending seventh is slurred and marked *jauchzend* ("exultant").

16. In the last instance, Strauss introduced trills on parallel thirds in the accompaniment at the mention of birds. This device of musical description was one of his favorites, reappearing in many songs from his childhood *Waldkonzert* (1871?) to *Im Abendrot* of the *Four Last Songs;* see p. 58.

17. Actual pitches of notes are given throughout this study according to method 3 in the article "Pitch names" in the *Harvard Dictionary of Music,* edited by Willi Apel, second edition (Cambridge, Massachusetts, 1969), p. 679. In this method, middle C is c^1, the octave above c^2, etc. For all songs, Strauss's original tonality (as first engraved and as reprinted in GL) is retained.

18. In opp. 10 to 32, the average span is an eleventh or twelfth with the extremes being a ninth (three songs) and fourteenth (three songs). From opp. 36 to 56 most ranges fall between a twelfth and fourteenth; only one song is limited to a tenth, while eight have a two-octave compass. From op. 66 to the *Four Last Songs,* the average is a thirteenth to a fifteenth. (The ranges in the early songs could be added to this progression: they vary from an octave to a fourteenth, the majority limited to a tenth.)

19. Written on Christmas Day 1922, *Erschaffen und Beleben* was originally dedicated to—and perhaps written specifically for the virtuosity of—Michael Bohnen, a bass at the Berlin Opera. In 1945 Strauss changed the dedication to Hans Hotter when he added it to the three Rückert songs (with *Vom künftigen Alter* also dedicated to Hotter) to form op. 87 of his *Nachlass.* It was the only one of the four songs to be published prior to GL (by Oertel in 1951).

20. Kravitt, "The Late Romantic Lied," p. 236.

21. Kravitt (ibid.) and others claim that Strauss as well as Wolf used analytic description less often in his later songs. Such a generalization is risky with Strauss: while certain later songs (e.g., op. 71 or 77) have hardly any examples of word painting, others from op. 66 to the *Four Last Songs* are full of such descriptive music. Often the contents of the poem itself determine the extent of the pictorialism. The flower songs in op. 22, for instance, have almost no examples of word painting because there are few words in them that can be readily translated into music.

22. Karl Straube, "Max Reger," *Die Gesellschaft,* XVIII/1 (1902), 178 (where he compares the two composers' settings of Liliencron's *Glückes genug*).

23. Werner Bollert, "Bermerkungen zu Richard Strauss Opus 68 and 69," IRSGM, no. 57/59 (December 1968), p. 11, cites the music of these two settings as having the closest and most sympathetic relationship to their poems and laments the continuing neglect by singers of *Waldesfahrt.*

24. Kravitt, "The Late Romantic Lied," p. 257, makes this claim, supporting it with several examples (pp. 254–57 and elsewhere).

25. GL II, 359.

26. In this study when an entire word is quoted but only one syllable thereof referred to or stressed, that syllable is italicized.

27. Kravitt, "The Late Romantic Lied," p. 257.
28. DM III, 269; Desmond Shawe-Taylor, notes to Elisabeth Schumann's recording of Strauss's lieder on Angel COLH-102 (p. 12); et al.
29. The unpublished manuscript in an unidentified hand—certainly not Strauss's—is preserved in the Österreichische Nationalbibliothek, S.m.30.084. The erroneous designation "op. 37" on the first page of music and the fact that no others of Strauss's orchestrations exist in copyists' copies speak out against its being his. On the other hand, references in three letters suggest that it may be a copy of his own orchestration, or at least one that he supervised and approved. Two early references to the orchestration of *Der Arbeitsmann* are, according to the file in the Strauss Archive, in unpublished letters to Strauss from Leo Kestenberg (1911 or 1919) and the Fürstner firm (25 December 1918). Both letters are reportedly in the Strauss Archive, where the card file gives conflicting dates for the former. I have not been able to ascertain more about the contents of either. In a published letter (Grasberger, *Briefe,* p. 408) of 9 September 1941 Strauss recommended the orchestration to Hans Hotter: " . . . I also have as suitable for you *Der Arbeitsmann* (Forberg), which is orchestrated, but only in a manuscript in Vienna, from where I will gladly send you the material." The orchestral forces are of typically Straussian proportions for the early decades of the twentieth century: full winds (including two basset horns—which Strauss also used in *Elektra* and *Das Thal,* op. 51, no. 1—six horns, and two tubas), percussion, and strings (all *divisi* except the double basses). Jefferson, *Richard Strauss* (London, 1975), includes the orchestration in a list of works (p. 110), but provides no documentation or other information on it. Schuh, *Lebenschronik,* p. 467, lists it as now lost ("verschollen") but dating from 12 December 1918. This new information seems to support the suggestion that the Fürstner letter concerns the orchestration of the song. (Schuh, in his foreword, p. 10, declares that—unless otherwise stated—his documentary evidence comes from originals or photocopies in the Strauss Archive; he makes no reference to the surviving copy of the orchestration.)
30. Uhland's poem describes the giant elms at Hirsau which break through and tower over the ruins of a former Benedictine monastery. In the eighth stanza he compares their struggle to dominate the ruined walls and roof with a similar conflict at Wittenberg which "with giant branches broke out of the cloister roof." Strauss makes it clear that Uhland's reference is to Martin Luther by quoting the first phrase of *Ein feste Burg ist unser Gott* in bass octaves at the start of the postlude.
31. Grasberger, *Briefe,* pp. 94–95 (letter of 12 December 1895). Henckell cited particularly the passages "stiehlt sich lichter Sonnenschein" and "wie die Brandung wenn sie schwillt," where word painting is quite vivid.
32. In Ex. 17c Strauss indulges in a bit of *Augenmusik* as well: the "Lobgesang" was rising from the bug ("Wanze," m. 56) as it died and began to stink. Since "Wanzen" is also the German nickname for sharps ("Flöhen und Wanzen" are flats and sharps), he uses an abundance of sharps in this passage. "Wanze" is also a colloquial word for bloodsucker, by which Kerr and Strauss mean their greedy publishers.
33. This fugal section contains a literal quotation from two songs in *Krämerspiegel* as well as parodies of other vocal styles. Originally an important instrumental theme in op. 66, nos. 8 and 12, in the final scene of the opera (on the moonlit terrace, hence its nickname, "moonlight theme") it is developed more fully. DM III, 214, suggests that the Countess's description of the stage as a magic mirror ("Zauberspiegel") of reality is responsible for the quoting of this melody. The composer's son, Franz, claims to have convinced his father to re-use the beautiful theme rather than let it lie fallow; see Franz Grasberger, "Hüter der Tradition," in *Festschrift Dr. Franz Strauss zum 70. Geburtstag,* edited by Hans Schneider (Tutzing, 1967), p. 23.
34. DM III, 285 and 343.
35. Max Steinitzer, *Richard Strauss in seiner Zeit* (Leipzig, 1914), p. 34. The example given here, however, calls into question the accuracy of his claim: Steinitzer says that Strauss did not include two lines in his setting of Gilm's *Geduld* (op. 10, no. 5), thinking they were ridiculous and would be laughed at. The lines he cites are

"So lebe wohl, ich seh' Dich nimmer wieder, so will's mein unerbittliches Geschick!" ("And so farewell, I will never see you again; my relentless fate wills it so!") They do, however, appear in measures 84–90, where they are set in a rather dramatic arioso manner that contrasts with all the preceding phrases. In fact, Strauss's setting of this poem retains all three of the poet's original eight-line strophes intact.

36. There are a few small exceptions, such as *Traum durch die Dämmerung,* where he added "hin" in line 3, and *Ständchen,* where he changed " . . . die über die Blumen hüpfen" to " . . . um über die Blumen zu hüpfen." See 220, n. 48.

37. Strauss/Hofmannsthal (1964), pp. 22–23 (Strauss's letter of 5 June 1906) and 25 (Hofmannsthal's reply of 16 June 1906). Strauss mentions his source of *Saul und David* as volume IX of the Rückert edition he owned; the planned opera is catalogued as AV 240.

38. Ibid., p. 124 (letter of 27 May 1911); see also p. 539 (Hofmannsthal's letter of 4 May 1925, referring to "Rückertsche Schnörkel" in his *Ariadne* libretto).

39. The original ghasel (*ghazal* in Arabic) appeared in about the eighth century; it is found in various Oriental literatures, including Persian, Arabic, and Turkish. It was usually made up of five to twelve couplets on the subject of love and wine; the poet signed his name in the final couplet. For further information on the Oriental ghasel and its poets, see the *Princeton Encyclopedia of Poetry and Poetics,* edited by Alex Preminger, enlarged edition (Princeton, 1974), under "Ghasel," "Arabic Poetry," and "Persian Poetry."

40. *Vom künftigen Alter* was published only posthumously (GL III, 113 ff.) from the manuscript now in the Munich Städtische Musikbibliothek (MprL). The text appears under the music as well as in Strauss's hand inside the back cover; both places should be checked to verify this point, since the confusion of "ac" with "we" in his hand would not be difficult. In another song, op. 31, no. 1, Strauss breaks the rhyme of Carl Busse's *Blauer Sommer* by substituting "Frucht" for "Birne" (which rhymed with "Stirne" as the second *c* of the *aabbccdd* rhyme scheme). In this case, his setting obliterates the rhyme anyway, since the music continues with the next syllable on the second eighth note of the measure instead of pausing on a longer note as at the end of other lines.

41. Other examples of the ghasel in the German lied include Schubert's *Du liebst mich nicht. Ghasele,* D. 756 (Platen), Brahms's *Der Strom, der neben mir verrauschte,* op. 34, no. 1 (Platen), and Wolf's *Sie haben wegen der Trunkenheit* (Goethe). According to Stein, *Poem and Music,* p. 134, Brahms successfully matches the form of his music to the structure of the poem. In Stein's opinion (pp. 94 and 185–86) neither Schubert's nor Wolf's setting serves its poem well since the music obscures the rhyme scheme. Stein does not mention Strauss's ghasel settings at all. DM III, 386, calls Strauss's *Erschaffen und Beleben* (AV 106) a ghasel, but this poem does not really fit the requirements of the form. Del Mar does not mention the ghasel in connection with any of Strauss's Rückert settings.

42. This article also appeared, in H. C. Robbins Landon's translation, as "The Sonnet in Richard Strauss's Opera 'Capriccio.' A Study in the Relation between the Metre and the Musical Phrase," *Tempo,* no. 47 (spring 1958), pp. 7–11.

43. This preponderance of five-measure phrases is rare even in Strauss's settings of pentametric verse. Rufus Hallmark, Jr., points out in "The Genesis of *Dichterliebe:* A Source Study" (Ph.D. dissertation, Princeton University, 1975), pp. 133–35 and 227, that composers who set verses in pentameters—whether in lieder, hymns, dramatic works, or other genres—most often set the five poetic feet in four-measure units. (This is probably attributable to the conventions of musical phrase structure; within a four-measure phrase the five poetic accents can, of course, still be given five musical stresses.)

44. Roland Tenschert, "Verhältnis von Wort und Ton. Eine Untersuchung an dem Strauss'schen Lied 'Ich trage meine Minne,' " *Zeitschrift für Musik (Regensburg),* CI (1934), 591–95.

45. Strauss used this title according to the folk dialect, i.e., without the usual umlaut on "funfzehn."

46. I have been unable to locate a printed source for this statement in Strauss's own words. It is quoted or paraphrased (without acknowledgement of date or source) in DM III, 271; Krause, *Richard Strauss, Gestalt und Werk*, p. 274; and Otto Erhardt, *Richard Strauss. Leben, Wirken, Schaffen* (Olten and Freiburg im Breisgau, 1953), p. 275; and elsewhere.

47. Edmund von Freyhold, "Die Technik der musikalischen Deklamation," *Die Musik*, IV (1905), 3–16, 115–34, and 147–64.

48. Ibid., p. 122. Freyhold's "lange und kurze Silben" are actually strong and weak (rather than long and short) syllables.

49. Ibid., p. 125.

50. Max Steinitzer, *Richard Strauss* (Berlin, 1911), p. 159, claims that "um über die" consists of four unaccented syllables of which Strauss incorrectly emphasized the second. For this line Trenner (GL I, 345) lists a variant from Schack's text, citing the poet's original as "die über die Blumen hüpfen." The difference in the two versions is more in structure than in meaning. Had Strauss used the original words, he would probably have set the line as follows:

Ex. 26, *Ständchen*, op. 17, no. 2 (mm. 29–30, reconstruction of the vocal line using Schack's original text):

die ü- ber die Blu- - men hüp- fen.

Strauss's version actually makes the poetic accents of the second line of each of the first two stanzas identical: ‿‿‿‿‿‿‿‿. I have not been able to locate the original edition of Schack's poem. The version "die über die Blumen hüpfen" was, however, set by F. Otto Dessoff, one of over a dozen obscure composers who also used this poem. His setting from ca. 1878 (op. 6, no. 3) is the only other setting I have been able to consult. Most anthologies of German lieder texts give the reading "die über die Blumen hüpfen" or call attention to Strauss's version as a variant of the original.

51. Another example of Strauss's adding a syllable to the poet's original text for a main motivic idea is in *Schwung* (op. 77, no. 2). Here he changed the original first line of each of the three stanzas, "Gebt meinen Becher!" to "Gebt mir meinen Becher!"

52. Richard Strauss, *Betrachtungen und Erinnerungen,* edited by Willi Schuh, second edition (Zurich, 1957), p. 146 (hereafter this collection will be cited as Strauss, BuE; all references are to the second edition).

53. Dietrich Fischer-Dieskau's recording of *Gestern war ich Atlas* (Electrola C #163–50047) provides an exaggerated example of consonants as weapons, particularly on the ascending leaps in mm. 35–36 ("je *banger*, je *lieber*").

54. Three of the songs have durations of approximately one minute, Strauss's *Du meines Herzens Krönelein* of about two minutes.

55. Reger's *Wiegenlied* (op. 43, no. 5) was composed between the fall of 1899 and summer of 1900, and was published by Aibl in 1900. Strauss's setting of the same Dehmel poem as *Wiegenliedchen* (op. 49, no. 3) dates from 20 September 1901; it was in print before the end of 1901. In all other pairs, the composition and publication of Strauss's setting appear to predate the composition of Reger's. Few of Reger's individual lieder are dated in the manuscripts; one must therefore rely on the date of completion of the opus or its publication in establishing a chronology. The information on dates and the editions of Reger's songs used in the present study are found in *Max Reger. Sämtliche Werke. Unter Mitarbeit des Max-Reger-Institutes, Sologesänge mit Klavier,* edited by Fritz Stein, volumes 31–34 (Wiesbaden, [1955–67]).

56. Wehmeyer, *Max Reger,* p. 289, estimates that one third of Reger's lieder have examples of word painting. For Strauss, I estimate the figure as approximately half of the songs.
57. Straube, "Max Reger," p. 178.
58. According to Elisabeth Schumann, Strauss wanted the singer to emphasize this pictorial phrase by holding back on each of the four quarter notes. Her statement is confirmed by her recording of this passage (Seraphim set IC-6041) and by her edition of *Morgen!* in her *Liederbuch/Favorite Songs,* new revised edition (London, [1952]), p. 87.
59. Strauss and Reger used the same version of Mackay's poem, which had first appeared in his *Dichtungen* (Berlin, 1886) and continued to be re-used in several later editions. In *John Henry Mackays Werke in einem Band,* edited by Leo Kasarnowski with Mackay (Berlin, 1928), p. 56, and subsequent editions, "stummes Schweigen" was altered to "grosses Schweigen," presumably by the poet himself. Another alteration incorporated, apparently at an earlier time, was the change from "wird uns, die Glücklichen" to "wird uns, die Seligen" in line 3; Strauss and Reger both used the former. I have been unable to locate a version of the poem published before 1909, i.e., one that would have been available to Strauss in 1894 or to Reger in 1902.
60. In *Freundliche Vision* Reger sets fifty of the seventy-two syllables in Bierbaum's text to ♪♪♪ (or ♪♪♪♪) patterns, even where the poem does not call for trochaic rhythms. See Kravitt, "The Late Romantic Lied," pp. 46–47 (including Exx. 8 and 9), for an evaluation of Strauss's setting of *Freundliche Vision* as superior to Reger's in terms of rhythm.
61. The 1928 edition of *Mackays Werke* mentioned in n. 59 is the first to omit the dots. The edition of Reger's song in his *Sämtliche Werke* does not include them, while that of Strauss's setting in GL I has them at the end and after "Erde" (end of line 4), the midpoint of the poem.
62. Although he did not make a solo piano transcription of Strauss's *Ich schwebe* (or of *Morgen!*), Reger may have gotten to know it shortly before creating his own lied on the text. Strauss's setting was composed on 25 September 1900 and published by Fürstner in 1901. Reger's was written in the second half of 1901 and published by Aibl in 1902. (Strauss's popular *Morgen!* dates from 1894 and must certainly have been familiar to Reger, whose *Morgen!* dates from early August 1902.)
63. Concerning the importance of this line to Strauss, see p. 27.
64. *Max Reger, Briefe eines deutschen Meisters,* edited by Else Hase-Koehler (Leipzig, 1928), p. 66 (letter from Reger to Frau Felix Schmidt-Koehne dated 7 December 1899, quoting the *Heidelberger Tageblatt* of 7 November 1899).
65. Straube, "Max Reger," p. 178.

CHAPTER IV

1. Ernst Roth, *Musik als Kunst und Ware. Betrachtungen und Begegnungen eines Musikverlegers* (Zurich, 1966), p. 189. (These comments do not appear in Roth's *The Business of Music. Reflections of a Music Publisher* [London, 1969], a translation of the second [1969] edition of this book.)
2. Arthur M. Abell, *Talks with Great Composers* (New York, 1955), p. 99. Abell first met Strauss in Weimar in 1890; in that and the following winter they saw each other nearly daily. While Abell (1868–1958) noted down his conversations at this time (without, however, recording exact dates), they were not published until much later.
3. Here and elsewhere in this study I have retained my original numbering of the sketchbooks, which coincides with the sequence on the Bayerische Staatsbibliothek microfilms (Mus. Fm. 1, Nr. 1–5).
4. In almost every book containing lieder sketches, at least one opening was filmed twice; the duplicates are not counted in my numbering system. That this happened

causes one to wonder how many openings might have been omitted from the films, and whether some might not be in the wrong order.

5. The films are not in good condition, nor are the originals particularly good candidates for facsimiles because of their faint pencil annotations, pin-point-sized noteheads, yellowed paper, hasty and abbreviated texts, and nearly indecipherable comments. Samples of a few of the better pages are included here as Illustrations 5–8.

6. Kravitt, "The Late Romantic Lied," p. 257. Kravitt discovered this incomplete Heine setting in one of the sketchbooks at the Strauss Archive. I have not yet been able to locate it in the films which I have ordered. The song is not indexed in Asow, nor, so far as either Kravitt or I can tell, is it mentioned elsewhere in the literature.

7. Willi Schuh, "Unvollendete Spätwerke von Richard Strauss," *Schweizerische Musikzeitung,* XC (1950), 399–400; see also Asow, pp. 1481–82. At some point before writing his article, Schuh had seen a complete version (draft?) of *Malven* in a sketchbook; this version is apparently now owned by Maria Jeritza-Seery. Repeated attempts by the editors of Asow III to obtain information about the song from her met with no success. In a letter of 6 March 1976 addressed to me, Miss Jeritza's lawyers stated that she does indeed own a copy of *Malven,* but is unable to give out any information about it because of copyright uncertainties and claims to ownership by Boosey & Hawkes which are currently being questioned. In 1971 the composer's daughter-in-law, Alice Strauss, told me that Jeritza claimed to have an unpublished Hesse song. (Jefferson, *Lieder,* p. 112, footnote, reports that Jeritza announced this to the press in 1968.) In a letter of 19 March 1949 the singer thanked Strauss for the gift of two lieder manuscripts he had sent her, unfortunately without mentioning their titles. One song is certainly *September* (with a text by Hesse), which Strauss dedicated to Jeritza and her husband. The other is probably *Malven* (text by Betty Knobel). It is doubtful that Jeritza would also have a setting of Hesse's *Nacht,* since there is no evidence that Strauss went beyond the first fifteen measures sketched in book 141. No other Hesse fragments are known to be among the sketches (but see *Höhe des Sommers* in Appendix B). Jeritza's letter is in Grasberger, *Briefe,* p. 469.

8. They are all too late to be included in *Lebenschronik,* which ends with 1898. In this volume, Schuh gives dates of some of the sketches for completed songs (especially on pp. 465–66), but does not discuss any incomplete sketches, sources for the sketches, or Strauss's working method.

9. Strauss/Eltern, p. 279. A footnote by the editor (Schuh) indicates that only *Gefunden* was completed. He does not refer here to the two other songs, which are among those listed in his *Goethe-Vertonungen,* pp. 27 and 42. (*Goethe-Vertonungen* dates from 1952, Strauss/Eltern from 1954.)

10. It is possible that Strauss decided that a group of six songs would be the best number to publish. The majority of his opus groups contain either four, five, or six songs: there are five, ten, and six groups of each type, respectively; only three groups each with two and three songs; two groups with eight; and one with twelve. Perhaps he or his publishers were sometimes influenced by the eighteenth-century practice of issuing six numbers in an opus. One is reminded of the ninth Gilm song which was left out of op. 10, perhaps by the publisher for the sake of balancing the two *Hefte.*

11. According to a notice in the *Vossische Zeitung* (Berlin), no. 308 (12 August 1904), as mentioned in Asow, p. 1230.

12. In a letter of 6 April 1976, Trenner informed me that Mrs. Ursula Fürstner had recently given most of her firm's Strauss manuscripts to the Bayerische Staatsbibliothek, with a few to the Munich Städtische Musikbibliothek. The exact disposition of these manuscripts should be made known in the forthcoming *Straussiana in Münchner und Wiener Bibliotheken,* the third (1979) volume in the series *Veröffentlichungen der Richard-Strauss-Gesellschaft München.*

13. In his afterword to *Richard Strauss. Wer hat's gethan (H. v. Gilm). Erstausgabe des Liedes mit vollständigem Faksimile . . .* (Tutzing, 1974), pp. 14–15. (Strauss's title includes the question mark, which I have retained in my references; the modern edition does not use it.) Unlike any of its companions in op. 10, *Wer hat's gethan?*

has a change of key signature after the text concludes [three of the songs have changes during the declamation of the text] and a long postlude of nineteen measures, or nearly one third the length of the entire song. The C-major postlude, growing out of a modulation from C minor in the final line of text, develops its own independent character and motives in a manner not encountered again in Strauss's lieder until much later (e.g., in *Die heiligen drei Könige aus Morgenland* or in several songs of *Krämerspiegel*).

14. On a visit to Scientific Library Service, I was told that Maria Jeritza had once submitted for appraisal an autograph copy of one of the tone poems dating from this period (possibly *Tod und Verklärung*) and was disappointed to learn that its value was nowhere equal to that of an original manuscript dating from the time of composition. On the other hand, in 1975, Hans Schneider's *Katalog Nr. 194. Richard Strauss,* p. 14, offered for sale four pages of the original autograph score of *Don Juan* for approximately $7,000; two pages of the score copied by Strauss in 1944 were priced at nearly $4,000.

15. The copy is now in the library of the Paris Opéra. (I am grateful to Professor Edward Kravitt for this recent information.)

16. The earlier date seems more likely to me, although Schuh, *Lebenschronik,* p. 34, suggests (without citing evidence) that some of them disappeared during World War II. Even if they did survive that long; there is no new mention of them in the Strauss literature during the decades between the wars; if they survived, they remained in private collections.

17. See Steinitzer's chapter 31, "Ungedruckte Jugendwerke," especially pp. 177–81. In subsequent editions of the book (1914, [1919], and 1927), Steinitzer moved this material to the end, as part of his index of compositions. He did not indicate any change in the existence or whereabouts of the manuscripts.

18. Johannes Oertel, for example, refers to copyists' versions for the use of the engraver in "Richard Strauss und der Verl[a]g Joh. Oertel, Berlin (früher Adolph Fürstner)," *Musikhandel,* I (1949), 34.

19. This manuscript survives as Frankfurt am Main, Stadt- und Universitätsbibliothek, Manskopfisches Museum, Mus. HS 1075.

20. "Richard Strauss und Anton Kippenberg. Briefwechsel," *Richard Strauss Jahrbuch 1959/60* (Bonn, 1960), p. 139. Strauss also wrote a short piece for unaccompanied bass voice (AV 126) expressing gratitude to Kippenberg (ibid., p. 132).

21. *Richard Strauss/Stefan Zweig. Briefwechsel,* edited by Willi Schuh (Frankfurt, 1957), p. 42. The text, in translation, reads "Yes, that I found you, you dear child, makes me glad all my days."

22. Grasberger, *Briefe,* p. 434. The text of the excerpt translates "Yes, you know it, dear soul . . . give thanks!"

23. Asow, p. 1642, indicates that the latter version did not actually appear until 1900, although both score and reduction bear the copyright date 1899.

24. The undated manuscript, now in the Carl Haverlin/BMI Archives of Broadcast Music Inc., New York, bears Schumann-Heink's annotation "written for me, when I sang it at the Berlin Royal Opera in 1902—he wanted me to sing it. . . ." I have not found any announcement or review of a performance by her. The song is not mentioned in her [auto]biography *Schumann-Heink, the Last of the Titans,* as told to Mary Lawton (New York, 1928). The manuscript, not known to the editors of GL or Asow, is mentioned in Harold C. Schonberg, "A Fantastic Collection of Americana," *The New York Times,* 4 May 1975, sec. D, p. 17. It is further described in my article "Ein ungewöhnliches Strauss-Autograph im New Yorker Rundfunk-Musik-Archiv/An Unusual Strauss Manuscript in the BMI Archives, New York," *RSB,* no. 12, pp. 24–26.

25. Strauss/Schuh, p. 14 (12 June 1936), and *Richard Strauss/Ernst von Schuch und Dresdens Oper,* edited by Friedrich von Schuch, second edition (Leipzig, 1953), p. 139 (12 October 1946).

26. I visited the Strauss Archive in 1971. The invitation for an afternoon's "Besichti-

gungsbesuch" was upon arrival extended to another day for examining sketches and manuscripts. Some of the orchestral songs which I asked for were said by Frau Dr. Alice Strauss to be unavailable, although listed in Asow and GL as at the Archive. Had they been in either the house or the local bank, I believe I would have been able to see them because she was very willing to fill my other requests for items in both places.

27. See "Strauss Society issues first report," *Musical America,* LXXIII (1953), 27, and appeals in early numbers of the IRSGM.

28. During my 1971 visit, I was able to examine only cursorily the Strausses' card files of correspondence, diary entries, manuscripts et al. I did not see the diaries themselves, also in the Archive, which would have been particularly interesting. A few writers such as Schuh have referred to Strauss's extensive diaries, in which he noted titles of the compositions he was working on and quoted from his correspondence. To my knowledge, the only excerpts from these diaries to have appeared in print are those from his winter 1892 trip to Greece and Egypt (which contain references to the composition of *Guntram*) and short passages in Schuh's *Lebenschronik.* The 1892 diary entries appear in the *Richard Strauss Jahrbuch 1954* (Bonn, 1953), pp. 89–96. The Richard-Strauss-Gesellschaft München intends to make available its editions of Strauss's diaries beginning in 1984.

29. Considering that several decades of engraving are represented, the variety is not surprising. The format of op. 22, the first group of songs published by Fürstner, is most obviously different from the others. Most of the engraving (including that of op. 22) was originally done by the Leipzig firm of C. G. Röder, which also did much of the design and lithography for the original covers.

30. Opp. 17 and 27 (both in GL I) are particularly difficult to read. Two of the composer's most popular lied groups, they and op. 10 (which fares somewhat better in GL I) are the most frequently reprinted.

31. Norman Del Mar, "Confusion and Error (II)," *The Score,* no. 22 (February 1958), p. 40.

32. Punctuation and the spelling of words such as "Wirthe"/ "Wirte" also vary between editions, but these discrepancies are not necessarily attributable to Strauss. The early setting, once numbered by Strauss op. 1, no. 2, was erroneously indexed in the first volume of Asow (p. 6), where the reason for its inclusion in *Die Musik* is given: *Einkehr* was at the time thought by some to be the earliest of Strauss's lieder. It is actually predated by *Weihnachtslied* (AV 2), from the previous Christmas, and may also have followed after at least three or four other songs the boy sketched during 1871. (See n. 35 below.)

33. A facsimile of the letter appears in Strauss/Thuille, p. 71, with transcription on p. 180. *Waldesgesang* is printed in GL III, 269, and NL, p. 70.

34. Steinitzer, *Richard Strauss* (1911), p. 180.

35. Steinitzer does not mention that Strauss's first song, *Weihnachtslied,* was printed for the first time in the Christmas 1898 supplement of the *Berliner Lokalanzeiger.* It appeared again in *Die Woche,* III (1901), a fact of which Steinitzer was aware. See his *Richard Strauss* (1911), p. 177, and plate 6 of the picture supplement, which is one of several facsimiles of the original manuscript available today.

36. One might argue that in the new version he took away one means of emphasis, that of delaying the high a^2 of "heilig" in a syncopated figure.

37. DM III, 264–65, makes the matter of the added text seem more problematic than it really is. The singer merely needs to omit the notes in measures 28–29; the orchestral music here is basically unchanged from the piano version. Some singers have chosen not to use the expanded version of the vocal line at all, keeping instead to the original rhythms (which are also those of Robert Heger's earlier orchestration).

38. No sketches for these orchestrations are listed in GL, Asow, or elsewhere in the Strauss literature. In the card file at the Strauss Archive, however, sketches of these five songs are listed together as belonging to the Archive. Although the card file gives no details of format, date, extent of sketch, or whether for piano or orchestra,

it seems that these might be orchestral sketches. The five songs were originally composed at different times, but orchestrated together between 15 June and 1 July 1918. I have been unable to obtain copies of these sketches.

39. These annotations are taken from the Strauss Archive card file. At the time of my visit, the diary entries covered only the years 1896 to 1901.

CHAPTER V

1. The orchestras required for these songs are no less large than those of Strauss's 1897 and 1900 orchestrations, but none of them calls for an orchestra as large as those required for the tone poems or for *Salome* and *Elektra*. Strauss did not go so far as Schoenberg or Stravinsky in writing for smaller chamber ensembles instead of full orchestra in the post-war years.

2. She gave op. 68 in the opening concert accompanied by her husband, Karl Alwin, and was highly acclaimed. See Roland Tenschert, "Richard Strauss und die Salzburger Festspiele," *Richard Strauss Jahrbuch 1954* (Bonn, 1953), p. 152, for the summary of a local review of the songs.

3. Jefferson, *Lieder,* p. 19, indicates that they did perform op. 68 on this tour, while DM III, 378, claims "It is not even sure that Elisabeth Schumann herself ever performed them; she certainly never sang them all." Michael Kennedy, in his *Richard Strauss* (London, 1976), p. 215, echoes Del Mar's statement. Jefferson is not always the most reliable source: for example, he claims that op. 68 was dedicated to Schumann (*The Life of Richard Strauss* [Newton Abbot, Devon, 1973], p. 164). It was indeed written for her voice, but never actually dedicated to her in manuscript or in print. I have located a reference to only one song from op. 68 (no. 2, *Ich wollt ein Sträusslein binden*) in programs, announcements, and reviews of her many American lieder recitals. Although I do not yet have documentary evidence that other songs in op. 68 were performed in the U. S., it does seem likely. Op. 69, nos. 1, 3, and 5, were in her tour repertoire. Antoine Goléa, *Richard Strauss* (Paris, [1965]), p. 206, mentions having heard Schumann and Strauss perform songs from both groups at about this time.

4. DM III, 358. Several other authors relate the story of the Bote & Bock problems and the creation of op. 66. In few of them has it been suggested that the return of Strauss's interest in the lied at this period is attributable solely to the publisher's demands.

5. Many biographers and cataloguers err in giving dates for opp. 66–69. The incorrect Asow dates for opp. 66, 68, and 69 (pp. 723, 734, and 739, respectively) are rectified on pp. 1645–46. Jefferson (*Life,* p. 164) states that these groups were written in numerical order; DM III, 366, is slightly more accurate in claiming that "many" of the songs in op. 68 were created before op. 66 was complete.

6. Jefferson, *Life,* p. 164, refers to the Ophelia songs as "very short and spiky" and the Goethe settings as "very depressing," while DM III, 366, calls the first three "mad" and the others "bad-tempered." Ernst Krause (*Richard Strauss. The Man and His Work,* p. 59) considers them "uncomfortable, spiky, and as short as possible." Robert Craft, in his " 'Elektra' and Richard Strauss," p. 32, goes so far as to suggest that in op. 66 the "split" emotions might be symptomatic of an actual breakdown on the part of the composer. Craft refers here to the opposition of the composer as artist and publisher as shopkeeper. One wonders what Craft's judgment on the texts chosen for op. 67 would be! (On the Ophelia songs, also see p. 45 of the present study.)

7. In op. 67 Strauss writes floridly only at the end of the sixth song. In contrast to the melismas which he usually used to highlight works such as "Blümlein," "lächelt," or "Elysium," the words emphasized here are " . . . und trockenen *Kot,* lass sie *drehn* und *stäuben.*" (The italicized words are given melismas; the passage translates " . . . and dry *dirt,* let them *whirl about* and *create dust.*")

8. Craft, " 'Elektra' and Richard Strauss," p. 32, criticizes Dietrich Fischer-Dieskau for having included op. 66 in his multi-volume recording of 131 (correctly 134) Strauss songs, finding the musical quotes "embarrassing." In the baritone's defense, it must be stated that he was one of the first two artists to record this cycle (both in 1964), thus making available to the public a work unlikely to be heard in performance. These songs can be quite effective in live performance if the singer is at ease and does not distract (or is not distracted) during the long piano solo sections, and if the audience is alerted to the story behind the satirical text and its references. The songs cannot be listened to, however, as an ordinary cycle of lieder, for that they are not. A recent New York performance meeting the above-mentioned requirements was that of Janet Steele and Fritz Jahoda in Carnegie Recital Hall on 19 November 1974.

9. Translation in the preface to the 1959 Boosey & Hawkes edition of op. 66. The anonymous author continues with his own judgment that it is "indeed music which belongs to the most attractive and harmonically most interesting among all his vocal works. The words are a mere pretext. . . ."

10. DM III, 367, in a typical and somewhat contemptuous judgment, declares that ". . . Strauss was nothing if not fluent and moreover, as we know from the operas, madness and the grotesque never failed to stimulate his imagination."

11. My no. 39 is the same as AV sketchbook 41, the Strauss Archive's no. 41, and Trenner's no. 41 in *Die Skizzenbücher von Richard Strauss,* pp. 57–58. On the film this book is not numbered, but falls in sequence as no. 39. The outside cover, in black oilcloth, has only the identification "Skizzen" stamped in gold. The inside cover is blank except for the title "Lieder." The outside cover was not filmed, nor was a blank section toward the end of the book. The fifty-three filmed openings include one hundred pages of sketches.

12. Here my no. 42 is the same as AV sketchbook 42, the Strauss Archive's no. 42 and Trenner's no. 42 (p. 58). On the film it is not assigned a number. The black oilcloth cover is again stamped "Skizzen." The size and format are similar to those of no. 39. Of the original 64 pages, only 44 are filled (and filmed) here.

13. Jefferson, *Life,* p. 162, and references in Strauss's correspondence of the period. An avid reader, the composer often referred to what he was reading at the moment, requested books from friends in the publishing business, and maintained a large library, including many works with inscriptions from their authors.

14. *Ich wollt ein Sträusslein binden* had been set at least twice before 1918. Louise Reichardt's setting dates from before 1815; it was published in Erk's *Deutscher Lied-erschatz,* II (Leipzig, [187–]). Strauss's boyhood friend Thuille set the poem as no. 3 of his Brentano lieder, op. 24. Although Strauss is known to have owned some of Thuille's youthful manuscripts, he may not have known of this setting (which was published in 1902) or have remembered the work of his late friend at this time. New settings of *Als mir dein Lied erklang* and *Säusle, liebe Myrte* were later created by Hermann Reutter and Arnim Knab, respectively.

15. On *Abendständchen,* see p. 97.

16. Jefferson, *Strauss* (1975), pp. 86–87, refers to Strauss's "note-spinning" as composing under pressure rather than from inspiration. On p. 42 of this book, Jefferson attributes the phrase "note-spinning" to Pauline, who reputedly used it in reference to Strauss's periods of "automatic" composition or scoring.

17. Such re-use of a lied melody—aside from undeveloped quotations as in *Ein Heldenleben*—is unique in Strauss's works. Franz Strauss, the composer's son, claims to have encouraged his father to re-use the melody in *Capriccio;* see Grasberger, "Hüter der Tradition," p. 23.

18. Here and in the examples all measures are counted as in the final version. Where it is necessary to refer to partial measures (i.e., the 2/4 measures of the sketch), the sketch measures are identified with a and b (and c for m. 18). Other meter changes between the sketch and final version can be found in op. 67, nos. 2 and 5, and in numerous passages of *Intermezzo.* In sketchbook 41 (opening 23), op. 67, no. 2, is written in 3/4, while the final version is in 3/8. In book 18 (openings 3^r–4^r), op. 67,

no. 5, has several measures that are not in agreement with the alternating 3/4 and 4/4 meter of the final version (see Ex. 19b).

19. Missing from *Amor* in sketchbook 39 are these measures (numbers after the decimal point refer to beats within the 3/4 measure): 12.1–13.3, 16.3–17.2, 36.2–38.1, 49.2–50.3, 66.1–3.

20. Strauss's incomplete sketch for *In tausend Formen* (see Appendix B) is a good example of this: on opening 3^r he marked off ten measures over which he wrote the text of stanza 5 but did not fill in either vocal line or accompaniment. Another example is his sketch for *Einerlei* (op. 69, no. 3); in sketchbook 17 (opening 15^v) there is no vocal line for the text of measures 46–57. The vocal melody is, however, written in for sections both before and after this passage.

21. After opening 53, where the Bayerische Staatsbibliothek film ends, sketchbook 39 contains several more blank pages and then six pages filled with only a few scattered chords and melodies which I have been unable to connect with any completed composition.

22. *Richard Strauss/Clemens Krauss. Briefwechsel,* selected and edited by Götz Klaus Kende and Willi Schuh, second edition (Munich, 1964), p. 148 (letter of 29 June 1940).

23. Ibid., p. 28 (letter of 10 September 1933).

24. Ibid., p. 27 (letter of 9 September 1933). The other two songs are obviously not included because Strauss had not yet orchestrated them.

25. Ibid., p. 152 (letter of 29 July 1940).

26. The copyright date of 1941 can be more precisely limited to early in the year by two of Strauss's letters to Rose Pauly, which are included in Alfred Frankenstein, "Richard Strauss und die Sängerin," IRSGM, no. 20 (February 1959), pp. 6 and 7.

27. Strauss/Krauss, p. 172. Although I have not yet found evidence of a performance by the Krausses, they may well have given some or all of the songs since both performed frequently at this period. A letter of Krauss's to the composer on 2 March 1942 indicates their intention to perform op. 68 with orchestra at the Berliner Kunstwoche in June 1942 (Strauss/Krauss, p. 230).

CHAPTER VI

1. "Er ist kein Liednatur" is quoted in reference to Strauss by Oscar Bie, *Das deutsche Lied* (Berlin, 1926), p. 257, and by other writers in reference to Strauss, Max Reger, and other composers.

2. Bie uses the terms "Vorklang" and "Nachklang" for the childhood songs and for those written after 1918, respectively, in his "Richard Strauss' Lieder," *Blätter der Staatsoper, Berlin,* VII/4(1926), 15, and in *Das deutsche Lied,* p. 258.

3. An eccentric article by Frank Merry, "The Publishing Problem: What Shall We Do After the War," is said to have been printed in a London journal *Music* for October [1917]; it accused Strauss of writing and publishing his songs in England under several English names "as familiar as Thomson or Baker." Merry also suspected that other German composers were posing as Russians or Norwegians in order to get their works published by English publishers with connections abroad. Reference to this article and a partial quotation of it (with a suggestion of doubt concerning its accuracy) appear in "Is Strauss Camouflaging under English Name?" *The Musical Leader,* XXXIV (1917), 508. I have been unable to locate a London periodical called merely *Music* for that year, nor have I seen other references to such activities (which seem highly unlikely on Strauss's part).

4. Six other songs written during this period stand outside the mainstream of Strauss's lieder. They include *Wer hat's gethan?* (originally intended as op. 10, no. 6); two that appeared in periodicals (1896 and 1899); the two written for Calderón's play (1904); and a final example for textless voice and piano (1906). These are listed in Asow as AV 84A, 90, 94, 96 (nos. I and II), and 102, respectively. To these should be added several of the sketches in Appendix B of the present study.

5. These are Kravitt's "The Late Romantic Lied" and the article drawn from his dissertation, "The Lied in 19th-Century Concert Life," *Journal of the American Musicological Society,* XVIII (1965), 207–18.

6. Ernst Roth, *The Business of Music,* pp. 182–83. Roth gives this goal as her reason for retiring from singing some ten years after her marriage. Other writers also (including Strauss himself) cite this as the explanation for her retirement; as suggested here, other factors were probably also responsible.

7. Johanna von Rauchenberger-Strauss, "Jugenderinnerungen," p. 17. A letter from Richard to his father that is printed here mentions one of Aunt Johanna's concerts on the previous Tuesday at which he, his sister, and four Pschorr cousins all sang and played. The compositions included a folksong, duets by one "M. B.," piano works of Mendelssohn and Weber, and Strauss's own *Hochzeitsmusik für Klavier und Kinderinstrumente* (AV 163) for cuckoo, quail, cymbals, triangle, etc. The original letter is dated only "July 31"; the editor's suggestion of 1878 as the year should be changed to 1879. See Strauss/Thuille, p. 184 (letter of 22 July 1879); the cousin's wedding for which this work was intended took place on 11 August 1879. There are no known documents to confirm its performance on that occasion.

8. Concerning these songs, see Strauss/Thuille, p. 180 (letter of 8 May 1879), and Chapter IV, p. 106, of the present study.

9. Strauss can be heard as a piano soloist on the following recordings, most of which were made from player-piano rolls: Columbia ML 4295, "Great Masters of the Keyboard," vol. 5 (from an original roll of 1906); Telefunken HT-18, "The Definitive Piano: Famous Composers Play Their Own Music"; and Telefunken HT-38, "Great Pianists of the 19th and 20th Centuries." The works represented are *Salome* (excerpts, including Salome's Dance); *Ein Heldenleben* (love scene); from the *Stimmungsbilder,* op. 9, nos. 3 *(Intermezzo)* and 4 *(Reverie);* and the song *Heimliche Aufforderung* (op. 27, no. 3). The original rolls also included the love scene from *Feuersnot* and op. 9, no. 2 *(An einsamer Quelle),* excerpts which have not been reissued. For recordings of Strauss as an accompanist, see pp. 157 ff. in this chapter, and Chapter I, p. 13.

10. Strauss, BuE, p. 203.

11. Finck, *Richard Strauss,* p. 290, et al. Erhardt *(Richard Strauss,* p. 177) describes this as one of Strauss's "orchestrally conceived" songs; the composer, however, never orchestrated it.

12. "Strauss in West Virginia," *Musical Courier,* XLVIII/12 (23 March 1904), 31.

13. Strauss/Eltern, p. 52 (letter of 18 March 1884). He asked specifically for three of his early songs (composed in 1880–81) and his sister's *Sturm.* His request for such early works supports the evidence of the dated manuscripts that op. 10 was not composed until 1885. If op. 10 had been written as early as 1882–83, as many writers have assumed, Strauss might not have bothered with these early songs.

14. Ibid., p. 72 (letter of 12 December 1885). He does not mention the names of the songs, which are probably from op. 10. (The last of its songs was written on 13 November 1885.)

15. Ibid., p. 88 (letter of 24 February 1886). The songs, he says, were *Begegnung* (from 1880) and *Rosenzeichen.* This choice would seem to contradict evidence for the 1885 date of op. 10, particularly since its eight songs were written for the tenor voice. But Strauss's letters to his parents and to Eugen Spitzweg in January and February 1886 show that the songs may have been in the press at that time and thus would have been unavailable. (No manuscript other than the *Stichvorlage* is known to have existed.) *Rosenzeichen* is identified by Willi Schuh as one of the two songs to which Strauss refers in his letter of 12 November 1885 (Strauss/Eltern, p. 70, footnote). Here Strauss states that he has just completed two songs; when editing Strauss/Eltern, Schuh was not aware of the precise dates in the manuscript for op. 10 and on the basis of the other letter suggested one song as *Rosenzeichen.* As a result of his footnote, the Asow listing for *Rosenzeichen* (AV 180) includes quotations from this letter (p. 1352) and refers to Strauss/Eltern, p. 70. It is now clear

that the songs were from op. 10, probably nos. 6 and 7 (*Die Verschwiegenen* and *Die Zeitlose*), which were composed on 11 and 12 November, respectively. Strauss himself made no other reference to a song called *Rosenzeichen;* it is my opinion that there was none. He may have been referring to *Der Dorn ist Zeichen der Verneinung* (a lost song written in 1884), *Die erwachte Rose* (1880), or *Rote Rosen* (1883).

16. Ibid., pp. 116, 117, and 118–19 (three separate letters). Strauss does not indicate whether or not he played the piano for the songs. That he did is quite likely, since it was his practice to accompany lieder that were given during orchestral concerts at which he conducted. His own song, if not the others, must have been sung with piano rather than orchestral accompaniment.

17. Kravitt, "The Late Romantic Lied," p. 9. Discussing typical nineteenth-century concert programs on pp. 2–13, he delineates three periods with regard to content of the programs: before 1830 (lieder rarely found on orchestral concerts, but arias frequently encountered), 1830–75 (lieder appear with increasing frequency as arias disappear), and after 1875 (lieder given in orchestral concerts as well as in recitals of instrumental chamber music). Much of the same discussion appears in the article mentioned above in n. 5.

18. Julius Stockhausen had given complete performances of Schubert's *Die schöne Müllerin* in 1860 and 1862; the critics looked on these concerts as experimental. The Viennese singer Gustav Walter and the concert manager Albert Gutmann were largely responsible for the blossoming of Viennese lieder recitals, when Walter began his annual evenings in 1876. In 1879 he increased the number to three each year, in 1884 to four. In addition to lieder, chamber music was performed at these evenings.

19. Albert Gutmann, *Aus dem Wiener Musikleben,* p. 99.

20. Berlin, Deutsche Staatsbibliothek, Mus. ms. autogr. Richard Strauss 3. The song, *Für funfzehn Pfennige* (op. 36, no. 2) is a setting of a humorous poem from *Des Knaben Wunderhorn.* (In folk dialect, "funfzehn" lacks its usual umlaut.) Several other amusing comments appear in the score, e.g., "Oktaven zwischen Melodie und Bass!! Oh!!!"

21. Roland Tenschert, *Richard Strauss und Wien. Eine Wahlverwandtschaft* (Vienna, 1949), p. 124.

22. Strauss/Eltern, p. 220 (27 January 1899); pp. 237–38 (24 November 1900).

23. Ibid., p. 235. This letter (dated 14 October 1901) contains another reference to Giessen's second recital. Strauss dedicated three of the songs in his op. 36 (nos. 2–4) to Walter.

24. Ibid., pp. 249, 250 (7 and 29 November 1901).

25. *Richard Strauss und Franz Wüllner im Briefwechsel,* edited by Dietrich Kämper (Cologne, 1963), p. 54. Ludwig Wüllner had established his fame as an actor before devoting himself to lieder ca. 1897. He sang in the premiere of *Feuersnot* shortly before the tour and was known as the best interpreter of Strauss's Dehmel settings *Der Arbeitsmann* and *Lied an meinen Sohn* (op. 39, nos. 3 and 5).

26. According to a report from Berlin in the *Monthly Musical Record,* XXXIII (1906), 96.

27. On a recital tour in Spain, she did sing two Wagner excerpts, Elisabeth's *Gebet* and Isolde's *Liebestod,* for three concerts in Madrid. See Strauss/Eltern, pp. 208–09 (letter of 24 February 1898). For another exception to her custom of singing only Strauss's music, see n. 29 below. In the *Revue de Paris* for 15 June 1899, Romain Rolland wrote of Pauline as a faithful wife "who has since her marriage devoted herself to the interpretation of her husband's *Lieder.*" This article appears in English translation in *Richard Strauss and Romain Rolland. Correspondence . . . Fragments from the Diary . . . Essays,* edited and annotated by Rollo Myers (Berkeley, 1968), pp. 184–85.

28. For most of Strauss's orchestral lieder, versions with piano accompaniments were published along with the original orchestral score and parts. Piano reductions of op.

33 were prepared by Hermann Bischoff (nos. 1 and 2) and Otto Singer (3 and 4). Bischoff, a pupil of the composer, later wrote a monograph *Das deutsche Lied* (Berlin, 1905) for a series *Die Musik,* of which Strauss was editor. Singer (1863–1931) prepared many piano reductions of Strauss's operas, songs, and orchestral works.

29. The listing in Asow (p. 1376) for the *Ganymed* orchestration attributes it to Strauss. This information is provided by Schuh, who in his *Lebenschronik* (p. 467) still credits Strauss with the work. In the Asow corrections (p. 1660), however, it is stated on the evidence of the manuscript (now owned by Franz Trenner), that Strauss's manuscript score is merely his own copy of an orchestration by the French composer H. A. J.-B. Chélard (1789–1861), who was active in both Munich and Weimar before Strauss's birth.

30. The first reference I have seen to the orchestration of *Ich liebe dich* is in Schuh's *Lebenschronik,* p. 467. It should not be confused with the 1943 orchestration of Strauss's song by the same title (op. 37, no. 2).

31. This program is reproduced in Franz Grasberger, *Kostbarkeiten der Musik. Erster Band: Das Lied. Mozart. Beethoven. Schubert. Brahms. Schumann. Wolf. Strauss* (Tutzing, 1968), p. 193.

32. Strauss/Eltern, p. 242 (letter of 17 March 1901). Strauss does not state whether the accompaniments for the Mahler songs were for piano or orchestra. A year before, Strauss had conducted a program at the Wagnerverein in Berlin, at which a Frau Herzog (Emilie?) sang three Mahler songs (see Strauss/Eltern, p. 233). These are the only two references I have found to his performance of Mahler's songs. A champion of Mahler, Strauss conducted his first four symphonies. Mahler in turn directed performances of *Feuersnot* (in 1902) and several of the tone poems.

33. Strauss/Wüllner, p. vii (see also pp. 49 and 50). As well as being the father of the lieder singer Ludwig, Franz Wüllner was important to Strauss because he conducted the premieres of *Till Eulenspiegel, Don Quixote,* and *Der Abend* (no. 1 of op. 34, *Zwei Gesänge für 16stimmigen gemischten Chor a cappella*).

34. Grasberger, *Briefe,* p. 118.

35. Ibid., pp. 333 and 375–76. At a dinner party in Paris in 1930, Maria Ivogün sang Zerbinetta's aria from *Ariadne auf Naxos.* (She had sung the role for many of Strauss's performances of the 1916 version of the opera.) Some of his lieder were sung at a party for fifty people given by "the richest man in Antwerp" in 1936. Other references to informal evenings of music from 1885 to 1900 can be found in Strauss/Eltern, pp. 72, 88, 117, 200, 216–17, and 220.

36. *Richard Strauss. Dokumente seines Lebens und Schaffens,* edited by Franz Trenner (Munich, 1954), p. 53. Strauss names these songs frequently in his references to Pauline's performances. Only *Morgen!* was orchestrated.

37. Willi Schuh and others use the term "Drei Mutterlieder." Richard Specht, in his *Richard Strauss und sein Werk* (Leipzig, 1921), II, 21, calls them "Privatlieder" or "lyrica domestica."

38. The diary entries are unpublished. Whether or not the three songs were sung together as a unit is unclear; the annotation for *Meinem Kinde* gives the date 9 July 1900, those for the other two, 8 July.

39. Strauss/Eltern, p. 236 (see also p. 238, reporting on a rehearsal for one of the concerts).

40. Asow and GL are both inconsistent about reporting copyright dates. In many cases (as here), their dates do not seem to be those of the earliest edition. The earliest editions of the orchestrations I have located are as follows: *Wiegenlied* (Leuckart, 1901, a further aid to the dating), *Meine Kinde* and *Muttertändelei* (Universal and Challier, respectively, 1911).

41. Several letters in Strauss/Eltern, pp. 236–41.

42. Hanslick's criticisms are quoted in Tenschert, *Strauss und Wien,* p. 23; in this review he made his much repeated reference to Pauline as Strauss's "better half." The other

favorable reviews were of the premiere performance of Strauss's Violin Concerto, op. 8 (given in its version for violin and piano by Strauss and Benno Walter on 12 December 1882) and of the Strausses' *Liederabend* in the Bösendorfer Saal on 31 January 1902; see Tenschert, pp. 9–10 and 33.

43. Strauss/Eltern, p. 241, footnote.
44. His *Taillefer*, op. 52 (an Uhland ballad for chorus, soloists, and orchestra written in 1902–03), was dedicated to the Faculty of Philosophy at the University. It received its premiere under Strauss at the same Heidelberg festival.
45. Evidence of this performance is provided by Heinrich Bihrle, editor, *Die musikalische Akademie, München, 1811–1911. Festschrift zur Feier des hundertjährigen Bestehens* (Munich, 1911), p. 152.
46. They include Hermann Gura, Ernst Kraus, Lillian Nordica, Anton van Rooy, Marcella Sembrich, and others.
47. *Musical Courier*, XLVIII/11 (16 March 1904), 24, and XLVIII/12 (23 March 1904), 31.
48. Karl Wolff, " 'Macbeth' von Richard Strauss," *Neue Musik-Zeitung (Stuttgart)*, XXI (1901), 45.
49. *Musical Courier*, XLVIII/10 (9 March 1904), 26. Several of the other critics who expressed similar opinions are quoted in Robert Breuer, "Richard Strauss in Amerika. Teil I: 1904," RSB, no. 8 (December 1976), pp. 1–17 (see especially pp. 13, 15, and 17).
50. Similar statements are made in Jefferson, *Lieder*, p. 17; in Thomas, *Richard Strauss*, p. 26; and elsewhere.
51. Specht, *Richard Strauss*, II, 21.
52. Reinhold Muschler, *Richard Strauss* (Hildesheim, [1925]), p. 339.
53. DM III, 314.
54. Elena Gerhardt, "Strauss and his Lieder. A Personal Reminiscence," *Tempo*, no. 12 (summer 1949), p. 10.
55. Ibid.
56. Jefferson, *Life*, p. 178.
57. Alexander Dillmann, "Sinfonia Domestica," in *Richard Strauss und seine Vaterstadt*, edited by Egid Gehring (Munich, 1934), p. 50. Dillmann's comments were originally recorded in his diary on 26 February 1911, on a day when Pauline had sung some lieder at a private gathering in a friend's home.
58. Roth, *Musik als Kunst und Ware*, p. 192; see Chapter IV, n. 1.
59. See Jefferson, *Life*, p. 98.
60. "Richard Strauss Matinee," *The Musical Leader*, VII/10 (10 March 1904), 5.
61. "The Strauss Orchestral Concerts," *The Musical Leader*, VII/10 (10 March 1904), 3.
62. "The Strauss Concerts," *The Musical Leader*, VII/10 (10 March 1904), 13.
63. "The Strauss-Bispham Concert," *The Musical Leader*, VII/14 (7 April 1904), 11.
64. The single most repeated incident about Pauline's temper is probably that of the *Guntram* rehearsal in 1894 during which Strauss kept stopping to correct and help the tenor Heinrich Zeller. Feeling neglected because he did not stop her, Pauline eventually threw her score at the conductor. While the orchestra feared for his safety, Strauss proceeded to her dressing room at the end of the rehearsal to ask her to marry him. Strauss himself tells of this scene in BuE, p. 221 (in "Erinnerungen an die ersten Aufführungen meiner Opern," AV 376 [1942]). Other versions can be found in Asow, pp. 143–44, DM I, 93–94, Kennedy, *Richard Strauss*, pp. 26–27, etc.
65. "Strauss the Composer Here," *The New York Times*, 25 February 1904, p. 9.
66. Alfred Orel, "Richard Strauss als Begleiter seiner Lieder," *Schweizerische Musikzeitung*, XCII (1952), 13. Orel's account of his experience as Strauss's page turner is retold in Trenner, *Dokumente*, pp. 82–83.
67. Ibid. DM III, 353, claims (without documentation) that Strauss used the *Rosenkavalier* duet theme in a similar function during a recital with Pauline. This is unlikely, since she did not perform in public after the completion of the opera.

68. The use of this theme is reported in two reviews of the Town Hall Recital by Schumann and Strauss on 15 December 1921: *Musical Courier*, LXXXII/25 (22 December 1921), 27; and *Musical America*, XXXV/9 (24 December 1921), 9.
69. Goléa, *Richard Strauss*, p. 206.
70. Richard Aldrich, "Dr. Strauss Plays Chamber Music," *The New York Times*, 19 November 1921, p. 11; and "Dr. Strauss Accompanies His Own Songs," *The New York Times*, 16 December 1921, p. 24.
71. Owen, "Elisabeth Schumann," p. 226.
72. Rococo 5217, a reissue of the ca. 1921–22 recordings, includes *Zueignung, Die Nacht, Heimkehr, Das Geheimnis, Ruhe, meine Seele!*, and *Ich liebe dich* by Schlusnus, with *Breit über mein Haupt* and *Morgen!* by Hutt. Rococo 5350 contains six songs each by Reining (*Zueignung, Cäcilie, Meinem Kinde, Freundliche Vision*, and *Waldseligkeit*) and Piltti (*Heimkehr, Ständchen, All mein Gedanken, Schlagende Herzen, Ich schwebe*, and *Kling!*), with eight by Dermota (*Zueignung, Die Nacht, Seitdem dein Aug', Breit über mein Haupt, Du meines Herzens Krönelein, Heimliche Aufforderung, Ich trage meine Minne*, and *Glückes genug*). Recordings supposedly made by Strauss and Elisabeth Schumann during their U. S. tour were never issued; whether or not they survive in an archive today is not known. For a brief review of the circumstances of these recordings, see Morse and Norton-Welsh's discography in *RSB*, no. 5, p. 84. The recordings made by Richard Tauber and once thought to have been accompanied by Strauss are now known not to be the composer's; see Robert Jones, "The Authenticity of the Alleged Strauss-Accompanied Tauber Records," *The Record Collector*, XIX (1970), 76–81.
73. *Ruhe, meine Seele!* would be a suitable companion for the *Four Last Songs* in both its text and its accompaniment; see Chapter VII, p. 178.
74. The orchestral version of *Cäcilie* is shortened by one measure; Strauss may have felt its original ending lacking in interest. One is tempted to ask how much singers' stage behavior influenced Strauss in his playing of the songs. According to Lotte Lehmann, Pauline's actions were designed to obscure the postlude or coda and to begin the applause immediately after the last word was sung. (See Lotte Lehmann, *Five Operas and Richard Strauss*, translated by Ernst Pawel [New York, 1964], p. 31, as well as Jefferson, *Lieder*, p. 17). Most of the songs that were in Pauline's repertoire end with a postlude of two to six measures. There is no evidence that she ever sang *Die heiligen drei Könige aus Morgenland* (op. 56, no. 6), of which the instrumental ending takes up thirty of the song's ninety-seven measures.
75. DM III, 271.
76. In the following songs, Strauss's tempo is approximately that of the other performers': *Die Nacht, Ständchen, Das Geheimnis, Cäcilie, Morgen!, Ich liebe dich, Ich schwebe, Kling!*, and *Waldseligkeit*. (E.g., in his tempos *Die Nacht* is approximately ♩ = 50 and ♩ = 60; other versions with piano accompaniment are ♩ = 48, 53, and 54).

CHAPTER VII

1. Kravitt, "The Late Romantic Lied," p. 103.
2. Ernst Challier, Sr., "Die Wirkung des Urheberrechts vom 19. Juni 1901. Ein statistische Skizze," *Die Musik*, IV (1905), 404.
3. Specht, *Richard Strauss*, II, 25. Matters have changed somewhat with the availability of almost every published song in recordings and of studies of the lieder such as those by Jefferson and Del Mar.
4. Newman, *Richard Strauss*, p. 99.
5. Ibid., p. 90.
6. Ibid. Elsewhere, Newman cites examples of these categories. For instance, these songs are "dull": *All mein Gedanken, Du meines Herzens Krönelein, Muttertändelei, Des Dichters Abendgang, Einkehr, Wer lieben will muss leiden*, and *Mit deinen blauen*

Augen (p. 99). The "pretentiously empty" songs include *Mein Auge, Auf ein Kind,* and *Frühlingsfeier* (p. 95).

7. Ibid.; the three statements are discussed on pp. 97, 90, and 100–01, respectively.
8. Finck, *Richard Strauss,* pp. 284 and 287.
9. Ibid., pp. 285–86. Richard Batka, Rudolf Louis, Leopold Schmidt, and Arthur Seidl were among those to credit Strauss with too much because he chose to set contemporary verses; the use of new poetry did not always guarantee a new musical style (as Louis tries to argue), nor was Strauss alone in setting the works of Dehmel, Gilm, Henckell, Liliencron, Schack, and other living writers.
10. Arthur Elson, *Modern Composers of Europe* (Boston, 1905), p. 25.
11. Newman, *Musical Studies* (London, 1905), p. 257.
12. E. A. Baughan, "The Bristol Festival," *Monthly Musical Record,* XXXV (1905), 204.
13. "In the Concert Room," *Monthly Musical Record,* XXXV (1905), 77.
14. "Dr. Richard Strauss to be in Boston," *The Musical Leader,* VII/9 (3 March 1904), 9.
15. Frederic S. Law, "Richard Strauss," *The Musician,* IX (1904), 48.
16. Richard Saville, "Songs of the Twentieth Century: II. Richard Strauss," *The Musician,* X (1905), 19. The first part of this article, also devoted to Strauss, appeared in *The Musician,* IX (1904), 430–31; the third part concerned the songs of the English composer Cyril Scott.
17. Mrs. Olin S. Johnson, "Richard Strauss," *The Musician,* IX (1904), 53.
18. This song was published by Fürstner along with the others in op. 31, also in 1896. The footnote appears in subsequent editions as well as in *Jugend;* see GL I, 166. In *Jugend* the song was in D-flat (ending in D) major. Strauss's *Die Frauen sind oft fromm und still* (op. 21, no. 5) also ends out of the original key, but without a change of key signature, which there is in *Wenn.* The original G-major version of *Die Frauen* ends on the first inversion of an A major triad.
19. Rudolf Louis, *Die deutsche Musik der Gegenwart* (Munich, 1909), p. 222.
20. See Chapter III, pp. 72 ff., and Steinitzer, *Richard Strauss* (1911), p. 159, for further discussion of the text setting and Strauss's dissatisfaction with it.
21. Theodor Schäfer, *Also sprach Richard Strauss zu mir. Aus dem Tagebuch eines Musikers und Schriftstellers* (Dortmund, [1924]), p. 109.
22. DM III, 271.
23. James Husst Hall, *The Art Song* (Norman, Oklahoma, 1953), p. 129.
24. Radcliffe, "Germany and Austria," p. 260. Although a predominantly lyrical song, *Ständchen* does have a few declamatory passages. Elena Gerhardt suggested that sudden changes to recitative-like lines in both Strauss's songs and his operas emphasize all the more the surrounding melodic richness ("Strauss and his Lieder," p. 10).
25. J. A. Fuller-Maitland, "Strauss, Richard," *Grove's Dictionary of Music and Musicians,* second edition (London, 1908), IV, 719.
26. James Huneker, *Overtones. A Book of Temperaments* (New York, 1904), p. 30.
27. Gerhardt, "Strauss and his Lieder," p. 10.
28. Elisabeth Schumann, "Richard Strauss. Morgen. A Master Lesson by Elisabeth Schumann," *Etude,* February 1951, pp. 26 and 56. (The music, with German and English text, appears on pp. 38–39 of this issue.) Schumann's recording of *Morgen!* (Seraphim set IC-6041), although made twenty-four years before the article was printed, exquisitely illustrates all of her points.
29. "In the Concert Room," *Monthly Musical Record,* XXXI (1901), 276.
30. "Letter from Leipzig," *Monthly Musical Record,* XXXI (1901), 56; the review of Wüllner's recital appears on p. 32 of the same volume.
31. Eugen Segnitz, "Kritik. Lieder und Gesänge von Richard Strauss," *Musikalisches Wochenblatt,* XXXII (1901), 647.
32. Ibid., 648.
33. Strauss's letter of 18 November 1944 to Tenschert is transcribed in IRSGM, no. 24 (March 1960), pp. [6]–7 under the title "Richard Strauss schüttet sein Herz aus." The variety in Strauss's lieder was recognized during his lifetime by Gysi and others as

well as by Segnitz. More recently, it has been acknowledged by writers such as Del Mar, Erhardt, Jefferson, and Krause.

34. Newman, *Richard Strauss* (p. 91), includes these songs in this group: *Wozu noch, mädchen; Ach, weh mir unglückhaftem Mann; Für funfzehn Pfennige; Herr Lenz; Wiegenlied; Von den sieben Zechbrüdern; Junggesellenschwur;* and *Ach, was Kummer, Qual und Schmerzen.*

35. J. M. P. Steinhauer, "Zwei grössere Gesänge . . . von Richard Strauss," *Neue Musik-Zeitung (Stuttgart)*, XXI (1900), 163 (a review of the first performance at the Aachen Festival of 1900, a premiere not noted by Asow).

36. Alfred Kalisch, "Strauss, Richard," *Grove's Dictionary of Music and Musicians*, third edition (London, 1927), V, 165. The main body of Kalisch's article remains unchanged in the fourth edition of *Grove's.*

37. Ibid.

38. Erich Urban, "Richard Strauss in neuen Liedern," *Die Musik*, I (1902), 2140.

39. "Richard Strauss Appears," *The New York Times*, 28 February 1904, p. 7 (unsigned review of his first American concert in Carnegie Hall on 27 February 1904).

40. Arthur Smolian, "Kritik: Konzerte. Berlin," *Die Musik*, V (1906), 13 (Tenth Philharmonic Concert of the Winderstein Orchestra).

41. Bernhard Schuster, "Kritik. Konzerte. Berlin," *Die Musik*, I (1902), 632.

42. Strauss/Rolland, p. 19 (letter of 1 June 1901). Published in 1900 and 1901, these songs were written in May–June 1900 (op. 47), and September–October 1900 (op. 48).

43. As an example of the latter, Hermann Bischoff, *Das deutsche Lied* (Berlin, 1905), p. 93, claims that Schumann and his entire circle of successors never had the slightest influence on Strauss.

44. Strauss's comment to Thuille, in Strauss/Thuille, p. 174, was made in a letter of 28 October 1878, just after he had first heard *Die Walküre* and had begun to study the score of *Siegfried.*

45. Louis, *Die deutsche Musik*, p. 223.

46. "Hamlin and Strauss," *The Musical Leader*, VII/9 (3 March 1904), 10.

47. Richard Aldrich, "Richard Strauss the Composer. Some Facts About the Famous Musician Who Is Coming to New York This Week," *The New York Times*, 21 February 1904, sec. III, p. 5.

48. "Kleine Mitteilungen von hier und dort," *Signale für die musikalische Welt*, LXXVI (1918), 546–47.

49. Florence Ffrench Lester, "Here and There," *The Musical Leader*, XLII (1921), 590.

50. Tenschert (quoting an unidentified critic of a Salzburg newspaper), "Richard Strauss und die Salzburger Festspiele," p. 152.

51. "Strauss' New 'Hymns' True to His Genius," *Musical Courier*, LXXXII/26 (29 December 1921), 13.

52. Ernst Rychnovsky, "Richard Strauss. Gesänge des Orients, op. 77," *Die Musik*, XXIV (1932), 383.

53. Curtin's recording, with the Boston Symphony Orchestra under Erich Leinsdorf, was a private pressing of concert excerpts from 29 August 1964. Fischer-Dieskau's recording with Gerald Moore forms part of his nine-record set *Richard Strauss: Das Liedschaffen* (Electrola C 163-50043/51).

54. Richard Aldrich, "Richard Strauss's Sixtieth Birthday," *The New York Times*, 20 July 1924, sec. VII, p. 5.

55. Grasberger, *Kostbarkeiten*, p. 192.

56. Henrietta Straus, "Fifteen Minutes with Richard Strauss," *The Nation*, 3 August 1921, p. 127. Strauss claimed that the reporter's inaccuracy resulted from her imperfect knowledge of German and that when agreeing to speak with her he had stated that he must not be quoted. He did not consider their meeting an official "interview." Subsequent letters to the editor and articles in *The New York Times* and other journals continued in the weeks before Strauss's arrival in the U. S.

57. Richard Aldrich, "The Return of Richard Strauss," *The New York Times*, 29 May 1921, sec. VI, p. 3.

58. Owen, "Elisabeth Schumann," p. 226. There is other evidence that Strauss was fond of Schubert's lieder at this time. Elena Gerhardt reports that Strauss once asked her to do a group of Schubert songs (instead of giving an all-Strauss program) on a recital they were to give together in Manchester. Of the eight Schubert works she remarked "And how beautifully he played them, with all the tenderness and devotion he has for the old masters." (Gerhardt, "Strauss and his Lieder," p. 9.)

59. At least sixteen of the same songs were performed on both tours. As a sampling of Strauss's lieder appearing on other New York concerts (none of which he accompanied) for the week of 31 October 1921, his first week in the U. S., the *New York Tribune's* "Programs of the Week" lists at least nine of the same songs that were sung by Schumann or other artists with the composer during the following two months. A Richard Strauss evening was given by Leon Rains at the New York Institute of Musical Art in November 1921; the composer apparently did not attend. The program is described in Dorothy J. Teal, "Rains' Strauss Program," *Musical America*, XXXV (1921), 21. It included the well known *Der Arbeitsmann* and *Das Lied des Steinklopfers* as well as two lieder from op. 56, *Im Spätboot* and *Mit deinen blauen Augen. Im Spätboot*, which was encored, was thought to be new to American audiences.

60. J. P. Nolan, "Richard Strauss: Giant of Modern Music," *Musical America*, XXXV (1921), 3. The reference here is unclear; it may mean the five songs orchestrated for Schumann in 1918 (see Table 3) or op. 71, a group definitely not performed on this tour. It is almost certainly not a reference to op. 68, which was not orchestrated until much later.

61. *Musical America*, XXXV (1921), 48 (signed merely "J. A. H.").

62. "Strauss Closes Second Tour Here . . . Faces $8,000 Income Tax. Conductor's Earnings Put at $50,000 . . . ," *The New York Times*, 2 January 1922, p. 17.

63. Strauss intended for most of the works written after *Capriccio* to form his *Nachlass* and to be published posthumously without opus numbers. He assigned no title or order to this group of four songs and left no written instructions concerning their publication, either separately or together. The order of their appearance in print—*Frühling, September, Beim Schlafengehn, Im Abendrot*—was determined by Ernst Roth, the dedicatee of *Im Abendrot* (for which he prepared the piano reduction himself). As the director of publications for Boosey & Hawkes, Roth oversaw their production and release. Although sung in a different order at their premiere, they are usually performed and recorded today in the order cited above, which is certainly a logical one in relation to their texts. In GL, however, both piano and orchestral versions are printed in the order in which the compositions were completed.

64. Yet another intended lied composition (from slightly before these others) is suggested by the presence of Brentano's *Wiegenlied* on the back covers of two sketchbooks otherwise devoted to instrumental works and dating from ca. 1944–46; see Appendix B.

65. Willi Schuh, "Die vier letzten Lieder von Richard Strauss," *Schweizerische Musikzeitung*, XC (1950), 302, n. 1 (including a list of titles and page locations of these poems in *Die Gedichte*, second edition; one of these is *Höhe des Sommers*).

66. For example, Hans F. Redlich, "Aus dem Nachlass von Richard Strauss," *Das Musikleben*, III (1950), 226.

67. "New Music Listing," *Monthly Musical Record*, LXXX (1950), 162.

68. A description of the music performed at Strauss's funeral is provided in Strauss/ Schuch, pp. 147–48. The *Rosenkavalier* trio was sung by the singers in the new Munich production mounted for Strauss's eighty-fifth birthday.

69. IRSGM, no. 17 (May 1958), p. 212.

70. Alan Frank, "Strauss's Last Songs," *Music and Letters*, XXXI (1950), 305. Frank's criticism may result from his having heard (or imagined) a particularly slow performance of the group: he gives the duration as twenty-nine minutes. The score indicates a total duration of twenty-two minutes; most recordings keep within nineteen to twenty-three minutes. I have not been able to hear the recording made by Flagstad at the dress rehearsal of the premiere, but on the basis of her recording of *September*

(made in 1951 with piano accompaniment) doubt that it could have been her performance that lasted twenty-nine minutes. No other reviewers comment on this point or criticize the songs for their sameness or slow pace.

71. Mosco Carner, "Strauss's 'Vier letzte Lieder,'" *Monthly Musical Record,* LXXX (1950), 173.
72. Ibid., p. 177.
73. Otto Erhardt, "The Later Operatic Works of Richard Strauss," *Tempo,* no. 12 (summer 1949), p. 30.
74. Boosey & Hawkes is not among the publishers named in op. 66, since Strauss did not have any dealings with that firm until the 1940's. As an example of the changed attitudes toward the songs, Asow reports that when seven of the twelve songs were broadcast over the Berlin radio network on Strauss's eighty-fifth birthday, the publishers Lienau and Reinecke complained that the songs in which they were mentioned had been omitted (Asow, p. 725)!
75. IRSGM, no. 39 (December 1963), p. 22.
76. Kennedy, *Richard Strauss,* p. 208.

SELECTED BIBLIOGRAPHY

Abell, Arthur M. *Talks with Great Composers.* New York, 1955.

Aldrich, Richard. "The Return of Richard Strauss." *The New York Times,* 29 May 1921, sec. VI, p. 3.

————. "Richard Strauss's Sixtieth Birthday." *The New York Times,* 20 July 1924, sec. VII, p. 5.

————. "Richard Strauss the Composer. Some Facts About the Famous Musician Who Is Coming to New York This Week." *The New York Times,* 21 February 1904, sec. III, p. 5.

Asow, E. H. Mueller von. *Richard Strauss. Thematisches Verzeichnis. Nach dem Tode des Verfassers vollendet und herausgegeben von Alfons Ott und Franz Trenner.* 3 vols. Vienna, 1955–74.

————. "Zu Richard Strauss's unveröffentlichtem Opus 81." *Wiener Figaro,* XXVIII/2 (June 1960), 7–8.

Batka, Richard. *Richard Strauss.* Berlin-Charlottenburg, 1908.

Baum, Günther. "Hugo Wolf und Richard Strauss in ihren Liedern." *Neue Zeitschrift für Musik,* CXXX (1969), 575–79.

Baum, Richard, and Wolfgang Rehm, editors. *Musik und Verlag. Karl Vötterle zum 65. Geburtstag am 12. April 1968.* Kassel, 1968.

Berg, Alban. *Letters to His Wife.* Edited, translated, and annotated by Bernard Grun. New York, 1971.

Bie, Oscar. *Das deutsche Lied.* Berlin, 1926.

————. *Die moderne Musik und Richard Strauss.* Berlin, [1906].

————. "Richard Strauss' Lieder." *Blätter der Staatsoper, Berlin,* VII/4 (1926), 15–17.

Bihrle, Heinrich, editor. *Die musikalische Akademie, München, 1811–1911. Festschrift zur Feier des hundertjährigen Bestehens.* Munich, 1911.

Bischoff, Hermann. *Das deutsche Lied.* Die Musik, 16–17. Berlin, 1905.

Blom, Eric. "Strauss, Richard." *The International Cyclopedia of Music and Musicians.* Edited by Oscar Thompson. Sixth, revised edition. New York, 1952.

Bock, Gustav. "Richard Strauss und der Verlag Ed. Bote & G. Bock, Berlin." *Musikhandel,* I (1949), 35–36.

Böhm, Karl. *Begegnung mit Richard Strauss.* Introduction by Franz Eugen Dostal. Vienna, 1964.

Bollert, Werner. "Bermerkungen zu Richard Strauss Opus 68 und 69," *Internationale Richard-Strauss-Gesellschaft. Mitteilungen,* no. 57/59 (December 1968), pp. 9–11.

Brecher, Gustav. *Richard Strauss. Eine monographische Skizze.* Leipzig, [1900].

Breuer, Robert. "Drei 'neue' Lieder von Richard Strauss." *Schweizerische Musikzeitung,* XCIX (1959), 10–15.

————. "Richard Strauss in Amerika. Teil I: 1904." *Richard Strauss-Blätter,* no. 8 (December 1976), pp. 1–17.

————. "The Richard Strauss Villa at Garmisch—A National Shrine." *Musical America,* LXXVI (1956), 31 and 211.

Brody, Elaine, and Robert A. Fowkes. *The German Lied and Its Poetry.* New York, 1971.

Brosche, Günter, editor. *Richard-Strauss-Bibliographie, Teil 2. 1944–1964.* Vienna, 1973. (See Ortner for *Teil 1.*)

Cardus, Neville. *Talking of Music.* New York, 1957.

Carner, Mosco. "Strauss's Vier letzte Lieder." *Monthly Musical Record,* LXXX (1950), 172–77.

Castelnuovo-Tedesco, Mario. "Music and Poetry: Problems of a Song-Writer." *The Musical Quarterly,* XXX (1944), 102–11.

Chadwick, Nicholas. "Berg's Unpublished Songs in the Österreichische Nationalbibliothek." *Music and Letters,* LII (1971), 123–40.

Craft, Robert. " 'Elektra' and Richard Strauss." *The New York Review of Books,* XXIII/10 (10 June 1976), 30–32.

D., M. "Les lieder de Richard Strauss." *S. I. M. Revue musicale,* VII (1911), 85.

Dehmel, Richard. "Offenherzige Erklärung." *Die Musik,* I/15–16 (May 1902), 1461–62.

Del Mar, Norman. "Confusion and Error (II)." *The Score,* no. 22 (February 1958), pp. 28–40.

———. *Richard Strauss. A Critical Commentary on His Life and Works.* 3 vols. London, 1962–72.

Deppisch, Walter. *Richard Strauss in Selbstzeugnissen und Bilddokumenten.* Reinbek bei Hamburg, 1968.

Dillmann, Alexander. "Sinfonia Domestica." *Richard Strauss und seine Vaterstadt.* Edited by Egid Gehring. Munich, 1934. pp. 49–52.

Domin, Brigitte. *Richard Strauss in Würdigung seines 100. Geburtstages am 11. Juni 1964. Eine Auswahl aus den Beständen der Stadtbibliothek Koblenz, Musikbücherei.* Edited by Hildegard Trapp. Koblenz, 1964.

Elson, Arthur. *Modern Composers of Europe.* Boston, 1905.

Erhardt, Otto. "The Later Operatic Works of Richard Strauss." *Tempo,* no. 12 (summer 1949), pp. 23–31.

———. *Richard Strauss. Leben, Wirken, Schaffen.* Olten and Freiburg im Breisgau, 1953.

Ernst Challier's grosser Lieder-Katalog. Giessen, 1885; supplements, 1888–1914.

Ewing, Douglas C., Otto E. Albrecht, and Herbert Cahoon, compilers. *The Mary Flagler Cary Music Collection.* New York, 1970.

Federhofer, Hellmut. "Die musikalische Gestaltung des Krämerspiegels von Richard Strauss." *Musik und Verlag. Karl Vötterle zum 65. Geburtstag am 12. April 1968.* Edited by Richard Baum and Wolfgang Rehm. Kassel, 1968. pp. 260–67.

Finck, Henry T. *Richard Strauss. The Man and His Work.* Boston, 1917.

———. *Songs and Song Writers.* New York, 1905.

———. *Success in Music and How It Is Won.* New York, 1909.

Frank, Alan. "Strauss's Last Songs." *Music and Letters,* XXXI (1950), 305–06.

Freyhold, Edmund von. "Die Technik der musikalischen Deklamation." *Die Musik,* IV (1905), 3–16, 115–34, and 147–64.

Fuller-Maitland, J. A. "Strauss, Richard." *Grove's Dictionary of Music and Musicians.* Second edition. London, 1908. IV, 717–20.

Fürstner, Ursula. "Richard Strauss und der Fürstner-Verlag." *Internationale Richard-Strauss-Gesellschaft. Mitteilungen,* no. 50 (September 1966), pp. 9–10.

Gavoty, Bernard. *Walter Gieseking.* Geneva, 1955.

Gehring, Egid, editor. *Richard Strauss und seine Vaterstadt.* Munich, 1934.

Gerhardt, Elena. *My Favorite German Songs.* Boston, 1915.

———. "Strauss and his Lieder. A Personal Reminiscence." *Tempo,* no. 12 (summer 1949), pp. 9–11.

Gieseking, Walter. *Ausgewählte Lieder. Richard Strauss. Freie Bearbeitungen für Klavier von Walter Gieseking.* Berlin, 1923.

———. *So würde ich Pianist.* Wiesbaden, 1963.

Goléa, Antoine. *Richard Strauss.* Paris, [1965].

Goodwin, N. "A Composer's Farewell." *Music and Musicians,* XII/6 (1964), 21.

Grasberger, Franz. *Die Handschriften der Meister. Berühmte Werke der Tonkunst im Autograph . . . Catalogue.* Vienna, [1966].

———. "Hüter der Tradition." *Festschrift Dr. Franz Strauss zum 70. Geburtstag.* Edited by Hans Schneider. Tutzing, 1967. pp. 17–23.

———. *Kostbarkeiten der Musik. Erster Band: Das Lied. Mozart. Beethoven. Schubert. Brahms. Schumann. Wolf. Strauss.* Tutzing, 1968.

———. *Richard Strauss. Hohe Kunst. Erfülltes Leben.* Vienna, 1965.

———, and Franz Hadamowsky. *"Göttlich ist und ewig der Geist." Richard-Strauss-Ausstellung zum 100. Geburtstag. . . .* Vienna, 1964.

———, in collaboration with Franz and Alice Strauss. *"Der Strom der Töne trug mich fort." Die Welt um Richard Strauss in Briefen.* Tutzing, 1967.

Gregor, Joseph. *Richard Strauss. Der Meister der Oper. Mit Briefen des Komponisten und 28 Bildern.* Munich, 1939.

Gudewill, Kurt. "Das Kunstlied im deutschen Sprachgebiet." Section A of the article "Lied," *Die Musik in Geschichte und Gegenwart.* Kassel, 1949–. VIII, cols. 746–75.

Gura, Eugen. *Erinnerungen aus meinem Leben.* Leipzig, 1905.

Gutmann, Albert. *Aus dem Wiener Musikleben. Künstler-Erinnerungen 1873–1908.* Vienna, 1914.

Gysi, Fritz. *Richard Strauss.* Potsdam, 1934.

Hall, James Husst. *The Art Song.* Norman, Oklahoma, 1953.

Hallmark, Rufus Eugene, Jr. "The Genesis of *Dichterliebe:* A Source Study." Ph.D. dissertation, Princeton University, 1975.

Hamburger, Paul. "Strauss the Song Writer." *Music and Musicians,* XII/10 (1964), 14 and 35.

Herrmann, Joachim. "Das letzte Lied von Richard Strauss. Eichendorffs 'Im Abendrot.' " *Aurora. Eichendorff-Almanach,* XIX (1959), 79–80.

———. "Mit Eichendorff beschloss Richard Strauss sein Schaffen. . . ." *Schlesien,* IX (1964), 107–08.

Hoffmann, Baptist. *Ein Leben für die Kunst.* Edited by G. Hoffmann-Küsel. Berlin, 1949.

Holde, Artur. "Unbekannte Briefe und Lieder von Richard Strauss." *Internationale Richard-Strauss-Gesellschaft. Mitteilungen,* no. 19 (November 1958), pp. 2–6, and no. 20 (February 1959), pp. 8–15.

Huder, Walter. "Alfred Kerr und Richard Strauss." *Internationale Richard-Strauss-Gesellschaft. Mitteilungen,* no. 48 (March 1966), pp. 18–20.

Huneker, James. *Mezzotints in Modern Music.* Third edition. New York, 1905.

———. *Overtones. A Book of Temperaments.* New York, 1904.

———, [compiler and editor]. *Richard Strauss. Forty Songs.* Boston, 1910.

Hutchins, Arthur. "Strauss's Four Last Songs." *Musical Times,* XCI (1950), 465–68.

Internationale Richard-Strauss-Gesellschaft. Mitteilungen. Nos. 1–62/63 (October 1952–December 1969).

"Is Strauss Camouflaging under English Name?" *The Musical Leader,* XXXIV (1917), 508.

Jefferson, Alan. *The Lieder of Richard Strauss.* London, 1971.

———. *The Life of Richard Strauss.* Newton Abbot, Devon, 1973.

———. *Richard Strauss.* London, 1975.

Jones, Robert. "The Authenticity of the Alleged Strauss-Accompanied Tauber Records." *The Record Collector,* XIX (1970), 76–81.

Kalisch, Alfred. "Strauss, Richard." *Grove's Dictionary of Music and Musicians.* Third edition. London, 1927. V, 160–68.

Kelletat, Alfred, and Maria Kohler. "Bibliographie der Vertonungen von Dichtungen Hölderlins." *Hölderlin-Jahrbuch,* VII (1953), 119–35.

Kennedy, Michael. *Richard Strauss.* London, 1976.

Kerr, Alfred. "Richard Strauss, menschlich." *Die neue Weltbühne,* XXXIV (1938), 263–67.

Krause, Ernst. *Richard Strauss. Gestalt und Werk.* Fifth edition. Leipzig, 1975.

———. *Richard Strauss. The Man and His Work.* Translated by John Coombs from the third edition of *Richard Strauss. Gestalt und Werk* (Leipzig, 1955). London, 1964.

Kravitt, Edward F. "The Ballad as Conceived by Germanic Composers of the Late Romantic Period." *Studies in Romanticism,* XII (1973), 499–515.

———. "The Late Romantic Lied. Performance, the Literary Approach, and the Naturalistic Movement." Ph.D. dissertation, New York University, 1960.

————. "The Lied in 19th-Century Concert Life." *Journal of the American Musicological Society*, XVIII (1965), 207–18.

Kreinitz, Willy. "Richard Strauss in Münchner Konzertleben." *Richard Strauss und seine Vaterstadt.* Edited by Egid Gehring. Munich, 1934. pp. 27–34.

"Krise der Internationalen Richard-Strauss-Gesellschaft?" *Musica*, VII (1953), 280–81.

Kusche, Ludwig. *Richard Strauss im Kulturkarussell der Zeit 1864–1964.* Munich, 1964.

Langer, Susanne. *The Problems of Art.* New York, 1957.

Lehmann, Lotte. *Five Operas and Richard Strauss.* Translated by Ernst Pawel. New York, 1964.

————. *My Many Lives.* Translated by Frances Holden. New York, 1948.

Leider, Frida. *Playing My Part.* Translated by Charles Osborne. New York, 1966.

Lindner, Adalbert. *Max Reger. Ein Bild seines Jugendlebens und künstlerischen Werdens.* Third edition. Stuttgart, 1938.

Louis, Rudolf. *Die deutsche Musik der Gegenwart.* Munich, 1909.

Mann, William. *Richard Strauss. A Critical Study of the Operas.* London, 1964.

Marek, George R. *Richard Strauss. The Life of a Non-Hero.* New York, 1967.

Marschalk, Max. "Richard Strauss über das Lied." *Oesterreichische Musikzeitung*, XVI (1961), 220. (Reprinted from Max Marschalk. "Gespräche mit Richard Strauss." *Vossische Zeitung*, 15 October 1918.)

Mathis, Alfred. "Elisabeth Schumann." *Opera*, XXIV (1973), 672–80, 783–93, and 968–79, and XXV (1974), 22–28.

Mauke, Wilhelm. "Liliencron als Befruchter der musikalischen Lyrik." Statistics compiled by George Brandes. *Die Musik*, III (1904), 438.

————. "[Richard Strauss.] Vier Gesänge für 1 Singstimme mit Orchester, op. 33. Erläutert von Wilhelm Mauke." *Der Musikführer*, no. 187. Leipzig, 1903.

————. "[Richard Strauss.] Zwei Gesänge, op. 34. Erläutert von Wilhelm Mauke." *Der Musikführer*, no. 188. Leipzig, [1903].

Mercier, Adalbert. "Richard Strauss et ses nouveaux lieder." *Revue d'histoire et de critique musicale*, IV (1904), 418–21.

Merry, Frank. "The Publishing Problem: What Shall We do After the War?" *Music*, October 1917.

Monthly Musical Record. XXX–XXXVI (1900–06).

Morse, Peter, and Christopher Norton-Welsh. "Die Lieder von Richard Strauss—Eine Diskographie/The Songs of Richard Strauss—A Discography." *Richard Strauss-Blätter*, no. 5 (August 1974), pp. 81–123.

Moser, Hans Joachim. *Das deutsche Lied seit Mozart.* Second, revised edition. Tutzing, 1968.

————. *Das deutsche Sololied und die Ballade.* Das Musikwerk, XIV. Cologne, 1959.

————. "Gesangskunst." *Die Musik in Geschichte und Gegenwart.* Kassel, 1949–. IV, cols. 1899–1908.

————. *Richard Strauss. Leben und Werk.* Krakow, 1944.

Müller, Günther. *Geschichte des deutschen Liedes vom Zeitalter des Barock bis zur Gegenwart.* Munich, 1925; reprint Darmstadt, 1959.

Müngersdorf, Theodor. "Richard Strauss als Vokalkomponist, I." *Die Stimme. Centralblatt für Stimm- und Tonbildung*, XVIII (1924), 125–26.

Muschler, Reinhold. *Richard Strauss.* Hildesheim, [1925].

Music and Musicians. Strauss Centenary Number. XII/10 (June 1964).

Musical America. XXXIV–XXXV (1921–22).

Musical Courier, The. XLVIII (1904) and LXXXII–LXXXIII (1921–22).

Musical Leader, The. VII–VIII (1904), XXXI (1916), XXXIV (1917), and LXI–LXIII (1921–22).

Musician, The. IX (1904).

Musik, Die. I–VI (1900–06).

Musik, Die. Richard-Strauss-Heft, IV/8 (January 1905).

Musik, Die. Richard-Strauss-Heft Nr. 2, XIII (June 1914).

Musik, Die. Edited by Richard Strauss, Arthur Seidl, et al. Vols. 1–32. Berlin, 1904–09.

Mutzenbecher, Hans-Esdras. "Marginalien um Richard Strauss/Marginal Jottings on Richard Strauss." *Richard Strauss-Blätter*, no. 8 (December 1976), pp. 18–21.

Neue Meister-Lieder. Sammlung berühmter Lieder der Neuzeit. New edition. Leipzig, [ca. 1894].

Neue Musik-Zeitung (Stuttgart). XXI–XXII (1900–02).

New York Times, The. 1899–1906 and 1911–25.

Newman, Ernest. *Musical Studies.* London, 1905. Second edition, London, 1910.

———. *Richard Strauss.* With a Personal Note by Alfred Kalisch. London, 1908.

———. "The Songs of Max Reger." *The Musician,* X (1905), 454–55.

Oertel, Johannes. "Richard Strauss und der Verl[a]g Joh. Oertel, Berlin (früher Adolph Fürstner)." *Musikhandel,* I (1949), 34–36.

Oesterreichische Musikzeitschrift. "Salzburg und Richard Strauss." XIX/8 (August 1964).

Orel, Alfred. "Richard Strauss als Begleiter seiner Lieder." *Schweizerische Musikzeitung,* XCII (1952), 12–13.

Ortner, Oswald. *Richard-Strauss-Bibliographie, Teil 1. Aus dem Nachlass herausgegeben von Franz Grasberger.* Vienna, 1964. (See Brosche for *Teil 2.*)

Ott, Alfons. "Documenta musicae domesticae Straussiana." *Festschrift Dr. Franz Strauss zum 70. Geburtstag.* Edited by Hans Schneider. Tutzing, 1967. pp. 65–81.

Ott, Alfons. *Richard Strauss—Festjahr München 1964 zum 100. Geburtstag von Richard Strauss.* Munich, 1964.

———. "Richard Strauss und sein Verlegerfreund Eugen Spitzweg." *Musik und Verlag. Karl Vötterle zum 65. Geburtstag am 12 April 1968.* Edited by Richard Baum and Wolfgang Rehm. Kassel, 1968. pp. 466–75.

Owen, H. G. "Elisabeth Schumann." *The Record Collector,* VII (1952), 221–28.

Pamer, Fritz Egon. "Das deutsche Lied im neunzehnten Jahrhundert." *Handbuch der Musikgeschichte.* Edited by Guido Adler. Berlin, 1930. II, 939–55.

Panofsky, Walter. *Richard Strauss. Partitur eines Lebens.* Munich, 1967.

"Persönliche Erinnerungen deutscher Musikverleger." *Musikhandel,* I (1949), 34–36. (Consists of the articles by Bock, Oertel, and Zentner cited here.)

Petersen, Barbara A. "Ein ungewöhnliches Strauss-Autograph in New Yorker Rundfunk-Musik-Archiv/An Unusual Strauss Manuscript in the BMI Archives, New York." German translation by Günter Brosche. *Richard Strauss-Blätter,* nc. 12 (December 1978), 24–26.

———. "Richard Strauss und die Aufführung seiner Lieder/Richard Strauss and the Performance of His Lieder." German translation by Helga Dostal. *Richard Strauss-Blätter,* no. 5 (August 1974), 79–81.

Petzoldt, Richard. *Richard Strauss. Sein Leben in Bildern.* With commentary on the illustrations by Eduard Crass. Leipzig, 1962.

Pfannkuch, Wilhelm. "Strauss, Richard." *Die Musik in Geschichte und Gegenwart.* Kassel, 1949–. XII, cols. 1474–85 and 1495–99. (Biography and bibliography; for works, see under Schuh.)

Pfister, Kurt. *Richard Strauss. Weg, Gestalt, Denkmal.* Vienna, 1949.

R., B. "Richard Strauss' Liederkompositionen." *Neue Musik-Zeitung (Stuttgart),* XXII (1901/02), 157–58, 173–74, and 202–03.

Radcliffe, Philip. "Germany and Austria." *A History of Song.* Edited by Denis Stevens. New York, 1961. pp. 228–264.

Rauchenberger-Strauss, Johanna von. "Jugenderinnerungen." *Richard Strauss Jahrbuch 1959/60.* Bonn, 1960. pp. 7–30.

Redlich, Hans. *Alban Berg. The Man and His Music.* New York, 1957.

———. "Aus dem Nachlass von Richard Strauss." *Das Musikleben,* III (1950), 226.

Reger, Max. *Max Reger. Briefe eines deutschen Meisters.* Edited by Else Hase-Koehler. Leipzig, 1928.

Reger, Max. *Richard Strauss. Ausgewählte Lieder. Piano Solo. (Mit beigefügten deutschen und englischen Text).* English translations by John Bernhoff. 2 vols. Vol. I: Vienna, 1899; reprint Vienna, 1904. Vol. II: Vienna, 1904. (The six works in each volume were also available separately.)

————. *Sämtliche Werke. Unter Mitarbeit des Max-Reger-Institutes. Sologesänge mit Klavier,* XXXI–XXXIV. Edited by Fritz Stein. Wiesbaden, [1955–67].

Richard Strauss-Blätter. Herausgegeben von der Internationalen Richard Strauss-Gesellschaft (Wien). Irregular; nos. 1–12 (June 1971–December 1978).

Richard Strauss Jahrbuch 1954. Edited by Willi Schuh. Bonn, 1953.

Richard Strauss Jahrbuch 1959/60. Edited by Willi Schuh. Bonn, 1960.

Riedel, Horst. "Dem Musikverlag Fürstner zum 100jährigen Bestehen." *Internationale Richard-Strauss-Gesellschaft. Mitteilungen,* no. 56 (October 1968), p. 19.

Rosenfeld, Paul. *Musical Chronicle (1917–1923).* New York, 1923.

Rostand, Claude. *Richard Strauss. L'homme et son oeuvre.* Paris, 1964. (New edition of his *Richard Strauss.* Paris, 1949.)

Roth, Ernst. *The Business of Music. Reflections of a Music Publisher.* London, 1969. (Translation of *Musik als Kunst und Ware. Betrachtungen und Begegnungen eines Musikverlegers.* Second edition. Zurich, 1969.)

————. "Gerechtigkeit für Pauline Strauss." *Internationale Richard-Strauss-Gesellschaft. Mitteilungen,* no. 36 (March 1963), pp. 21–22. (Reprinted from the *Münchner Merkur,* [2/3 February 1963].)

————. *Musik als Kunst und Ware. Betrachtungen und Begegnungen eines Musikverlegers.* First edition. Zurich, 1966. (Some of the anecdotes about Strauss are not repeated from one edition to the other; the second edition and the English translation of it do contain the same material. The English version of the second edition was used in the preparation of this study.)

Rudder, May de. "L'oeuvre lyrique de Richard Strauss." *Le Guide Musical,* LX (1914), 127–38.

Rychnovsky, Ernst. "Richard Strauss. Gesänge des Orients, op. 77." *Die Musik,* XXIV (1932), 383.

[Sabin, Robert.] "Recitals in New York." *Musical America,* LXXVIII (1958), 32.

Samson, Ingrid. "Richard Strauss. 'Ich wollt ein Sträusslein binden.' " *Neue Zeitschrift für Musik,* CXXV (1964), 288. (Notes accompanying the musical supplement, op. 68, no. 2.)

Saville, Richard. "Songs of the Twentieth Century: I. Richard Strauss." *The Musician,* IX (1904), 430–31.

————. "Songs of the Twentieth Century: II. Richard Strauss." *The Musician,* X (1905), 19.

Scanzoni, Signe von. *Richard Strauss und seine Sänger. Eine Plauderei über das Musiktheater in den Wind gesprochen.* Munich, [1961].

————. *"Richard Strauss und seine Zeit." Katalog der Ausstellung München 1964.* Munich, 1964.

Schäfer, Theodor. *Also sprach Richard Strauss zu mir. Aus dem Tagebuch eines Musikers und Schriftstellers.* Dortmund, [1924].

Schmidt, Leopold. *Aus dem Musikleben der Gegenwart. Beiträge zur zeitgenössischen Kunstkritik.* Foreword by Richard Strauss. Berlin, 1909.

————. *Erlebnisse und Betrachtungen. Aus dem Musikleben der Gegenwart.* Berlin, 1913.

————. *Musikleben der Gegenwart.* Berlin, 1922.

Schmieder, Wolfgang. "57 unveröffentlichte Briefe und Karten von Richard Strauss in der Stadt- und Universitätsbibliothek Frankfurt/Main." *Festschrift Helmut Osthoff zum 65. Geburtstage.* Edited by Lothar Hoffmann-Erbrecht and Helmut Hucke. Tutzing, 1961. pp. 163–79.

Schneider, Hans, [editor]. *Festschrift Dr. Franz Strauss zum 70. Geburtstag.* Tutzing, 1967.

————. *Katalog Nr. 194. Richard Strauss. 1. Teil: Manuskripte und Briefe.* Tutzing, 1975.

Schoch, Rudolf. *Hundert Jahre Tonhalle Zürich 1868–1968.* Zurich, 1968.

Schuh, Willi. "Die vier letzten Lieder von Richard Strauss." *Schweizerische Musikzeitung,* XC (1950), 301–04.

————. "Ein vergessenes Goethe-Lied von Richard Strauss." *Schweizerische Musikzeitung,* LXXXIX (1949), 235.

————. *Goethe-Vertonungen. Ein Verzeichnis.* Zurich, 1952.

————. *Hugo von Hofmannsthal. Richard Strauss. Der Rosenkavalier. Fassungen, Filmszenarium, Briefe.* Frankfurt, 1971.

―――. "Pauline Strauss-de Ahna †." *Schweizerische Musikzeitung*, XC (1950), 329.
―――. *Richard Strauss. Jugend und frühe Meisterjahre. Lebenschronik 1864–98.* Zurich, 1976.
Schuh, Willi, editor. *Richard Strauss. Nachlese. Lieder aus der Jugendzeit und Verstreute Lieder aus späteren Jahren.* London, 1968.
―――. "Richard Strauss's *Four Last Songs.*" Translated by Max Loewenthal. *Tempo,* no. 15 (spring 1950), 25–30.
―――. "Strauss, Richard." *Die Musik in Geschichte und Gegenwart.* Kassel, 1949–. XII, cols. 1485–95. (Works; for biography and bibliography, see under Pfannkuch.)
―――. "Unvollendete Spätwerke von Richard Strauss." *Schweizerische Musikzeitung,* XC (1950), 392–402.
―――, and Ernst Roth. *Richard Strauss. Gesamtverzeichnis.* London, 1964.
Schuhmacher, Gerhard. *Geschichte und Möglichkeiten der Vertonung von Dichtungen Friedrich Hölderlins.* Regensburg, 1967.
Schumann, Elisabeth. *German Song.* Translated by D. Millar Craig. New York, 1948.
―――, [compiler]. *Liederbuch/Favorite Songs.* New, revised edition. London, [1952].
―――. "Richard Strauss. Morgen. A Master Lesson by Elisabeth Schumann." *Etude,* February 1951, pp. 26 and 56.
Schumann-Heink, Ernestine. *Schumann-Heink, the Last of the Titans.* As told to Mary Lawton. New York, 1928.
Schweizerische Musikzeitung. Sonderheft Richard Strauss zum 80. Geburtstag. LXXXIV/6 (June 1944).
Segnitz, Eugen. "Kritik. Lieder und Gesänge von Richard Strauss." *Musikalisches Wochenblatt,* XXXII (1901), 647–48.
Seidl, Arthur. *Richard Strauss. Eine Characterskizze.* Prague, 1896.
―――. *Straussiana. Aufsätze zur Richard Strauss-Frage aus drei Jahrzehnten.* Regensburg, [1913].
Spanuth, A. "Richard Straussens 'Krämerspiegel.' " *Signale für die musikalische Welt,* LXXVI (1918), 641–43.
Specht, Richard. *Richard Strauss und sein Werk.* 2 vols. Leipzig, 1921.
―――. *Richard Strauss. Vollständiges Verzeichnis der im Druck erschienenen Werke.* Vienna, 1910.
Stein, Jack M. *Poem and Music in the German Lied from Gluck to Hugo Wolf.* Cambridge, Mass., 1971.
―――. "Was Goethe Wrong about the Nineteenth-Century Lied? An Examination of the Relation of Poem and Music." *Publications of the Modern Language Association,* LXXVII (1962), 232–39.
Steinhauer, J. M. P. "Zwei grössere Gesänge . . . von Richard Strauss." *Neue Musik-Zeitung (Stuttgart),* XXI (1900), 163.
Steinitzer, Max. *Richard Strauss.* Berlin, 1911. (Also consulted were the second through fourth editions of 1914, [1919], and 1927.)
―――. *Richard Strauss in seiner Zeit.* Leipzig, 1914.
―――. *Straussiana und andres. Ein Büchlein musikalische Humors,* . . . . Stuttgart, 1910.
Straube, Karl. "Max Reger." *Die Gesellschaft,* XVIII/1 (1902), 169–81.
Straus, Henrietta. "Fifteen Minutes with Richard Strauss." *The Nation,* 3 August 1921, p. 127.
Strauss, Richard. *Betrachtungen und Erinnerungen.* Edited by Willi Schuh. Second, enlarged edition. Zurich, 1957.
―――. *Briefe an die Eltern 1882–1906.* Edited by Willi Schuh. Zurich, 1954.
―――. *A Confidential Matter. The Letters of Richard Strauss and Stefan Zweig, 1931–1935.* Translated by Max Knight with foreword by Edward E. Lowinsky. Berkeley, 1977.
―――. "Correspondence with Dr. Roth and 1) Richard Strauss." *Tempo,* no. 98 (winter 1972), 9–17.
―――. *Cosima Wagner/Richard Strauss. Ein Briefwechsel. Veröffentlichungen der Richard-Strauss-Gesellschaft München,* 2. Edited by Franz Trenner. Tutzing, 1978.
―――. *Im Abendrot. Particell.* Darmstadt, [1967].

———. *Morgen.* Facsimile edition of the autograph with afterword by Franz Grasberger. Vienna, 1964.

———. *Recollections and Reflections.* Translated by J. L. Lawrence from the first edition of *Betrachtungen und Erinnerungen* (Zurich, 1949). London, 1953.

———. *Richard Strauss and Romain Rolland. Correspondence . . . Fragments from the Diary . . . Essays.* Edited and annotated by Rollo Myers. Berkeley. 1968.

———. *Richard Strauss. Briefwechsel mit Willi Schuh.* Edited by Willi Schuh. Zurich, 1969.

———. *Richard Strauss/Clemens Krauss. Briefwechsel.* Selected and edited by Götz Klaus Kende and Willi Schuh. Second edition. Munich, 1964.

———. *Richard Strauss/Ernst von Schuch und Dresdens Oper.* Edited by Friedrich von Schuch. Second edition. Leipzig, 1953.

———. *Richard Strauss/Hugo von Hofmannsthal. Briefwechsel. Gesamtausgabe.* Edited by Willi Schuh in collaboration with Franz and Alice Strauss. Fourth, enlarged edition. Zurich, 1970. (Some references are to the third, enlarged edition [Zurich, 1964].)

———. "Richard Strauss/Ludwig Karpath. Briefwechsel 1902–1933." Edited by Günter Brosche. *Richard Strauss-Blätter,* no. 6 (December 1975), 2–29; no. 7 (May 1976), 1–18.

———. "Richard Strauss/Roland Tenschert. Briefwechsel 1943–1949." Edited by Günter Brosche. *Richard Strauss-Blätter,* no. 10 (December 1977), 1–10.

———. *Richard Strauss/Stefan Zweig. Briefwechsel.* Edited by Willi Schuh. Frankfurt, 1957.

———. "Richard Strauss und Anton Kippenberg. Briefwechsel." *Richard Strauss Jahrbuch 1959/60.* Bonn, 1960. pp. 114–46.

———. *Richard Strauss und Franz Wüllner im Briefwechsel.* Edited by Dietrich Kämper. Cologne, 1963.

———. *Richard Strauss und Joseph Gregor. Briefwechsel 1934–1949.* Edited by Roland Tenschert. Salzburg, 1955.

———. *Richard Strauss und Ludwig Thuille. Briefe der Freundschaft, 1877–1907.* Edited by Alfons Ott. Munich, 1969.

———. *Wer hat's gethan (H. v. Gilm). Erstausgabe des Liedes mit vollständigem Faksimile. . . .* Afterword by Willi Schuh. Tutzing, 1974.

———. *Wir beide wollen springen. Ein Meisterlied aus der Zeit des Jugendstils. . . .* Edited and with introduction by Alfons Ott. Tutzing, 1968.

———. *A Working Friendship. The Correspondence between Richard Strauss and Hugo von Hofmannsthal.* Edited by Willi Schuh in collaboration with Franz and Alice Strauss. Translated from the second edition (1955) of *Richard Strauss/Hugo von Hofmannsthal. Briefwechsel* by Hanns Hammelmann and Ewald Osers. New York, 1961.

[Strauss, Richard. Unsigned reviews of works by.] [Drei Hymnen] "Strauss' New 'Hymns' True to His Genius." *The Musical Courier,* LXXXII/26 (29 December 1921), 13. [Four Last Songs] *Monthly Musical Record,* LXXX (1950), 162. *Music Review,* XI (1950), 328–29. *Musical Opinion,* LXXI (1951), 281.

"Strauss Society Issues First Report." *Musical America,* LXXIII (1953), 27.

Taubmann, Otto. *25 Lieder von Richard Strauss für Klavier (mit beigefügtem deutsch-englischen Text).* Berlin, 1903.

Tempo. Strauss Centenary Number. no. 69 (summer 1964).

Tenschert, Roland. *3 × 7 Variationen über das Thema, Richard Strauss.* Vienna, 1944.

———. "Freundliche Vision. Betrachtungen zu dem Lied op. 48, Nr. 1 von Richard Strauss." *Allgemeine Musikzeitung,* LXII (1935), 303–05.

———. "Der 'Krämerspiegel' von Richard Strauss." *Oesterreichische Musikzeitschrift,* XVI (1961), 221–23.

Tenschert, Roland. 'Richard Strauss's Schwanengesang." *Oesterreichische Musikzeitschrift,* V (1950), 225–29.

———. *Richard Strauss und Wien. Eine Wahlverwandtschaft.* Vienna, 1949.

———. "Das Sonett in Richard Strauss' Oper 'Capriccio.' Eine Studie zur Beziehung von Versmetrik und musikalischer Phrase." *Schweizerische Musikzeitung,* XCVIII (1958), 1–5.

———. "The Sonnet in Richard Strauss's Opera 'Capriccio.' A Study in the Relation between the Metre and the Musical Phrase." Translated by H. C. Robbins Landon. *Tempo*, no. 47 (spring 1958), pp. 7–11.

————. "Verhältnis von Wort und Ton. Eine Untersuchung an dem Strauss'schen Lied 'Ich trage meine Minne.' " *Zeitschrift für Musik (Regensburg)*, CI (1934), 591–95.

————. "Versuch einer Typologie der Strauss'schen Melodik." *Zeitschrift für Musikwissenschaft*, XVI (1934), 274–93.

Thomas, Walter. *Richard Strauss und seine Zeitgenossen*. Vienna, 1964.

Trenner, Franz. *Die Skizzenbücher von Richard Strauss aus dem Richard Strauss-Archiv in Garmisch. Veröffentlichungen der Richard-Strauss-Gesellschaft München*, 1. Tutzing, 1977.

————, editor. *Richard Strauss. Dokumente seines Lebens und Schaffens*. Munich, 1954.

————, editor. *Richard Strauss. Gesamtausgabe der Lieder*. 4 vols. London, 1964–65.

Tuchman, Barbara W. *The Proud Tower. A Portrait of the World before the War, 1890–1914*. New York, 1966.

Urban, Erich. *Richard Strauss*. Berlin, 1901.

————. "Richard Strauss in neuen Liedern." *Die Musik*, I (1902), 2137–41.

————. *Strauss contra Wagner*. Second edition. Berlin, 1902.

Völckers, Jürgen. "Ein Richard-Strauss-Museum." *Musica*, V (1951), 438–40.

Wachten, Edmund. *Richard Strauss * 1864. Sein Leben in Bildern*. Leipzig, 1940.

Wehmeyer, Grete. *Max Reger als Liederkomponist. Ein Beitrag zum Problem der Wort-Ton-Beziehung*. Regensburg, 1955.

Wellesz, Egon. "Richard Strauss, 1864–1949." *The Music Review*, XI (1950), 23–33.

Wildgans, Lilly, editor. *Anton Wildgans. Ein Leben in Briefen*. 3 volumes. Vienna, 1947.

Wiora, Walter. *Das deutsche Lied . . . Zur Geschichte und Ästhetik einer musikalischen Gattung*. Wölfenbuttel, 1971.

Zentner, Wilhelm. "Richard Strauss und der Verlag F. E. C. Leuckart, Leipzig, jetzt München." *Musikhandel*, I (1949), 34.

INDEX

Unless otherwise noted in parentheses, all composition titles refer to works by Richard Strauss. Op. or AV numbers appear in this index in all references to the composer's instrumental, choral, and stage works as well as to collections of songs. The individual songs are given here without their op. or AV numbers since these can be found by referring to Appendix A, pp. 185-200.